D0208462

YANKEE CITY SERIES

VOLUME

II

PUBLISHED ON THE

Richard Teller Crane, Jr., Memorial Fund

The Yankee City Series Is Dedicated to

CORNELIUS CRANE

THE STATUS SYSTEM OF A MODERN COMMUNITY

BY

W. LLOYD WARNER

AND

PAUL S. LUNT

GREENWOOD PRESS, PUBLISHERS
WESTPORT, CONNECTICUT

Library of Congress Cataloging in Publication Data

Warner, William Lloyd, 1898-1970.
The status system of a modern community.

Reprint of the ed. published by Yale University Press, New Haven, which was issued as v. 2 of Yankee City series.
1. Cities and towns. 2. Social classes.
I. Lunt, Paul Sanborn, joint author. II. Title.
III. Series: Yankee City series, v. 2.
HT609.W32 1973 301.36'3 73-8153
ISBN 0-8371-6959-3

Originally published in 1942 by Yale University Press, New Haven

Reprinted with the permission of Yale University Press

Reprinted in 1973 by Greenwood Press, Inc.,
51 Riverside Avenue, Westport, CT 06880

Library of Congress catalog card number 73-8153
ISBN 0-8371-6959-3

Printed in the United States of America

10 9 8 7 6 5 4 3 2

THIS VOLUME IS DEDICATED TO

Robert Lowie

YANKEE CITY RESEARCH STAFF

Writer W   Analyst A   Field Worker F

W. Lloyd Warner	W A F	Fay Abrams	A
Leo Srole	W A F	Eve Goddard	A
Paul S. Lunt	W A F	Dorothy Jones	A
J. O. Low	W A F	Rosamond Brown	A
Eliot Chapple	A F	Margaret Mack	A
Buford Junker	A F	Viola Vanderhorck	A
Solon Kimball	A F	Grace Senders	A
Marion Lee	A F	Shirley Star	A
Conrad Arensberg	A F	Mildred Warner	A
Robert G. Snider	A F	Joseph Weckler	A
Allison Davis	A F	J. O. Brew	F
Elizabeth Davis	A F	Dorothea Mayo	F
Burleigh Gardner	A F	O. S. Lovekin	F
Dorothy Moulton	A	Gwenneth Harrington	F
Alice Williams	A	Hess Haughton	F
Sylva Beyer	A		

ACKNOWLEDGMENTS

THE research staff of the Yankee City Series are indebted to many people for aid in the inception, course of research, and publication of this work. We cannot thank all of them here.

Above all we wish to express our appreciation to the citizens of Yankee City who generously gave their knowledge of the community and maintained a coöperating interest in our work. We are grateful to the Committee of Industrial Physiology of Harvard University for sponsoring and financing the field research. Professor Elton Mayo and Dean Wallace Donham of the Graduate School of Business Administration of Harvard University have contributed incalculably to the study by their wise guidance, insight, and understanding. In simple expression of our gratitude we dedicated the first volume of the series to them.

The entire series is dedicated to our generous benefactor, friend, and colleague in social anthropology, Cornelius Crane, as an inadequate recognition of his deep and sympathetic interest in our work and of his consuming concern for the problem, the nature of man.

We are very grateful to the Social Science Research Committee of the University of Chicago, the Emergency Relief Administration, the National Youth Administration, and the Works Progress Administration, all of which have contributed aid in the laborious and expensive analysis of the data of these six volumes.

The authors are particularly indebted to Professors E. B. Wilson, Carl Doering, and Earnest Hooton, all of Harvard University, and Professor Samuel Stouffer of the University of Chicago, for advice and assistance on statistical problems.

We wish to thank Professor George Peter Murdock of Yale University for his interest in the publication of these volumes and for his unerring aid in the editing of the manuscripts.

Dr. Stephen Reed and Dr. Allan Holmberg of Yale University, Dr. Joseph Weckler of the Smithsonian Institution, and Mildred Hall Warner have contributed their skill in the preparation of the manuscripts for publication. It is evident to all of the research staff that without their aid we would have been heavily handicapped in completing our task.

We wish to thank our friend and colleague, Dr. Mark May, and his staff of the Institute of Human Relations at Yale University, for the encouragement they gave us by their critical and sympathetic interest.

To John Dollard of the Institute of Human Relations we owe a very special debt of gratitude for his recognition of the significance of the scientific problems we attacked and for his help in the solution of many of them. The searching questions he asked us and the generous acclaim he gave our research have been deep sources of scientific and spiritual strength to all of us.

CONTENTS

TABLES

CHARTS

PREFACE

THE "Yankee City Series," of which the present work is the second volume, will be completed in six volumes. Each will deal with a significant aspect of the life of a modern community as it has been recorded and analyzed by the combined and coöperative labors of a group of social anthropologists. The same techniques and viewpoints applied by them to the study of societies of simpler peoples are here subjected to empirical testing in a concrete case study in modern American society. The town chosen (for reasons given in Volume I) was an old New England community.

The first volume, *The Social Life of a Modern Community*, by W. Lloyd Warner and Paul S. Lunt, describes in detail the cultural life of the community, emphasizing particularly the way in which these people have been divided into superior and inferior classes. It also presents the reader with an interpretation of the systematic analysis of the techniques, methods, and conceptual framework used in the research, a summary of the findings, and a general orientation.

The present volume, *The Status System of a Modern Community*, by W. Lloyd Warner and P. S. Lunt, gives a detailed description and careful analysis of the social institutions of this community. It shows how our New England subjects live a well-ordered existence according to a status system maintained by these several social institutions.

The third volume, *The Social Systems of American Ethnic Groups*, by W. Lloyd Warner and Leo Srole, is a detailed study of the social life of a number of ethnic groups, including the Irish, French Canadians, Jews, Armenians, and Poles; it explains how they maintain their old cultural traditions but at the same time undergo social changes which make them more and more like the larger American community.

The fourth volume, *The Social System of the Modern Factory*, by W. Lloyd Warner and J. O. Low, is specifically concerned with the study of the social organization of the modern factory. It shows not only how industrial workers coöperate in producing manufactured goods, but also how they fit into the larger community.

The fifth volume, *American Symbol Systems,* by W. Lloyd Warner, deals with the conceptual processes which Americans use when they think about themselves and their own behavior. It analyzes the myth and ritual as well as the secular behavior of the members of Yankee City.

The concluding volume, *Data Book for the Yankee City Series,* by W. Lloyd Warner, supplies additional data for those who wish to examine the more detailed aspects of the subjects treated in the other volumes.

PART I
METHOD

I

THE STATUS SYSTEM OF YANKEE CITY

THE relation of social differentiation to rank and status in a modern community is the general subject of this volume.[1] Throughout the world complex communities like Yankee City always manifest rank orders composed of higher and lower social positions. All such complex social groups exhibit extreme differentiation of behavior between higher and lower social levels in which all the people within the community are hierarchically typed and ranked. If a science may be defined by the questions it asks, then any research made within its field should be capable of similar definition. Until that phase of the investigation represented by this volume began, the Yankee City research simply asked: What *similarities* exist among the members of the *same* class in the social hierarchy? What differences are found among the members of different classes? The total answer comprised a mosaic of many traits from which a portrait of each class was derived.

The research on which the present volume is based, however, was oriented around the following more inclusive questions: What is the nature of the social differentiation *within each* of the six classes? How are the classes interconnected? What are the nature and extent of the interconnections? Do they constitute a system? The answers to these more general questions constitute the principal portions of the present volume.

1. Why Do Members of the Same Class Behave Differently?

AFTER we had placed each individual in one of the several classes and completed the study of the specific characteristics of each class and of interclass relations, it still remained to

1. The term "rank" refers here to series of higher and lower statuses or positions; the term "status" is a more general word which applies to any social position and does not necessarily refer to higher and lower ranking. For example, several men may have the same class ranking but occupy different statuses within a class because of memberships in different social structures.

explain the not inconsiderable variations in behavior among members of a given class. Carrying the analysis further, therefore, we turned to a reëxamination of the separate structures (the family, the clique, the association, and the church and economic institutions) to interpret the behavior of individuals in interaction within these structures. However, analysis of the behavior of individuals within a family and analysis of these same individuals in the class system could not be synthesized; there was always the dichotomy of the structure and class concepts running through our interpretations.

In addition to this problem an even graver difficulty confronted us in our analysis of social behavior in Yankee City. We had gathered excellent, detailed interview material consisting of clear statements of how individuals had acted and what they had said in concrete situations. But when we attempted to relate specific behavioral observations to the general category of class, we found that the class concept, while suggestive in broad outline, did not give an infallible key to interpretation of the details and variations of the individual's behavior within the context of his class. The concept of the social personality[2] helped greatly in understanding the individual's participation in class and in the several social structures. The concepts of structure and class helped us make larger generalizations about Yankee City behavior as a whole. But we still lacked a construct which would draw together all our special findings into an internally coherent system.

Although we had discussed class as two-dimensional, we had treated it in only one dimension. We had seen one class as above or below the other but had not worked out systematically the range of variations within the lateral extension of each class. It became necessary, therefore, to reformulate the problem of interpreting our data, to attempt to solve the question of how we were to study class in other dimensions, and to create a new construct which would synthesize our findings on the social personality, the several structures, and the class hierarchy. The effort to accomplish this task resulted ultimately in the formation of what we have called the "positional system." This chapter will be devoted to stating how we arrived

2. See *The Social Life of a Modern Community,* "Yankee City Series," I, 26–28.

at this generalization and of what the positional system of Yankee City consisted when we had completed our research.

2. Reëxamination of the Distribution in Class of the Several Social Structures and Their Conversion into Class Types and Structural Positions

In the first volume we considered the problem of the relation of an organization like the family, the clique, or the association to the class hierarchy. These structures we placed in the class system by counting the number of institutions or individuals appearing in one or more of the strata. This method of analysis gave invaluable insight into how the various institutions were distributed and, by inference, some insight into how they affected, and were affected by, class considerations. We learned, for example, that the family did not tend to spread beyond one class; that the clique, although sometimes confined to only one class, was usually distributed in two; and that the association was seldom confined to one class, a little more frequently comprised two, and most often three or four. A comparison of the spread of these three types of institutions gave us a significant comprehension of how the various classes were interrelated.

A reëxamination of the distribution of the various social structures in the class hierarchy, however, yielded much better results for our understanding of institutional and class behavior and ultimately led us to discard these two types of behavior in favor of a system of relations whose ultimate units consisted of relative positions. There were some 357 associations on which we had accurate and approximately complete membership and activity data; the composition of these structures with respect to sex, age, ethnicity, religion, and class had already been determined. But the analysis of the distribution of the associations in class soon demonstrated that the various associations could be typed according to the range of their extension through the six classes. On the basis of the data collected in the field, the associations were typed finally into nineteen varieties which we shall call "class types." They were:

Type 1: associations comprised of upper-upper members only;

Type 2: upper-upper and lower-upper members only;

Type 3: upper-upper, lower-upper, and upper-middle individuals;

Type 4: upper-upper, lower-upper, upper-middle, and lower-middle individuals;

Type 5: upper-upper through upper-lower individuals;

Type 6: of individuals from every class in the society, upper-upper through lower-lower inclusive;

Type 7: lower-upper[3] and upper-middle individuals only;

Type 8: lower-upper, upper-middle, and lower-middle individuals;

Type 9: lower-upper, upper-middle, lower-middle, and upper-lower members;

Type 10: lower-upper through lower-lower members;

Type 11: upper-middle[4] and lower-middle members only;

Type 12: upper-middle, lower-middle, and upper-lower classes;

Type 13: upper-middle through lower-lower inclusive members;

Type 14: lower-middle members only;

Type 15: lower-middle and upper-lower members only;

Type 16: lower-middle, upper-lower, and lower-lower members;

Type 17: upper-lower individuals only;

Type 18: upper-lower and lower-lower members only;

Type 19: lower-lower members only.

In these nineteen class types of associations there were at least nineteen varieties of behavioral relations among the different members of the associational system of Yankee City. Hence the actual behavior of the people in these different types of associations would be expected to vary accordingly. For instance, a man or woman in Type 1 would, in all probability, behave very differently from a man or woman in Type 19. In the case of these two types we already knew this because the individuals in them were upper-upper and lower-lower respectively. However, when we examined the behavior of an upper-

3. There were no associations consisting only of the lower-upper.

4. There were no associations which were confined only to the upper-middle class.

upper person who belonged to associations of both Type 1 and Type 6, it immediately became apparent that his relations in the former were quite different from those in the latter. In the Type 1 association all relations are of approximate equivalence since they are all of one class, while the Type 6 relations are not equivalent because the upper-upper members are related to the members of all classes below them. More specifically, an upper-upper individual in Type 6 is related directly to a lower-lower individual and to members of any other interstitial class. The behavior of the same person in an association of Type 1 and an association of Type 6 is obviously quite different. This would also be true of a lower-lower individual belonging to associations of Type 19 and Type 6. In the first he would be with his equals and in the second with representatives of five other classes all superior to his own. A cursory comparison of such types as 11 (UM and LM) and 16 (LM through LL) illustrates the point again. In Type 11 a lower-middle member is subordinate to all other members, whereas in 16 he is superordinate to all the others. In other words, he occupies exactly the opposite position in each of the two types and will in all likelihood behave very differently.

Let us make one other comparison before continuing with more general statements about associational class types. An upper-middle person might belong to a Type 3 association (UU through UM), a Type 6 (UU through LL), and a Type 13 (UM through LL). In the first all his relations would be with people above him and to whom, as a member of a class, he would feel inferior. In the second he would have bilateral relations with people both above and below him. There would be two class positions above him and three below him. In the third type (UM through LL) he would occupy a class position superior to all others and inferior to none; consequently, he would constantly express superordinate class behavior and expect to receive subordinate behavior.

Considerations of this range of behavior exhibited within one class, but based on the relational position in the types of association, led to the formulation of two new hypotheses:

1. Wherever a person's relations with his own class or with other classes varied because of the types of association to which he belonged, there was a lateral extension of social behavior

at any one point in the vertical class hierarchy. This extension could be examined by the device of the class types of associations; and for our purposes such an extension at the six levels of the vertical hierarchy constituted a part of the horizontal, or lateral, extension of the society.

2. When the nineteen types of associations were seen as units in the lateral extension of each class, the two dimensions became fifty-four positions. For example, Class Type 2 (UU and LU) now became two positions, one of which consisted of upper-upper people who were in association with lower-upper, and the second of lower-upper people who were in association with upper-upper people. Chart I represents the two-dimensional system of positions worked out on the basis of the nineteen class types of associations.

	1	2	3	4	5	6	7	8	9	10	11	12	13	14	15	16	17	18	19
UU	1	2	3	4	5	6													
LU		7	8	9	10	11	12	13	14	15									
UM			16	17	18	19	20	21	22	23	24	25	26						
LM				27	28	29		30	31	32	33	34	35	36	37	38			
UL					39	40			41	42		43	44		45	46	47	48	
LL						49				50			51			52		53	54

I. *The Associational Positional System in Yankee City*

In this chart the positions are numbered from left to right beginning at upper-upper and ending at lower-lower so that Position 1 is at the top left-hand corner of the chart and Position 54 at the lower right-hand corner. A member in any one of these positions would exhibit a somewhat different type of behavior from that of a member in any other position. A glance back at what has been said about Class Type 1 and Class Type 6 will help to clarify this point.

We have already said that the behavior of an upper-class individual varies in each of these associational types. Because of this difference in behavior, we formulated the positional theory. The upper-middle person belonging to associational Types 3, 6, and 13 is now in Position 16 (formerly called Class Type 3), in Position 19 (spoken of above as Class Type 6), and in Position 26 (formerly Class Type 13). His behavior can now be examined and compared with that of other members of his various positions.

The fifty-four positions of the associational system are seen to extend laterally through nineteen class types. We have earlier examined the distribution of the several structures in class. With the discovery that the associations could be typed for a better understanding of the behavior of individuals in Yankee City, we applied the same conceptual scheme to the other structures of the society.

From the data collected on the several thousand families in Yankee City and their distribution in class, twenty-four class types of families were determined.

These twenty-four types were converted into fifty positions. Chart II represents all these family positions. There are, of course, twenty-four lateral positions. Of these, five include the upper-upper class, six the lower-upper class, twelve the upper-middle, eleven the lower-middle, eight the upper-lower, and eight the lower-lower. The lower-lower is more extended laterally in the family structure than it is in the association. There is a greater similarity of behavior among lower-lower people, judged by these measurements, in the associational structure than there is in the family structure, since only six associational positions appear as against eight family positions. This is reversed, however, in the upper-lower where there are ten associational and only eight family positions. In the lower-middle they are approximately equal: eleven family and twelve associational positions. The same is true for the upper-middle where there are twelve family and eleven associational positions. In the lower-upper there are nine associational against six family positions; in the upper-upper six associational against five family positions.

Of the five upper-upper family positions, none has relations which reach to the upper-lower; only one has relations with lower-middle; two have relations with upper-middle; and two with the lower-upper; naturally all five have relations among themselves. A glance at Chart II will show that the same analysis can be made of the positions in all of the other classes. For the present, however, we shall forego further analysis of this point; it will be somewhat more useful at a later stage of our exposition.

The difference between the relations of an associational position and of a family position is that a man can belong to only one family (as the family has been considered in this study)

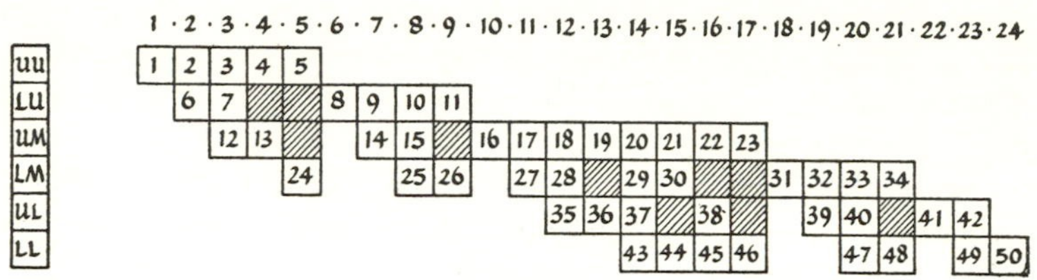

II. *The Family Positional System in Yankee City*

whereas he may belong to a number of associations. Consequently the associational membership can be interlocked because of the multiple membership of the various individuals in any given class. The family's extension depends on the extended kinship system for its horizontal spread; but membership in the association is characterized by interchangeability from one lateral position to another. The associational system allows the individual to occupy many places—six, for instance, if he is of the upper-upper class—but the family system allows him but one.

The family's usual system of superordinate, subordinate, and coördinate relations, with an ordered scheme of obligations, respect, rights, and duties, is greatly altered in places where the family type spreads over more than one class. Here a priori analysis would lead one to expect that in families where the members are in one class ordinary social relations will be little disturbed by the operation of class principles; but that where the members are distributed through two or more classes, ordinary family relations will be disturbed. In the father-son relation, for instance, the father is ordinarily superordinate and the son subordinate. This follows from the kinship organization. However, if the son's position is superordinate in class, there is a probability either of the son's being superordinate to the father or of a balanced equality because of the opposition of the kinship and class principles. Also, the father may still dominate the son through the strength of the kinship principles. The last possibility, however, is slight. The relation of father-daughter can be similarly deduced as can those of mother-son and mother-daughter.

Brothers of approximately the same age in this society tend to have equivalent relations; but this relationship is unbalanced through one brother's rising or sinking to a higher or lower position, and one may come to dominate the other. Approximately the same thing is true of sisters and brothers, and among sisters. While an older sibling ordinarily occupies a position of dominance over his juniors, the operation of social mobility may raise one of the younger siblings to a superior class position, with the probability of his dominating his elder. An examination of the positions occupied by any of these kinship personalities in the family positional system will give one a working hypothesis of the kind of behavior one might expect in any specific family under analysis.

The several thousand cliques studied (see Chart III) were also put in class types on the basis of the materials gathered in the field. Thirty-one class types of cliques were identified: nine upper-upper, eleven lower-upper, sixteen upper-middle, seventeen lower-middle, twelve upper-lower, and eight lower-lower.

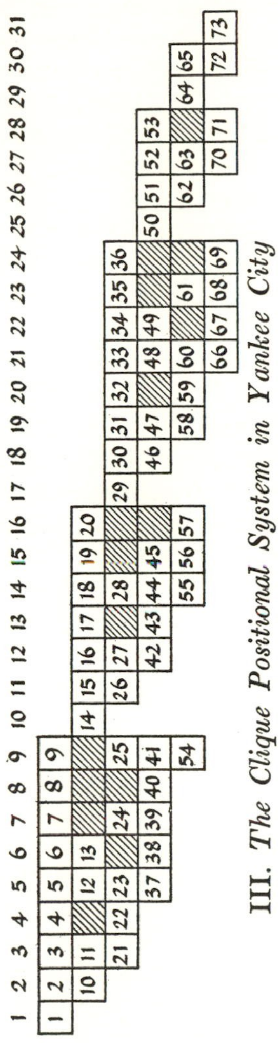

III. *The Clique Positional System in Yankee City*

Chart III presents the seventy-three clique positions and their interrelationships. Other institutions, including such economic organizations as the retail and wholesale stores, factories, and offices of professional men, were also examined and typed. There are twenty-six class types of economic organization, three church class types, two school class types, and one political class type. The political class type, having total class representation, is similar to Class Type 6 in the associational structure, i.e., all six classes are found in the political organizations of Yankee City. The church types include but three: (1) a class type distributed through all six classes; (2) a class type distributed from lower-upper to lower-lower; (3) a class type from upper-middle to lower-lower. The economic class types correspond more closely to the family and clique class types than to the associational class types, since they do not all have positions in sequence as do the associational class types.

3. The Conversion of Structural Positions into a General System of Positions

When the several internal structures of the community of Yankee City had been analyzed to determine the number and kind of positions and relations, we sought to convert all the relations and positions of the separate structures into one general positional system. If this were possible, we could dispense with the older class and structural analysis and depend entirely on the positional and relational system.

The relations of the family, the clique, and the association, each of which was distributed through one or more classes in the separate class types, were now converted into relations which had no references to the several structures but were seen as general relations or general class types. This was done by breaking down the class types of each of the structures into one general class type. Thus, whenever two or more of the structural types coincided, they were treated as one general class type; whenever only one structure occurred, this also was treated as one general class type. Thirty-four of these general class types were found, and these were converted into eighty-nine positions. However, the problem of actually studying hundreds of thousands of specific social relations which would constitute the general positional system we sought was a difficult one.

Looking at the problem as though we had started from the beginning, our task was to analyze the interview material, which consisted of observations of the acts of our informants and their verbalizations about their own and other people's behavior, into member relations. This we had already done for the relations within the immediate family, the clique, the association, and other structures. Meanwhile we had succeeded in putting each of the several thousand families into class types; and we had done the same for the cliques, associations, economic institutions, and other internal structures of Yankee City. We thus moved through four levels of abstraction: (1) gathering concrete factual interview material (the acts of individuals); (2) looking at all this material as constituting acts which belonged to different kinds of relations of members of the family, the clique, and the association (members in relation); (3) assessing the relations not as specific ones—e.g., husband-wife or father-son relations within the family—but in their *totality* of behavior and class alignments in the community; and (4) formulating the concept of the positional system of each structure and, ultimately, the positional system of the total community. As we progressed from the first to the last stages of the work we constantly reduced the number of items to which we applied our attention.

By means of this latter discipline the millions of social facts collected in our five years of field work were reduced first to several hundred thousand relations, and then to several thousand families, cliques, associations, and other institutions. From the latter we worked out the class types, of which there were thirty-one for the clique, twenty-four for the family, and nineteen for the association; and the class types were in turn reduced to the positional and relational system. Analysis of the chart of the positional system of Yankee City will be aided by first examining the accompanying diagram (Chart IV).

Chart IV shows how we reduced the material until we reached the idea of position (P). The two lines from the bottom of the diagram which converge on P indicate the simplification which took place, while the two lines which spread upward from P represent the smaller number of generalizations used for handling the data. CT, to be found also at the top of the chart of the positional system (Chart V), stands for the class types, of which there were some thirty-four in the community. The general class type is a composite formed by the combination of family, clique, association, economic, political, school, and church organizations. Above the class type in the diagram will be found the structural type, ST. The structural type indicates the kind of organizational behavior which can be found

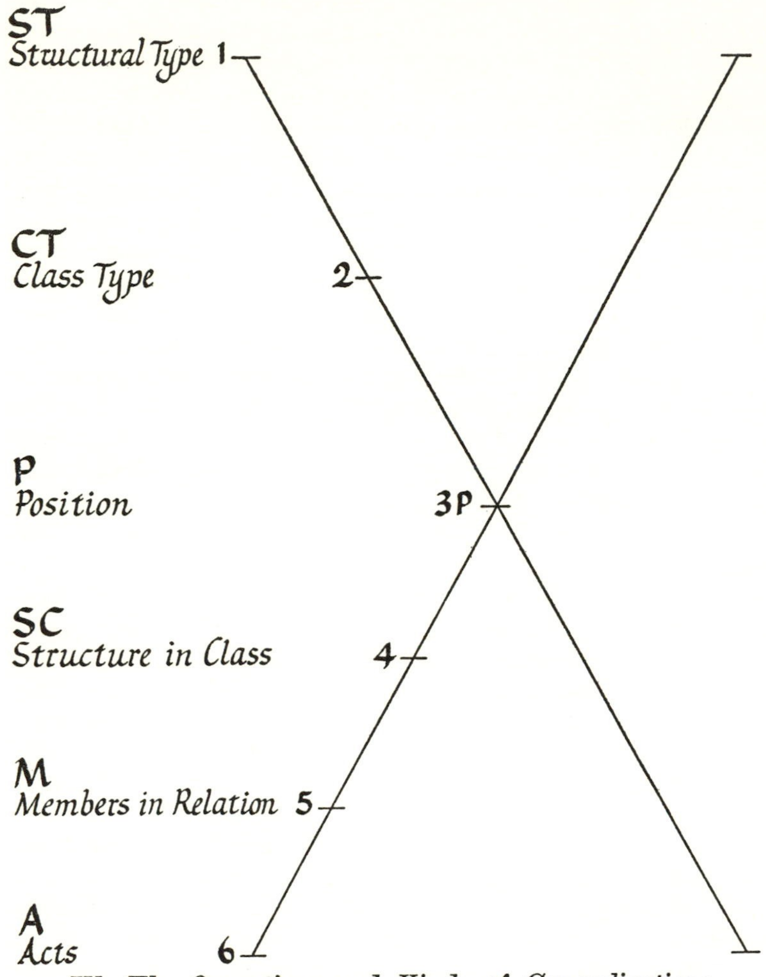

IV. *The Operations and Kinds of Generalizations*

in each of the eighty-nine positions. The structural type reduces the number of generalizations from thirty-four to eleven. ST1, for example, which is to be found a number of times across the distribution of the thirty-four class types in Chart

V, is composed of the family, clique, association, and economic groups. STII is composed of the family, association and the clique. STIII is composed of the clique and family. STIV includes clique and association. STV includes only the clique. The other types are listed in the legend of Chart V.

There has been no attempt here to study the actual number of relations involved among the positions. We have merely examined the number of types of relations and will leave until later chapters the determination of the actual number of relations within each type. There are, therefore, three kinds of enumeration which can and have been made:

(1) the number of types of relation;

(2) the number of institutions in each class type (number of associations distributed in UU and LU, for example);

(3) the number of relations found in each of the institutions and each of the types of institutions (for example, let us say there are thirty members of the Rotary Club, twenty of Kiwanis, and ten of Elks—making a total of sixty relations which are distributed in a particular class type).

The problem at the moment is not to describe the number of relations but to present the method and give the outline of the positional system of Yankee City.

4. General Description of the Status System

THE status system of Yankee City consists of interrelated social structures, differentiated by the class hierachy in which the individuals of the community are placed. There are six classes and seven different kinds of social structure. Each of the seven types of social structure is composed of one or more separate social structures. For instance, the family type is made up of thousands of single, elementary families, but the church and school types contain comparatively few structures. Each of the six classes and seven types of structure possesses hundreds or thousands of members. The 17,000 individuals who compose the total population of Yankee City are members of both the class and structural systems. An individual can be a member of only one class at a given moment in his life career and at a given moment in the history of Yankee City society. All individuals are treated as occupying but one class in the rank order of Yankee City.

However, a given individual is ordinarily a member of a number of kinds of social structure; and he may participate in all seven kinds of social structure while being a member of but one class. In a few of the seven types of institution he can belong to more than one structure: a man may be a member of two or more associations and several cliques. An individual usually belongs to but one church and school and ordinarily, by reason of his occupation, is a member of but one economic organization. All individuals in Yankee City belong to but one major political organization, the corporate township of Yankee City. For the purposes of this analysis we have placed the individual in but one family. If he is a parent and spouse, he is in his family of procreation (the family he creates by and after marriage). If he is a child or an adult living with his parents, or an adult living with his siblings—but not a parent—he has been placed by this study in his family of orientation (the family into which he was born).

Because an individual belongs to several kinds of separate structures which compose a type, he participates in a number of social situations at the same time. His rank remains unchanged, but his position within that rank is constantly changing. At all times the social statuses which compose the whole field of his participation influence his behavior; they are all interdependent in his life and in the lives of the other individuals who are members of the social system.

Since most of the members of associations, cliques, and families are members of other institutions, and the other members of these additional structures are also members of still other institutions, the whole community of individuals may be viewed as an interrelated, interconnected, and interdependent system of memberships.

We shall hereafter refer to the eighty-nine behavioral situations (or statuses) as social positions or statuses, and the total social system of Yankee City as the positional or status system (see Chart V).

In Chart V these positions are numbered as they are distributed through each class, beginning with the upper-upper and ending with the lower-lower.[5] Position 1 in the upper-upper

5. Throughout this part of the discussion the reader must refer to this master chart of the positional system.

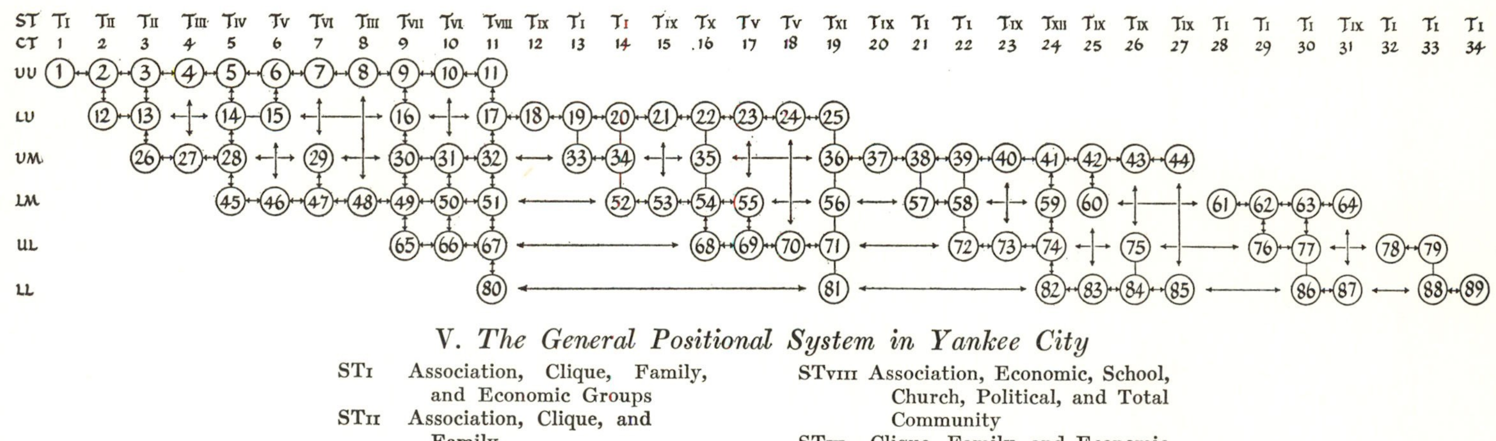

V. *The General Positional System in Yankee City*

STI	Association, Clique, Family, and Economic Groups
STII	Association, Clique, and Family
STIII	Clique and Family
STIV	Association and Clique
STV	Clique Only
STVI	Clique and Economic
STVII	Association and Economic
STVIII	Association, Economic, School, Church, Political, and Total Community
STIX	Clique, Family, and Economic
STX	Association, Clique, and Economic
STXI	Association, Economic, and Church

group has no positions directly below it; and the only connections between it and all the positions which are below it are through the other positions found in the upper-upper class, that is, Positions 2 through 11. Position 89, at the other end of the positional system, is the reverse of Position 1 in its relations to the rest of the society. Position 89 has no direct vertical connections with any positions above it, and must depend upon indirect connections through other positions in the same horizontal extension.

Position 11 functions in exactly the opposite manner to Position 1 in the upper-upper group positions. It is directly connected with the lower-lower Position 80 through Positions 17, 32, 51, and 67. This means that a man who belongs to an association such as the American Legion (which extends all the way through the society) has by virtue of his membership an internal membership relation with a man who is a member of the American Legion and who occupies Position 80. As defined here, these two memberships are in direct relation because they are in the same association and not dependent on some other group for their interconnections; they have direct, face-to-face relations within one specific social structure.

Position 80, as the reader may readily infer, is in the same functional position in the lower-lower group as Position 11 in the upper-upper group. A man in Position 89 cannot, by virtue of belonging to that position, be in direct relation with anyone above. However, this same lower-lower individual, by belonging to Position 80, can and does have direct relations with members of all five positions directly above. Not only does he have direct relations internally with the five positions above his own (i.e., 67, 51, 32, 17, and 11) but at the same time he is indirectly interconnected with every other position in the whole of the society. In other words, when a man is born into or joins Position 1 or 89, he tends to be isolated and only indirectly connected with the society which is above or below him, whereas an individual who has membership in Position 11 or 80 has direct relations with part of the members of all classes and indirect membership relations with all the rest. It might be further stated here that *by indirect relation we mean the relation that is, first, outside or external to the type of group to which a man belongs, and second, one of superiority and inferiority.* This last consideration must be added since a given position in any one of the six strata can directly combine with all the others at that level; not only can two positions at a given level be directly connected by virtue of a member of one being a member of another, but the same individual could and sometimes does have a membership in all the positions. A man, for example, may have a membership in all the positions from 80 through 89. This brings out very clearly a fundamental point in our method: we are dealing here not with individuals but with *memberships* in a positional system.

Although for the purposes of exposition we have confined our attention to Positions 1 and 11 in the upper-upper group and Positions 80 and 89 in the lower-lower group, we might just as easily have used Positions 18 and 25 in the lower-upper, 37 and 41 in the upper-middle, 61 and 63 in the lower-middle, and 78 and 79 in the upper-lower. Position 18 in the lower-upper class is almost analogous to Positions 1 and 89 in the upper-upper and lower-lower classes. A person who has membership only in Position 18 would have no direct relations up or down but only direct horizontal relations. The same is true of Positions 37 (UM), 61 (LM), and 78 (UL). There is, however, a difference between these four positions and the other two. Position 1, like all the other ten positions in its general vertical place, cannot be extended upward. Position 89, as well as all the other positions from 80 to 89, cannot be extended downward. However, Positions 18, 37, 61, and 78 are composed of members who are in the same lateral extension with other members in other positions which are capable of being extended up and down.

Positions 25, 41, 63, and 79 are approximately analogous to Position 11; and Positions 81, 82, 86, and 88 are approximately analogous to Position 80. The first series of positions is analogous to Position 11 because they extend their members throughout all the classes which are found between the two end positions. For example, Position 25 extends through 36, 56, 71, to 81, and obviously Position 81 extends internally, directly, and upward through all these positions.[6]

6. It is possible, by examination of the several types of relational situations of positions, to distinguish ten relational types, as follows:

(1) Type 1, positions which have no direct relations outside their own class. These positions are: 1, 18, 37, 61, 78, 89 (see Chart V). (2) Type 2, positions

Until now we have confined our attention almost wholly to the upward and downward extensions of the positional system. Positions 1 through 11 are *in relationship to each other directly and with unlimited interchangeability.* That is, an upper-upper man or woman, by virtue of status, may have direct relations with members of all positions at this level and can belong to all of them; there is no limit to an individual's right to join and participate in all eleven positions.

This is in contrast to the *limited interchangeability in the direct vertical relations.* A man in Position 11 may have direct relations with the members of the five positions below his but he could not join, let us say, Positions 17 or 80 because he is an upper-upper person and those positions are lower-upper and lower-lower respectively. However, as a member of an association which extends through all these positions and has members who have internal and direct relations with each other, he does have limited interchangeability with these other five positions. The rules governing such an institution as an association or a clique commonly declare that all the members are equal. This means that within the associational membership per se there is equality but that class attitudes still operate to differentiate the people who belong to the different positions within this structure. The direct behavior of the individuals in such relations clearly demonstrates this. Part of the behavior shows that the considerations of equality of membership are present. Any member from any stratum is eligible to office, for example. All votes are considered of *equal* value. However, while this is

which have direct relations with one adjoining class: 2, 12, 19, 33, 38, 57, 62, 76, 79, 88. (3) Type 3, positions which have vertical relations with two other classes in sequence: 3, 13, 26, 20, 34, 52, 39, 58, 72, 63, 77, 86. (4) Type 4, positions which are in a vertical relation with three other classes in sequence: 5, 14, 28, 45, 22, 35, 54, 68, 41, 59, 74, 82. (5) Type 5, positions which are related to four other classes in sequence: 9, 16, 30, 49, 65, 25, 36, 56, 71, 81. (6) Type 6, positions related to five other classes in sequence: 11, 17, 32, 51, 67, 80. (7) Type 7, two positions not in sequence, that is, skipping one class: 4 and 27; 21 and 53; 40 and 73; 64 and 87. (8) Type 8 extends across four classes but contains only three positions, since one is not in sequence. The positions are: 6, 15, 46, 7, 29, 47, 23, 55, 69, 42, 60, 83, 43, 75, 84. (9) Type 9 extends across five classes, skipping one: 10, 31, 50, 66. (10) Type 10 extends across four classes, skipping two: 8 and 48; 24 and 70; 44 and 85.

It will be noticed that these types are induced from observed relations among the eighty-nine positions. They do not exhaust the logical possibilities of combination.

true, class attitudes are still present and feelings of superiority and inferiority differentiate the members into several segments. There is, therefore, *limited* interchangeability in these vertical positions which are in internal relation as compared with the unlimited interchangeability in the direct external relations among the positions which are at the same horizontal level.[7]

Such positions as 13, 32, and 58, to choose three at random, place their members in relations very different from those which we have just discussed. An individual possessing membership in Position 13 would have relations both above and below himself. He would have direct relations with Positions 3 and 26. Positions 32 and 58, among others, also have these upward and downward relations. Obviously, the adjustments made by individuals in such memberships are very different from those made by an individual with a membership in Position 1, 11, or 80. A person in Position 13 is constantly adjusting himself in primary relations to persons above him while at the same time making adjustments in direct relation to persons below him. An individual in Position 11 is adjusting his relation only to those below him, while those with whom he has direct relations are adjusting themselves to positions both above and below. An individual in Position 80 adjusts himself only to persons above him whereas the persons above him with whom he has relations are adjusting themselves to positions both above and below their own. In Positions 1, 18, 37, 61, 78, and 89 there is no adjustment up or down, and all relations are those of equivalence.

We have now described and given examples of all the positions which are in sequence vertically and horizontally. There are, however, certain positions which are in direct relationship to each other vertically but are not in vertical sequence. Such positions as 4 and 27, 15 and 46, 8 and 48, 43 and 75, and 44 and 85, to choose several pairs of them, are in direct internal

7. The reader should not be confused by the term "external" as applied to the relations which exist between positions which are horizontally equivalent. It is sometimes confusing to think of one individual as having membership in all of the eleven positions and yet speak of these memberships as external relations. The memberships in the positions are external to each other since each membership is within a group which is within a type. For instance, the memberships of an upper-middle-class person in the Knights of Pythias and the Elks are external to each other, even though they are held by one individual.

relations but are not connected through members from all the intervening classes. Positions 44 and 85 are in direct internal vertical relation, which means that a man or woman in the upper-middle class is in direct relation with a man or woman in the lower-lower because they have membership in the same family or clique. There are greater differences between their positions than between two positions in a sequential relation. Ordinarily the adjustments necessary are much greater than between positions which are next to each other. This does not mean that the adjustments between the members of the two positions will always be more difficult since there are times when the superordinate-subordinate relationship may be sufficiently explicit and well organized to allow the individuals involved in the membership to accept this relation without thought and without a problem of adjustment.

Positions which are in horizontal relations cannot be out of sequence since they are interchangeable and all capable of direct relation.

In summary, the eighty-nine positions, operationally speaking, are a combination of the family, clique, association, school, church, economic, and political structures as they are found in the class system of Yankee City. There are thirty-one types of cliques, twenty-four types of families, nineteen types of associations, twenty-six economic types, three church, two school, and one political. Within each of these types there are a number of individual structures. That is to say, within one general class type there may be twenty or more associations, fifteen or more cliques, and one hundred families, as well as several stores and one or more factories or offices.

When the positions are examined from the point of view of the amount of segmentation that one finds in the various classes, one discovers that of the eighty-nine positions:

11 are upper-upper (P1–11)
14 are lower-upper (P12–25)
19 are upper-middle (P26–44)
20 are lower-middle (P45–64)
15 are upper-lower (P65–79)
10 are lower-lower (P80–89)

Chart VI presents the reader with the profile of the extension of the several classes when measured by the number of positions found in each class.

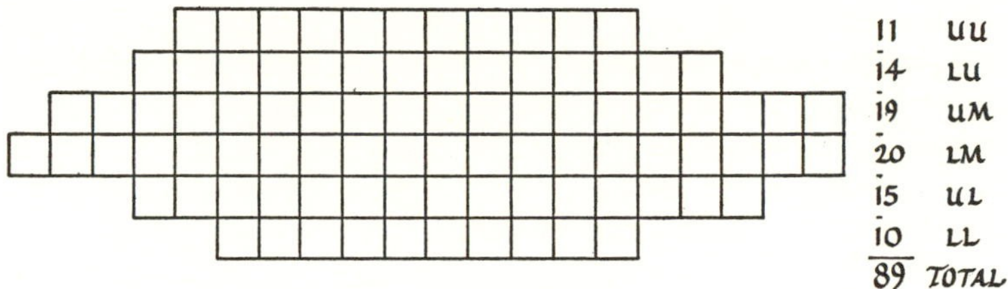

VI. *Profile of the Positions as Seen in Two Dimensions*

It shows clearly that the two middle groups are much more extended than the others and that the lowest group is the least extended. The extension or lack of extension of positions within each class shows that the lower-middle positions are twice as differentiated as the lower-lower, etc. From the point of view of an individual in any one of the six classes, it means that there is greater opportunity for the elaboration and extension of the social personality in the middle groups than there is in either end group. On the whole it confirms our original hypothesis that the lower-lower group is much less differentiated than the other groups, although it had been supposed that the upper-upper group would be more varied than these measurements have proved it to be. The middle groups, we had assumed from our first evidence, were more elaborated and varied than the others, and this measurement demonstrates that, as judged by the positional system, they are about twice as varied as the top and bottom groups.

When one examines the positional system in order to determine the extent of the interrelations of the several classes, it becomes evident immediately that each of the six classes has a degree of unity which sets it apart from any other class. The classes that are at the two ends of the vertical extension are shown to be much less related than those which are closer to each other. Each of the classes may be examined with the aid of the chart and the relations measured and enumerated.[8] As

8. By careful scrutiny of Chart V the reader may determine the number and type of relationships that each class manifests, internally and externally.

an example, let us take the lower-lower class. We will use family, clique, and association for illustrative purposes.

The lower-lower-class positions are internally related to the upper-upper only by Position 80 in Type 4 (see Chart V), which is composed solely of associational structures. The two lower-lower-class positions, 80 and 81, are internally related to the lower-upper Positions 17 and 25, again by associational relations. Lower-lower positions are related internally to upper-middle by Positions 80–85. These connections consist of Type 1, where family, clique, and association are found (once) : Type 2, family and clique (three times) ; and Type 4, association alone (twice). Lower-lower and lower-middle are related internally by Positions 80–83, 86, 87, which include Types 4, 1, and 2. Type 4 is represented twice, as are Types 1 and 2. This means that the lower-lower and lower-middle are interconnected twice by associational relations; twice by family, clique, and associational relations; and twice by family and clique relations.

The behavior in the positions will be described in the next chapter and illustrations will be given. Part of the data used will be selected from the sketches drawn of class behavior in Chapter VII, Volume I. As the analysis develops it will become clear that the positional system fits the data more precisely and, for most purposes, is a better instrument of analysis than a conceptual scheme of six classes.

PART II
RESULTS

II

THE EIGHTY-NINE POSITIONS AS BEHAVIORAL SITUATIONS

1. Description of Each Position

A DISCUSSION of the relative place and the expected attitudes of each of the eighty-nine positions is presented in this section. It is followed by an analysis of concrete events in the social interactions of certain Yankee City people. The chapter concludes with statistical statements of the size and social composition of each position.

The members of Position 1 consciously or unconsciously express the sentiments of the superordinate group in the community. Those who belong to associations and other structures in which only their own class is represented are aware that they are in a so-called "exclusive" group. The members of an upper-upper clique or association, when comparing themselves with other cliques and associations, are usually aware of their exclusiveness and of the fact that they occupy the superior position within the society. Of the several positions in the upper-upper class, Position 1 is viewed as being most satisfactory "socially." The members of a family in this position do not feel the strains present in family groups representing two or more classes. There is no feeling of inferiority about class position on the part of any of the members, and pride is manifested in the family heritage. The members of the upper-upper economic groups, usually office or professional people, are in a position in which the owner or manager is in an economically superior relation but in a coördinate or equal class position. There is a sense of social equality in their relations which is not found where the manager belongs to one class and the employees to another. An office in this position has "prestige."

Position 18 is in the lower-upper class. Its members consciously or unconsciously consider themselves superior to the members of the classes below them; but they feel they belong to the so-called "new people" in the upper class and they recognize the superior position of the members of the class above them (upper-upper). Their relations among themselves in the clique, family, and economic groups are of the same order as described for those same structures in Position 1. The relations of the members of Position 37 in the upper-middle class are all coördinate, and the attitudes expressed among the members of the clique, family, and economic groups are also the same as those found for the structures in Position 1. The members of Position 61 are also in coördinate relations. The fact that they belong to the lower-middle class means that they are aware of their lower status in the social system of Yankee City. The attitudes they express in their associations, clique, family, and economic relations indicate their awareness of being below the other three classes, yet they feel above the other two.

The members of Position 78 are in the upper-lower class. They enjoy a certain feeling of superiority to those in the bottom group, but they are also aware of their social inferiority to members of the classes above them. They are likely to be "pushy" and ambitious people. The members of Position 89, in the lower-lower group, are coördinate only with the other nine positions in the lower-lower group. The attitudes they express in the association, clique, family, and economic groups are indicative of this fact.

The members of Position 2 have direct and superior internal relations with the lower-upper members of Position 12, and of course the latter have a relation of subordinacy to Position 2. The superiority-inferiority relations are found in the association, clique, and family structures.

The cliques maintain generally friendly relations, but there is sometimes bitter talk by those in Position 12 of not being "fully accepted," and the people in 2 frequently insist that members of 12 "are nice people although they are newcomers." Class claims are made obliquely and with the aid of symbolic references.

The associations frequently include members who are mutually antagonistic on a class basis. Women are accused of being "pushy," of acting like "climbers," or their "faults" are underscored and their virtues ignored. Men are less likely to indicate such feelings, but "kidding" relations express the ambivalent feelings of unity in the club and difference in class.

The informal clique relations and associational relations among men and women of Positions 2 and 12 often account for the membership and protection of particular individuals in the lower class.

In Positions 19 and 33 members of two classes are in direct internal relations of superiority and inferiority, and the role of the lower-upper-class member is the reverse of that in Position 12, superior rather than inferior.

The families are those in which children have climbed above their parents, or which include grown siblings who have moved unequally up or down in the class hierarchy. The cliques are intimate but usually with the clear recognition that the members of Position 19 have intimate friends and acquaintances in the upper-upper class (ordinarily through 12) which people in 33 generally lack. The associations are small and ordinarily consist of formal committees which meet infrequently. Social relations in the last-mentioned organizations are not intimate. The lower-upper person, while feeling superior to his upper-middle clique and associational friends, is aware of the fact that he is not implementing his social position by such a relation. Occasionally an adult clique is a survival of an earlier clique when the person in 19 belonged to the class below. Our records show that certain people in a family occupying Position 18, formerly in both a family and a clique of 37, continued the earlier clique relation for a time. Once they had formed strong clique and associational relations of the 12–2 type, however, they began to withdraw from the 19–33 relation. Embarrassment and acrimony often arise from this sort of situation.

In Position 38 the upper-middle-class person is superior with relation to lower-middle-class Position 57, a direct reversal of his relative status in Position 33. The representative economic group here is usually a small store or office. Among the members of all structures there is recognition of the difference in status between the two classes. The members of 38 frequently participate in 33 with lower-upper Hill Streeters and infrequently with upper-upper Hill Streeters in 26. This is primarily done in cliques and associations.

The family in these two positions is usually a product of social mobility, the children having climbed to higher statuses than the parents, or having dropped, or siblings having fallen or risen to other social levels. This change of status within families is particularly frequent among ethnic groups.

In Position 62 the lower-middle-class person stands in a superordinate relation to the upper-lower-class person in Position 76; and in Position 79 the upper-lower-class member is superordinate to the lower-lower person in Position 88.

Associations covering this relationship tend to be cliquelike, as for instance subadult cliques which have little more than a name and an informal policy regarding membership. People in associations and cliques in 76 are often men and women with some prized talent or ability. The family members have fallen or risen in the social hierarchy and the usual defenses are present to explain, praise, or condemn the differences among the kindred. The economic groups are typified by small stores and retail establishments.

The family members of Position 79 are apt to be socially mobile ethnic children of parents in 88. The clique members are often courting couples, some of them Yankee Riverbrooker women in 88 who are "going around" with ethnic young men of 79.

We may turn now to the behavioral situations in positions lying in three adjoining classes. Positions 3, 13, and 26 include members in direct internal relation through the association, clique, and family. The upper-upper-class members of Position 3 express attitudes of superiority to the members of the other two positions, but the superiority is manifest with respect to the members of Position 26 more than to those of Position 13. When the members of such an association congregate, they often arrive and leave in cliques, and they frequently group themselves by cliques during the meeting. In these cliques the upper-middle people are often included with the two upper classes. Cliques form in all associations of three or more classes and organize more often than not on class lines.

The members of Positions 3 and 13 feel themselves members of the upper class in relation to the middle class, and a certain unity exists among them; but there is always an associated feeling of difference and opposition between these upper-class members. The members of the three positions, however, have a sense of unity among themselves and superiority to all other members of positions beneath them. This is particularly noticeable in associations where there is a definite recognition on the part of all the members that they are in some way superior to other associations which have members from positions beneath them. One group of men of this sequence is familiarly known as the "House of Lords"; a larger association with members from the lower-middle is called the "House of Commons." The sense of exclusiveness found in Position 1 and Positions 2 and 12 is still maintained in this three-class situation.

This means that while members of Position 26 feel socially inferior to members of the two superior positions, they can maintain feelings of superiority to members of lower positions or to those in their same class who are in lower types of associations.

Family behavior is extremely variant in this position. Many families of this kind are the result of downward mobility of the children, some of whom have dropped lower than others. The resulting strains on the family are severe. Different members participate in higher and lower cliques and find it difficult if not impossible to bring their friends home. The parents maintain a precarious hold on the old family status.

In Positions 20, 34, and 52 the lower-upper-class person's social place is changed and he is now in a position superior to that of members of the other two classes, whereas his status in Position 13 in the preceding sequence was one of superiority to the members of Position 26 and inferiority to Position 3. In the sequence of Positions 39, 58, and 72, the upper-middle-class person is in the superior position and the lower-middle and upper-lower people are in an inferior position.

The above positions are treated together because they present the same social situation. All include family, clique, association, and economic groups. The family in each is variant and a product of upward and downward mobility. Most of the cases are due to upward mobility of children and siblings. This is particularly true in the sequence of Positions 63, 77, and 86. The associational and clique behavior is much like that described in 13 and 26.

From this analysis of general behavioral situations it becomes clear that a member of a class is faced with a constantly shifting series of relative positions in the society. At one moment he may participate in relations which are entirely coordinate (see Relational Type 1, p. 19). At another time he is in a relation with a class above him, where his position is inferior. And shortly thereafter he may find himself in a superior relation with one class below him (see Relational Type 2, p. 19). Still later he may occupy positions in which he is for a time superior to the members of two other classes, inferior to the members of two other classes, or superior to members of a class below him and inferior to the members of a class above him. Such social contexts of behavior, at a given moment in time, may appear in direct face-to-face relations as, for example, in a meeting of an association, in day-by-day family life, or in little clique gatherings for purposes of pleasure; or this behavior may be expressed in the private reveries of the individual. He can feel inferior in his private thoughts and be either aggressive or submissive toward a member of the class above him; or he can feel superior and have reveries of bolstering his own ego by thinking of behavior in which he is always in a superior position. Such behavior in the same status may take forms as variant as snobbishness and openhearted philanthropy.

Let us examine the positions in Relational Type 4. In this sequence of Positions 5, 14, 28, and 45 the members still feel superior to persons in structures which extend to positions below them. The members of these positions are in associations and cliques. There is still conscious exclusion of certain members of the society because they are not considered desirable. The same thing is largely true in the sequence of Positions 22, 35, 54, and 68. Those positions in the sequence 41, 59, 74, and 82, however, belong to a different category; since the vertical extension runs from the lower-lower through the upper-middle classes, there is a feeling of belonging to the "whole" community. This is particularly true of the school and church groups. The very few families which belong to a positional sequence of this kind are highly disrupted by the factor of class, and economic groups ordinarily are strengthened by it. The families are largely ethnic and very mobile.

The schools are ethnic and parochial. The children form cliques which separate them by class, and their teachers recognize "better and poorer" family stock. The churches in this Relational Type (41, 59, 74, and 82) are regarded as inferior to some of those having representatives of the two upper classes in them. Within each church there is clear recognition of the higher and lower statuses of parishioners and clergy.

The positions belonging to Relational Types 5 and 6 tend to have relations which are very much of a kind: the members of the structures involved are either spread throughout the society, as in the case of the six-class type, or lack representation in only one class at the top or the bottom. The attitudes expressed in such associations, schools, and church or political groups in face-to-face relations accent the total-community symbols. There is much talk of "the flag," of "our city," or reference to religious symbols which include everyone in the democratic ideology of equality and fraternity among men and before God. However, differentiation still appears in the attitudes of members of the various positions among themselves. Although an association member of Position 11 in a patriotic organization is believed to be a "comrade" to a "buddy" in Position 80, and equal to him, there is always a clear recognition of their social differences. Each has but one vote in an election of officers, but the man in Position 11 is still a Hill Streeter and superior, and the man in Position 80 is still a Riverbrooker and believed to be inferior. The subtleties of status allow an expression of deference and inequality, but the demands of democracy insist they are "brothers in fraternity."

The control of churches lies in Positions 11, 17, and 25. The behavior of the ministers shows much more deference to members of these positions than to members in 80 and 81. When crises develop, Positions 11, 17, and 32, in the one sequence, and 25 and 36 in the other are clearly separated from the positions below them. The clique and associational behavior in churches and schools clearly expresses class attitudes.

Most of the economic members of these two sequences are employed in factories (see volume on factory systems).

The political statuses show the same formal recognition of equality and the informal recognition of rank. "That Wop," "those Kikes and Niggers," or "Riverbrookers" become Mr. This-and-That in the political meeting or courtroom, but the uncontrolled glance, the inflection of the voice, still say "Wop" and "Kike." When the meeting adjourns, the Riverbrooker in 80 does not go home with the Hill Streeter in 11.

The positions classified under Relational Types 7–9, where the classes are not in sequence, tend to emphasize differences in class feelings. In Positions 4 and 27 members of cliques and families are in direct relation with each other. Upper-middle-class persons in Position 27, while being pleased with their class relation with members of the upper-upper class, at the same time are aware of the great difference between themselves and the members of Position 4. The same is true of Positions 21 and 53. In Position 40 the place of the upper-middle-class person is the reverse of what it was in Position 27, and he is in a superior place to that of the members of Position 73, two classes below him. In Positions 64 and 87 the lower-middle-class person occupies an analogous place to the upper-lower member of Position 73.

In Relational Type 8 occurs a certain variation not found in Relational Type 7, since three positions are involved, extending through four classes but skipping one. This means that two positions will be in sequence and one out of sequence. The degree of unity and consciousness of kind will vary, of course, according to which positions are in sequence and which out of sequence within a given structure. In all these situations in Relational Type 8 economic organizations are found. Such a situation tends to strengthen the ordinary superordinate and subordinate relations found in economic organizations. In all these situations the clique is also found. Cliques of this type tend to be less intimate, usually quite large in membership, and frequently of a specialized kind, such as a group of men who hunt or play cards together but whose wives and families are not on intimate terms. Such class situations in a family tend to put special strains on the relations among its members. In the positions of Relational Type 9 the members act much as in the behavioral situations of Type 8.

Of the four positions involved, the three lower ones are in sequence and the top one (Position 10) is in the upper-upper class. Once again the clique and economic groups are found and conform to the rules stated for Relational Type 8 for these two structures.

Relational Type 10, where two classes intervene between the two positions, accentuates the situation found in Relational

Type 3, where there is but one intervening class. The clique is found in all six of the positions involved, the economic organization in two of them, and the family in one. What has been said of the clique, economic, and family organizations in Relational Types 7–9 also holds true for Type 10.

The foregoing analysis of behavioral situations found in certain of the eighty-nine positions of the six classes prepares us for variations in the behavior of a member of a given class from moment to moment. It gives, for instance, some foreknowledge of how a specific person will act as he moves from one position to another. Take one example of this. Mr. X and his family are all members of the upper-upper class. In fact, membership in the same class is the normal type of class affiliation for all families. One afternoon at cocktails he was heard discussing the lineages of certain old families with several of his intimate clique friends, also of the upper-upper class. Here all his relations were coördinate, as was obvious from the common attitudes expressed. In the evening he went to the Alpha Club to join some friends for dinner and to read the New York papers. There he was in Position 3. After dinner he attended a meeting of the Beta Club—where he was in Position 2—and discussed with members of his own and the class below him subjects of special interest to that group. On the following day he went to his factory office and conferred with the managerial group and then went out into the shop to consult with some of the men about working conditions. He was at this time in Position 11. That afternoon he went hunting with a few of his old high-school friends and was in Position 6; and on Sunday he attended church where he again was in Position 11.

During all these events Mr. X adapted his behavior constantly to fit the position in which he found himself. His behavior as a member of a factory in Position 11 was different from that as a member of a church; but nevertheless certain of his attitudes were common to both cases and certain attitudes expressed to him by the members of other positions were the same. His lower-upper-class minister, when shaking hands on Sunday morning, was just as aware of Mr. X's superior position as was his lower-upper-class manager when he walked into the factory on Monday morning. The constant factor here is the relationship of upper-upper to lower-upper, and the differences involved are primarily those attitudes which are appropriate to the two different kinds of social structure.

Mr. X is an adult male; his behavior in each of these situations is always conditioned by these factors. Were he subadult, or a woman, he would be expected, and expect, to behave differently. Mr. X is a Yankee by birth and tradition and of the Protestant faith; were he Irish and Catholic, he would be expected, and expect, to act differently in each of the positions in which he participates. These social characteristics—age, sex, ethnic affiliation, and religious faith—are also possessed by everyone he meets and modify their behavior. Plainly, in each position these factors in behavior must be accounted for if we are to understand what happens in the events which make up the life of the community.

2. The Positions in Social Interaction

The several sketches in Chapter VII, Volume I, will be used to illustrate how human behavior in Yankee City can be analyzed within the framework of the positional system. (The volume in this series which analyzes the symbol systems of Yankee City will devote more attention to this aspect of the research.)

It will be remembered that in the section entitled "They All Came" Mrs. Breckenridge (UU) had given a political tea, which was discussed, after the others had gone, by the hostess and her friend in the presence of a researcher. The members of the political association were from the three upper classes. They were, therefore, in face-to-face associational relations in Class Type 3. The upper-upper were in Position 3, the lower-upper members in Position 13, and the upper-middle members in Position 26 (see Chart V). They were gathered to promote morale and to advance the interests of their group in the general community. Yet despite the necessity of influencing large proportions of the voters, only members of the nonpopulous upper three classes were present. Such a committee was fashioned to contribute to the solidarity of the three top groups by attempting to ignore the antagonisms existing among the several strata. The attempt was only partially successful, for this reason: although the members of the committee were theoretically equal and had joined as citizens who were believed to be equal, they were all using the association for quite different purposes. Evidence from the conversation of the hostess may not be thoroughly reliable since it is inevitably biased, but it should be examined for the insight it gives. Granted such evidence is biased, the question is, why? The evidence is the expression of two women talking in a clique relation of Class Type 1 in Position 1, not of the same individuals talking in Class Type 3 in Position 3. These older upper-upper women were expressing some of the sentiments common to their class without the inconvenience of having to dissimulate these feelings because of the presence of others below their status. They felt superior to the classes lower than theirs, and their conscious and unconscious attitudes expressed this superiority. In Position 1 they freely manifested attitudes which were largely inhibited from direct expression when they were in Position 3. The "social rules" of Position 3 demanded semiformal, polite behavior; and the purpose of the committee's meetings, to promote solidarity and to control antagonisms, also made it imperative to mask "natural feelings." In each position the two upper-upper ladies were acting according to what was permitted and not permitted by social usage. When the visiting lady departed and Mrs. Breckenridge was left alone with the interviewer, she expressed another attitude, also characteristic of Position 1 (as well as of certain other positions). She felt guilty for the "catty remarks" about the lower-upper Starrs: "Every time Diane Wentworth and I talk like that I'm just a little ashamed afterward. Yet that's the way I honestly feel when I do it." The two women and others like them stimulate the expression of these sentiments in each other when they are meeting on their own plan and talking about people of social levels below them. This happens because they are in a class order and of the same rank; both have families which belong to Position 1; and at the moment of their conversation they are in a clique of the same status.

During the tea (one event in a series which make up the life of the social group) certain behavior is noted. The lower-upper Starrs (as well as other lower-uppers) in Position 13 at the tea act superior to the upper-middle Frenches and other upper-middles in Position 26. The upper-middle people tend to herd together. Ezra Rodgers, upper-middle and nonmobile, unlike the mobile Frenches, sits by himself and makes little or no attempt to ingratiate himself with those around him. Mrs. Starr talks to John Alton (UU) about sailing ships (13⟷3) and snubs Mrs. French (13⟷26). Mrs. French finds herself unable to compete with the other ladies who are talking to Mrs. Starr and Mrs. Frederica Alton (3⟷13⟷26) because they are all members of the House and Home Club (2⟷12) and she is not. Although at the moment they were all in positions of direct interaction with another class, the two upper-class women's membership in House and Home contributed to their feeling of being "nearer" and "having something to talk about." The sense of being excluded probably impelled Mrs. French to move to another part of the room where she conversed with a member of the upper-middle class who was a clique mate of hers (Position 37) and a member of the Woman's Club. Both Mrs. Camp and Mrs. French belonged to families in Position 37. Although the two women were now in 26, these extraneous factors also operated. It is a likely hypothesis that their clique affiliations and sense of being equal in an unequal situation contributed to their being together when their attempts to interact on a basis of semiequality with those above them had not succeeded. They felt safer. Past experience in this same position (26) had taught Mrs. French that she was likely to be defeated if she tried to exploit the situation for her own ends, because all her indirect efforts had met with failure when she had tried to enter the House and Home Club. Furthermore, her husband (Family: 37) in similar situations had met with similar unpleasantness. They both had reason to prefer withdrawal from too close interaction with such positions (3⟷13) when their own socially mobile attitudes were uppermost in their behavior. Mrs. Breckenridge declared that the Frenches were "pushers and climbers and always scheming to get into your house."

The presence of the Irish Catholic Flahertys introduces two variables into the event which present new problems for our analysis: the ethnic and religious affiliations of these two participants. It is clear from the conversation of Mrs. Breckenridge and Mrs. Wentworth that the ethnic and religious factors modify behavior in any position. The Irish Catholic Flahertys are "nice Irish" (3⟷26); they are "lace-curtain" and not "shanty Irish," and are present at a social event which includes most of the "better people of Yankee City." The fact that they are not excluded from a gathering to which "They All Came" indicates that they belong to the higher groups and not the lower ones, but their behavior at the party and their known class position indicate that they are on the periphery of the total group.

The ethnic affiliations of the Irish and the other nine ethnic groups (including the Yankees) are accounted for in our numerical analysis of the status system (Section 3 of this chapter). Age and sex factors are also considered.

The interactive situation so far considered in this analysis of the first sketch is represented in the following chart (Chart VII):

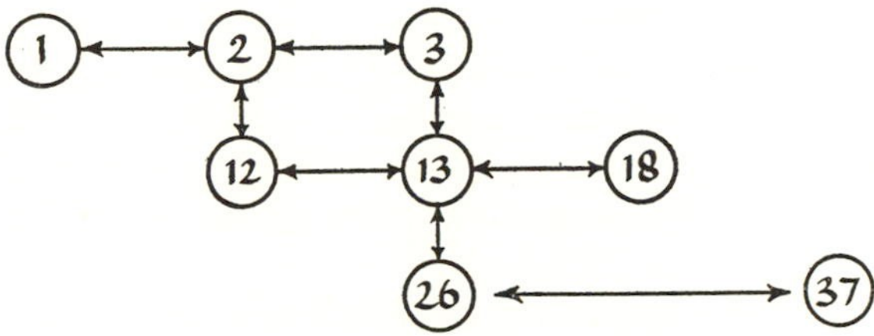

VII. *Interactive System of the Tea*

Only eight of the eighty-nine positions have been directly or indirectly involved; only part of the behavior in such systems of interaction is considered. But, of greatest importance, we *know* we are not taking account of the whole social system of Yankee City, and we are not considering all the types of social behavior for people in the upper classes because Positions 4–11 in the upper-upper class, Positions 14–25 in the lower-upper class, and Positions 27–36 and 38–44 in the upper-middle class are not considered. If we were studying nonhumans, we would say that we know what parts of the maze they were acting in and what parts of the maze were not involved.

When the memberships in the whole system are computed and compared with those just considered, the latter appear still smaller. Before starting the analysis of the rest of the positions of the higher classes, figures will be given for the membership in all classes. Of the total of 71,149 memberships in the seven structures of the status system, our highest number of memberships, 22,959 (32.3%), are in the upper-lower class; the next highest are in the lower-middle class, 22,228 (31.2%); the third highest, 12,432 (17.5%), in the the lower-lower class;

the fourth, 9,587 (13.5%), in the upper-middle class; the fifth, 2,079 (2.9%), in the lower-upper class; and the sixth, 1,864 (2.6%), in the upper-upper class. The individual percentages in each class follow: the highest number, 5,471 (32.60%), are in the upper-lower class; the next highest in the lower-middle, 4,720 (28.12%); the third highest, 4,234 (25.22%), in the lower-lower class; the fourth, 1,715 (10.22%), in the upper-middle; the fifth, 262 (1.56%), in the lower-upper; and the sixth, 242 (1.44%), in the upper-upper class. (There were 141 or 0.84% whose class membership was unknown.)

There are 522 members in Position 1, 361 in Position 2, and 399 in Position 3; about 1,300 of the approximately 1,900 members of the upper-upper class are in these three positions. A glance at Table 1 at the end of this chapter (from left to right at the top of the first page of the table) shows that these three positions are the largest in the upper-upper class and have no contact with the classes below upper-middle (see Chart V).

Position 26 with 632 members and Position 37 with 2,229 are large positions in the upper-middle class. Despite the high proportion of the membership of the three upper classes represented in them, the eight positions they include are but a small part of the total membership of the whole system.

Further scanning of Table 1 gives us more information on the representativeness of the sample under analysis. The 522 members of Position 1 constitute only 0.73% of the total membership, and the position ranks thirtieth in the total of eighty-nine.

In the left-hand column the seven types of institutions are listed and below them their several characteristics. Over half the members of Position 1 are in cliques (53.06%) and 45.02% are in family organizations. The remainder are in associations (0.77%) and economic organizations (1.15%). There are no school, church, or political members. Most of the members of Position 2 are in cliques (82.27%), and by far the largest proportion (83.46%) of Position 3 are associational members. (The figure at the top of each column [i.e., 522 for Position 1, 361 for Position 2, etc.] is the total or 100% for the structure found in each position. Instructions in the use of the table are contained in Section 3 of this chapter.)

Most of the members of Position 12 (88.46%) are clique members; in 13 they are in associations (71.65%); and in 18 in families (54.20%) or cliques (44.60%). Position 26 in the upper-middle class has almost 90% associational members and 10% clique. The principal structures considered in the analysis of the tea and the attendant events were the family and clique in Position 1, the clique and association in 2, the association in 3, and the most representative structures in the other positions. This brief review of the number of members in each position indicates that we have been dealing with the structural behavior which is characteristic of the position.

The presence of the Flahertys calls attention to the necessity for considering ethnic and religious as well as sex and age factors. In the three upper-class positions there are only Yankees. There are no other ethnic groups in the upper-upper class. In the lower-upper class about 4% of the members of 12, 3% of 13, and 6% of 18 are ethnics and the rest are Yankees. All the ethnics in each position are Irish (see left-hand column of Table 1). In the upper-middle class 90.35% of the members of 26 are Yankees and 9.65% are ethnics. Most of the ethnics are Irish since 8.22% of the 632 members in the position are of that group, and only 0.32% are French-Canadian, 0.95% Jewish, and 0.16% Greek. No other ethnic groups are represented. Eighteen per cent of Position 37 are ethnic; 15% Irish; and the remainder scattered through the French-Canadian, Jewish, Italian, Greek, and Armenian groups. The two Flahertys represent a fair sample of the Irish present in the two upper-middle positions. A glance at the percentages listed for religious faith shows a similar disproportion between Protestants and Catholics for these lower-upper and upper-middle statuses.

The second case study of class behavior sketched in Volume I telling how the upper-upper Breckenridge family behaved, and what sometimes happens to the daughters and sons of the upper-upper class, gives us further details of behavior in Position 1. The critical situation examined is that of the daughter and her relations with a man outside her own class (probably upper-middle). The relation, classed as a male-female clique (4⟵⟶27), terminated with her failure to marry the man. The third example, "Old Family," indicates how the upper-upper class (Position 1, in particular) is related back into the past through its knowledge of lineage. The graveyard "which is truly our home," the old houses with their memories, and the genealogical records are ever-present reminders of the class symbols of Position 1. Families in Positions 2 and 3 also use these symbols to maintain status, but their attitudes must necessarily vary because other members of the immediate family are below them in different positions (i.e., 2⟵⟶12 or 3⟵⟶13 ⟵⟶26) and need different attitudes for successful adjustments.

The "New Family" sketch presents a much more complex social situation and involves a larger number of positions. When the Starrs drove home and had dinner, they were in Position 18. The relations between the father and his son and daughter, as well as those of the mother and her child, mentioned throughout the narrative, are also in this context (Position 18). Some of the facts to be noticed in these relationships are the father's failure to get his son into his own business, the mother's trying to marry her daughter off or to get her in the House and Home Club, and the general situation indicated by their way of life.

After dinner Mr. Starr went down to the Lowell Club, an exclusively male association, where conversation similar to that at the tea took place. Mr. Starr was in Position 13 at the Lowell Club; Mr. French was again in 26; and the upper-upper members present were in 3. The manifest attitudes could not have been as freely and as explicitly expressed in the discussion had members of lower classes been present. For example, Mr. Flaherty's evaluation of what had taken place at the Veterans' meeting would have needed considerable revision had members of the lower-middle class who belonged to the Veterans been present. This becomes immediately apparent in the Veteran's sketch and indicates that because of difference in composition the behavior of Class Type 5 varies from that of Class Type 3.

When Mr. Starr left the Lowell Club he was accompanied by two lower-upper members. They were, then, an informal grouping in Position 18. The behavior of upper-middle Mr. French in 26, it seems likely, is understood by assuming from his other observed behavior that his frustrated desire to join the February Club was stimulated by the departure of the lower-upper members of the Lowell and February clubs. The statement that he was "too young," we find, is often used in our society as a convenient symbol of (and for) subordination.

At the February Club Mr. Starr and his companion found both upper-upper and lower-upper members present. He was now in Position 12, the upper-uppers in Position 2. This discussion group expresses the values of the two classes when they are together and indicates the type of interaction which occurs when the two levels meet and the participants are older men in a formal association. The upper-upper members tend to talk of family history, and the lower-uppers of history generally, when historical matters pertaining to the town are considered. On the other hand the lower-uppers when alone ordinarily discuss economic questions.[1]

Mrs. Starr's clique relations with Miss Churchill (2⟷12) were referred to in the first scene when the House and Home Club was said to be distressed by the controversy over the lower-upper woman's admittance into the association. The clique was strong but dependent, at least in part, on a reciprocity built up between these two women from unequal classes. It is true that Mrs. Starr's expensive gifts to Miss Churchill expressed her high esteem for her upper-upper friend (Family: Position 1) but they also functioned as symbols of the position of the two women. Equality in gift giving assumes some kind of exchange of objects of equal value. The value of Mrs. Starr's gifts lay not only in their price but also in their beauty and rarity, since they had been bought in Paris. Miss Churchill never returned objects of value. She had reciprocated through "her friendship" to Mrs. Starr. This seems an inadequate reward, but "her friendship" was a useful ladder for Mrs. Starr's social ambitions. Mrs. Starr's subordinate role, willingly played in all her clique relations with Miss Churchill, was the payment she

1. We have now discussed several situations of the Class Type 3 variety. Clearly, it is not difficult to acquire a large amount of data on: (1) behavior of different people in the same positions in the same event; (2) behavior of the same people in different events in the same position; (3) behavior of the same or different people in different events in the same or different structures.

A drawback in the present research is, however, that we acquired our interview material before arriving at our present knowledge of the positional system. We did not formulate the system as an analytical device until after the field work was completed.

made for advancement into the social world Miss Churchill had entered at birth. Probably Mrs. Starr was far more conscious of the realities of the situation than Miss Churchill. A mobile person tends to become conscious of social place by movement from one position to another, and as he or she moves through them is likely to develop a certain objectivity toward his or her own behavior. Mrs. Starr could exploit the clique relation only within limits. When she attempted to capitalize on her intimacy with Miss Churchill in a wider sphere, she was not wholly successful; for the social power of her upper-upper friend was controlled by the actions of the other upper-class women who were involved (1←→1; 1←→2; etc.). Miss Churchill alone could not swing open the social doors of the House and Home Club for Mrs. Starr's daughter. The jealous competition of the other lower-upper women also operated to prevent further consolidation of the social gains made by the Starr family.

Johnny Starr (Family: Position 18) visited his lower-upper friends (Clique: Position 18) the Uptons (Family: Position 18). His relations with the police indicated his superordinate position to the city's officers. The policeman, from one of the three lower positions in Class Type 11 (probably 67), was related to Johnny in Position 17 and acted accordingly. It is interesting to notice that in the sketches of the Riverbrookers the police behavior was very different, in fact almost opposite, since the truant officer was in Position 51 and the Riverbrooker in Position 81. Furthermore, the policeman threatened the Riverbrooker with an appearance before Judge Black (Family: 37; and political position: 32). The political position of Johnny, 17, would have been higher than the judge's had he been called before him.

The conversation in the Uptons' clique brings out some of the values and attitudes of the lower-upper people when there are no representatives of higher or lower classes present. Their conversation was very different from that of the upper-upper clique of Mrs. Breckenridge. Clique 18 expressed its opposition to the subordination of the upper-upper class through the antagonisms to the upper-upper reverence for things which are old. These antagonisms are the partial result of frustrating experiences of the lower-upper class with their class superiors.

The "poor Starr children" were the victims of the downward pressure of some of the upper-upper class. Johnny's behavior was filled with escape symbols. In all likelihood this symbolic behavior reflected his desire to free himself from a social maze in which he felt himself trapped. He went to Europe to be an artist. In this he tried to follow the path of upward mobility and escape by the use of his talent, but his talent failed him. The trip to Rome provided temporary release from the unpleasant realities of Yankee City. It was an escape. He dreamed of going to Tahiti—a popular European and American symbol of a place where the social restraints that control individuals are relaxed. He sought women below his own class and thereby escaped; and at the same time he drank enough for alcoholic release. Finally he threatened to go to a psychiatrist in the hope that he might be relieved of the painful social pressures which weighed down his life.

The Uptons belonged to a number of clubs which included Class Types 3, 5, 9, and 11.[2]

Katherine Starr's Girl Scout group was in Class Type 19. It included Positions 25, 36, 56, 71, and 81; however, the membership was drawn almost entirely from the last two positions in the lower class. Miss Starr was instructing the children in ethical and social codes of the middle and upper classes. Her superordinate role gave her a status which commanded respect from the lower groups and stimulated their mobile interests.

On the way home Miss Starr visited an upper-upper friend (2⟷12), and their conversation typified the interests of women of their age of the upper classes. The joking of the upper-upper women about the superfluity of men would not have been appreciated if the actual dearth of upper-class men in Yankee City had not been familiar to them all. Its significance would not have been understood by women of classes below them. When Katherine went home (Family: 18) she, too, symbolically expressed her desire to escape and thought of getting away from the immediate present. She read the *National Geographic* and wondered if she might not be able to take a trip to Egypt. Katherine Starr ultimately adjusted to Yankee City by becom-

2. The class composition of such associations as the Woman's Club, the Garden Club, the Rotary Club, etc., will not be given because of the authors' desire not to divulge the social ranking of these groups.

ing active in the philanthropic organizations of the town. These organizations do good to others and by so doing usually subordinate those they help. They put the lower-upper persons in such positions as 16, 17, 22, and 25.

The "New Family" system of interaction is more complex than the previous ones analyzed. Some of the important interactive situations are listed below in the chart (Chart VIII) which diagrams the behavior just analyzed.

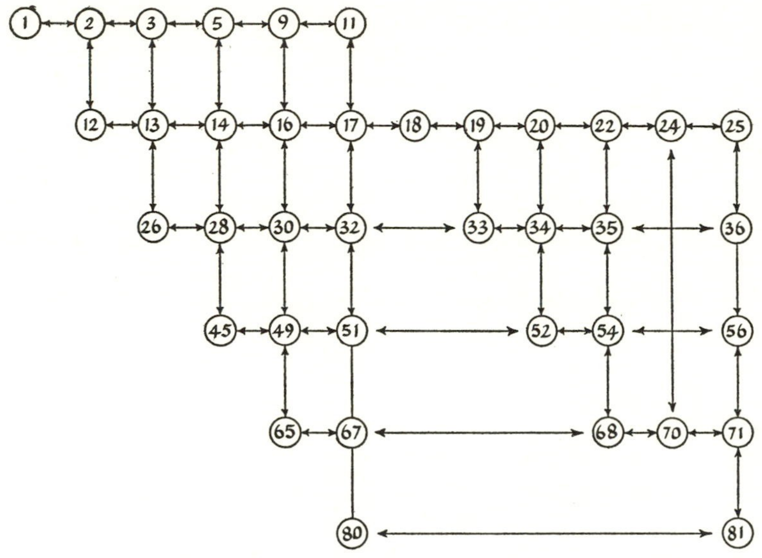

VIII. *Interactive System of the "New Family"*

Before referring to the size of the several positions involved in the interactive system of the "New Family" sketch we shall analyze the behavior at the election of the Patriotic Order of the United States Veterans of All Wars. The membership of this association extended from the upper-upper class through all the other strata (11, 17, 32, 51, 67, and 80). The evidence indicates that the most active members were from the three lower classes, principally from the lower-middle. The bulk of the membership also was from these three classes.

As in most of the associations with extended class membership, the officials of the Veterans' Order were not from the highest classes but from classes below the top. When the crisis occurred which threatened to develop into an open scandal, the members of the three upper classes organized as an informal group (3←→13←→26) to influence opinion within the association and change the officials in the Order. We learned that the ministers' association (3←→13←→26) had condemned the smokers, and one minister (Family: 1) had reported the happenings to Mr. Brooks Sinclair at a meeting of the February Club (2←→12). The ministers in their association had been influenced and were influencing their parishioners in Class Type 11 (11←→17←→32←→51←→67←→80), Class Type 19 (25←→36←→56←→71←→81), and Class Type 24 (41←→59←→74←→82). Through the ministers' association the leaders of the several church organizations were interrelated in one primary group. Their power in a small, well-integrated community was not inconsiderable. The members of the six classes came to a meeting of the Order from family positions which were largely 1, 18, 37, 61, 78, and 89. When they entered the club room they changed from their former positions to those appropriate to Class Type 11. Mr. Mather Blaisdail, Mr. Brooks Sinclair, and Mr. Edward Marshall (Family: 1) changed to an associational membership in Position 11; Travis Upton and Paul Foley from 18 to 17; and Alexander French from 34 to 32. Tim Pinkham changed from 61 to 51, and Patrick Donaghue and Tim Kelley from 78 to 67. The Greens, Joneses, and Tylers changed from 89 to 80.

The most pronounced division in the Order was between the upper-middle and lower-middle classes. Leadership in the lower-middle class had to be supplanted by the numerically less powerful three upper classes. The preparations by members of the three upper classes before the meeting included picking a lower-upper Catholic to run for president. Mr. Sinclair, informally representing the members from the higher strata, next saw the Reverend John Foreman (Clique: 2←→12) and asked him to intervene with the ministers' association (positions in Class Types 3, 11, 19, and 25). Because the minister (upper-upper) supported him, he was able to persuade his friend Flaherty (Clique: 4←→27) "to get hold of the boys at the Knights of St. Patrick's." Flaherty (Family: 37) went to the Knights (25←→36←→56←→71←→81) and "lined them up." French (Family: 37) was asked to see the Caribous (41←→59←→74←→82), and Flaherty the Antlers (5←→14←→28←→45), which had a large lower-middle-class membership. Thus Mr. Sinclair had access to a large number of members from all classes and was in a position of influence. His interactive situation is charted below (Chart IX).

Sinclair's Area of Participation

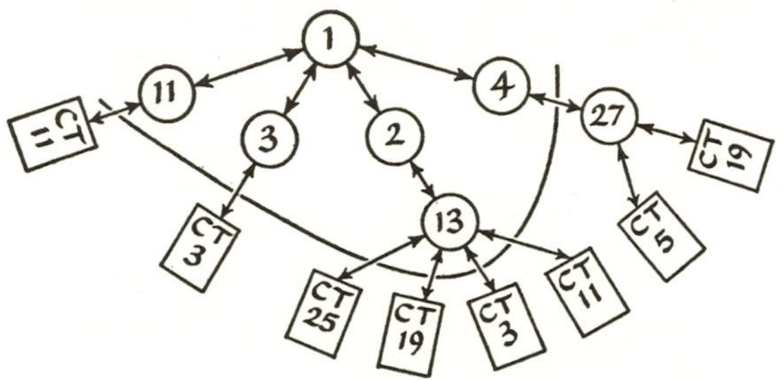

IX. *Interactive System of the Sinclairs*

Mr. Edward Marshall led the group publicly. He made the speech to sponsor Mr. Foley. He felt it his duty to come "at least for the elections." In Position 1 Mr. Marshall resembled Mr. Breckenridge in his behavior and expressed similar ideas, sentiments, and attitudes; but when his membership changed from 1 to 11 his behavior changed to fit the new social situation. He was now in an organization which extended throughout the society. The situation was one of explicit social equality and demanded democratic behavior. All the outward and more explicit behavior at the meeting was of this type, but other behavior betrayed the class situation. Some of the behavior indicative of this was the president's (51) getting up and going over to Marshall (11). Marshall, by the etiquette of politeness, indicated their equality by asking the president to sit down beside him. Mr. Pinkham entered the situation by offering a cigarette and having it accepted. Mr. Marshall reaffirmed the position of equivalence by lighting both their cigarettes with the same match (a reciprocal exchange).

The formal democratic and equalitarian symbols of the organization were expressed in the ritual preceding the election. Their comrades had sacrificed their lives in war for all our country. Bullets are no respecters of rank and kill rich and poor alike. And the dead men, whether rich or poor, were being equally honored. The symbols of equality included the flag, their country (in which they were all equal citizens), and a number of other integrating stimuli. The formal context for the election which followed was one of complete social equality.

Edward Marshall's speech emphasized these same elements. He was careful to insist that the former presidents (from lower classes) were all good men. He made a point of equality in race and creed. (The ethnic and non-Protestant religious groups are largely from the lower classes.) He emphasized the fact that a member of any ethnic or religious group could aspire to the highest office of the Veterans'—and that his candidate was an Irish Catholic, as well as a man for whom the Irish and the Catholics had great respect. He used status differences, however, to advance the election of his candidate when he said that "they must all pull together in times of crises" (here he identified the prevailing economic crisis with the moral one in the Order) and when he declared that Foley's business leadership (and higher status) could be used to their advantage were he elected president. Then the speaker once more returned to the theme of equality which is a fundamental fiction (and part truth) of all such organizations: "Since each man has only *one* vote, we are all equal." But the prestige of his own position was introduced under this ideology of equality when he said, "I am going to cast *my* one vote for Paul [Foley]."

On the whole Marshall's behavior accents democratic ideals. The general behavior at the meeting also emphasizes these sentiments and beliefs. When Mr. Marshall is interacting in Positions 1, 2, or 3, his behavior is quite different. (Compare, for instance, the Lowell and February Club meetings. He was a member of these organizations.) It is not necessary to impute insecurity or hypocrisy to him or to others like him. The behavior of an individual changes as he shifts his position in the social structure. Individuals incapable of such shifts are improperly adjusted. Perhaps the likeliest interpretations of certain forms of insanity, drunkenness, and other social and antisocial conduct rest on assumptions of the inability of some individuals to adjust to the necessities of all given social situations. Some individuals are consciously more aware than others of social situations. The conversation after the election at Mr. Breckenridge's (3⟷13⟷26) indicates that all of them were partially aware of what had been done. The sentiments shifted here and the feelings of group unity and the interactions permitted shifted from a 3- to a 6-positional situation. There was still faintly present the belief in democracy and equality. The equalities were greater among men who had fewer class differences and were aware that they were more alike than were all the members of the Veterans' organization.

When John Burke and Tim Pinkham were at the meeting of the Order, they were in Position 51. They left in the company of Tom Rafferty and Will Carlton (Family: 78) and were temporarily in an informal clique grouping (62⟷76). In Caribou Hall they were in a formal grouping of four positions (41⟷59⟷74⟷82) and part of their conversation expressed attitudes of people in such positions. They were antagonistic to upper-middle French who, except on special occasions, rarely appeared at the club. Although French was not there, the effect of his membership was felt in the group. The democratic ideology was still influential, but class antagonisms were present.

The clique, consisting of Jones, Green, and Tyler (89), went down to the Three Mast Hall (63⟷77⟷86) where their position changed to 86. They were influenced by their surroundings although much of their behavior was of the clique type. The feeling that everyone was equal and alike, stimulated and reaffirmed at the meeting of the Order, now changed. Anti-Jewish feelings, influenced in part by class differences, were expressed. Antagonisms toward the three upper classes were apparent and lower-middle Pinkham was under criticism because of his superior behavior in the Three Mast Club. Pinkham occupied the same relatively high position in the club as French did in the Caribou.

In the morning each is found in his family position (Blaisdail: 1; Starr: 18; French: 37; Pinkham: 61). Pinkham's wife, we learn, belonged to the Art Club, where she was in Position 45 (5⟷14⟷28⟷45), and to the Woman's Auxiliary (Position 63). Some of her behavior becomes meaningful in these two contexts.

The chart shows Mrs. Pinkham in her family position (61);

her membership in Position 63 placed her in a superordinate role to the other members. Here she indicated her intimacy with women from the higher classes who also belonged to the Art Club. In Position 45 in the Art Club her role was reversed to that of the most subordinate in this interactive group. In Position 45 she felt uneasy in the company of—say, Mrs. Upton (Position: 14).

Mr. Sam Jones (Family: 89) was in a very subordinate position, and his fears of "someone doing something to him" illustrate a certain type of "hybrid" interaction between different types of organizations. He and his wife (see also "Clam Flats") were afraid of the truant officer (51), a representative of the city government (Class Type 11) and of the S.P.C.C. In the latter case the social context was exceedingly complicated. The girl who was field representative of the society was in an associational membership situation, while Mr. Jones was in a family context and both of them were in a political situation. This means that politically he was in 80 and she in 32; in his family he was in Position 89 and was being controlled by threats of local action which would put him in Position 80. The interactive situation between the girl and him jumped several classes (44⟷85). They were in a "hybrid" relationship of an informal family associational grouping.

The chart below (Chart X) diagrams the positions involved in the incident of the election and the several events which precede and follow it.

Even a brief perusal of the memberships in the positions involved in the system of interaction analyzed in the Veterans' sketch demonstrates that we have been dealing with a very large proportion of the system's membership. For example, in Class Type 11, Position 11 has 272 members; Position 17 has 310; Position 32, 2,185; 51, 4,636; 67, 3,915; and 80, 2,025. A random sample of some of the other large positions in the two lower classes shows that many of them are equally large.

The system of vertical interaction becomes more complex with the introduction of new ethnic and religious factors which are not found in the higher classes. The positions at the top, largely Yankee, are in interaction with positions farther down where a large proportion of the members are ethnic and have different religious faiths. Yankee dominance and the mainten-

Class Type 1 2 3 4 5 8 11 12 13 14 16 19 20 21 22 24 27 28 29 30 32 33 34

X. *Structural Analysis of the Election of the War Veterans*

Class Type 1. Families of upper-upper participants
Class Type 2. Cliques of upper-upper and lower-upper members
Class Type 3. The meeting at the Blaisdail home; the ministers' association
Class Type 4. Clique of Sinclair and French, etc.
Class Type 5. Antlers, Art Club
Class Type 8. Implied informal relations between Pinkham and Marshall
Class Type 11. The Veterans' Order; the city of Yankee City; school; certain churches
Class Type 12. Lower-upper cliques; lower-upper families
Class Type 13. Lower-upper and upper-middle cliques
Class Type 14. Cliques
Class Type 16. Associations
Class Type 19. Knights of St. Patrick's; certain churches
Class Type 20. Upper-middle families and cliques
Class Type 21. Lower-middle and upper middle cliques
Class Type 22. Cliques
Class Type 24. Caribou, Woman's Auxiliary
Class Type 27. S. P. C. C. girl and lower-lower Sam Jones
Class Type 28. Lower-middle families and cliques
Class Type 29. Lower-middle to upper-lower cliques
Class Type 30. Three Mast association
Class Type 32. Upper-lower family and clique
Class Type 33. Upper-lower to lower-lower cliques
Class Type 34. Lower-lower clique and family

ance of Yankee tradition are greatly aided by the superordinate positions occupied by representatives of this group. All the 272 members of Position 11 are Yankees; but in Position 17, 4.84 per cent are Irish; and in Position 32 about 12 per cent of the members are ethnic. In addition to the Irish there are French Canadians, Greeks, Jews, Armenians, and Italians present. Twenty-nine per cent of the members of 51 are ethnic; in addition to the ethnics in 32, Poles and Russians are also present. In Position 67 the ethnic membership (56.14 per cent) is larger than the native membership; 48.99 per cent of the members of 80 are ethnic. In addition to the other ethnic groups, Negroes are also present in this position (see Table 1). These complicating factors, which all add to the social differentiation of the system, are treated in Chapter IV.

3. Composition of the Eighty-Nine Positions

THE eighty-nine positions constituting the Yankee City status system contain 71,149 memberships or "members." The present section will be devoted to an examination and classification of the gross numbers in terms of the eighty-nine positions. It is evident that the memberships are not evenly divided throughout the system, for some behavioral positions have very few, others several thousand members.

This measurement allows us to refine our knowledge of the quantitative differences among all positions while giving us an exact picture of the number and kinds of interclass connections and of the kind of behavior that is usual in each of the classes. It also tells us the amount of membership influence among the positions within a vertical extension (class type).

These statistics are all concerned with the *relative* number of the positions' members in the total system, in class, and in class type. The total of each position's membership is determined by the number of members in each of the structures represented in the position.

The number and per cent of the members of each structure give the reader the amount of each kind of behavior in a given status. They tell, for instance, that most of the behavior in Position 26 is not familial but clique and associational, and that in Position 1 most of the behavior is of a family type and not associational. Only such an accounting provides us with the comparative analysis of this kind of behavior within the

TABLE 1

Membership in the Eighty-nine Positions

Positions	1	2	3	4	5	6	7	8	9	10	11
No. of members	522	361	399	73	140	1	10	22	51	13	272
Per cent of grand total	0.73	0.51	0.56	0.10	0.20	0.001	0.01	0.03	0.07	0.02	0.38
Rank order	30	38	35	56	53	81	77	71	61	76	43
Association	0.77	16.07	83.46		95.71				92.16		17.65
Clique	53.06	82.27	16.04	98.63	4.29	100.00	90.00	86.36		92.31	
Family	45.02	1.66	0.50	1.37				13.64			
Economic	1.15						10.00		7.84	7.69	0.74
School											1.47
Church											51.10
Political											29.04
Adult	91.96	96.68	94.74	91.78	98.57	100.00	60.00	59.09	98.04	46.15	88.60
Subadult	8.04	3.32	5.26	8.22	1.43		40.00	40.91	1.96	53.85	11.40
Male	44.06	47.09	36.34	56.16	34.29		40.00	31.82	41.18	76.92	38.97
Female	55.94	52.91	63.66	43.84	65.71	100.00	60.00	68.18	58.82	23.08	61.03

TABLE 1 (Continued)

Positions	1	2	3	4	5	6	7	8	9	10	11
Catholic											
Protestant	65.71	74.79	70.43	71.23	76.43	100.00	60.00	86.36	74.51	76.92	87.87
Jewish											
Greek											
None*	34.29	25.21	29.57	28.77	23.57		40.00	13.64	25.49	23.08	12.13
Native	100.00	100.00	100.00	100.00	100.00	100.00	100.00	100.00	100.00	100.00	100.00

* In all tables "none" refers to "no religion."

TABLE 1 (Continued)

Positions	12	13	14	15	16	17	18	19	20	21	22	23	24	25
No. of members	364	395	162	4	43	310	417	189	53	30	27	17	5	63
Per cent of grand total	0.51	0.56	0.23	0.01	0.06	0.44	0.59	0.27	0.07	0.04	0.04	0.02	0.01	0.09
Rank order	37	36	52	79	62	40	34	48	60	67	69	74	78	57
Association	10.99	71.65	93.21		93.02	18.71		0.53	15.09		40.74			61.90
Clique	88.46	28.10	6.79	100.00			44.60	87.30	73.59	76.66	51.85	100.00	100.00	
Family	0.55	0.25					54.20	11.64	5.66	16.67				
Economic					6.98	0.97	1.20	0.53	5.66	6.67	7.41			12.70
School						2.26								
Church						45.48								25.40
Political						32.58								
Adult	98.08	94.94	98.15	100.00	100.00	88.39	87.05	86.77	71.70	76.67	77.78	29.41	40.00	68.25
Subadult	1.92	5.06	1.85			11.61	12.95	13.23	28.30	23.33	22.22	70.59	60.00	31.75
Male	42.58	50.38	51.23	75.00	67.44	49.68	54.20	64.02	66.04	73.33	74.07	52.94	20.00	60.32
Female	57.42	49.62	48.77	25.00	32.56	50.32	45.80	35.98	33.96	26.67	25.93	47.06	80.00	39.68
Catholic	1.65	2.28	6.79			2.90	3.60	2.41	11.32	10.00	3.41	5.88		23.81

TABLE 1 (Continued)

Positions	12	13	14	15	16	17	18	19	20	21	22	23	24	25
Protestant	76.92	70.88	77.78	50.00	88.37	86.45	64.03	65.61	60.38	40.00	62.96	52.94	80.00	58.73
Jewish														
Greek														
None	21.43	26.84	15.43	50.00	11.63	10.65	32.37	26.98	28.30	50.00	29.63	41.18	20.00	17.46
Native	96.43	96.71	91.36	100.00	100.00	95.16	94.24	90.48	86.79	90.00	92.59	94.12	100.00	76.19
Ethnic(Irishonly)	3.57	3.29	8.64			4.84	5.76	9.52	13.21	10.00	7.41	5.88		23.81

TABLE 1 (Continued)

Positions	26	27	28	29	30	31	32	33	34	35	36	37	38	39	40	41	42	43	44
No. of members	632	90	585	19	230	37	2,185	232	311	125	524	2,229	1,063	634	204	419	22	33	13
Per cent of grand total	0.89	0.13	0.82	0.03	0.32	0.05	3.07	0.33	0.44	0.18	0.74	3.13	1.49	0.89	0.29	0.59	0.03	0.04	0.02
Rank order	27	55	28	72	45	64	11	44	39	54	29	10	23	26	47	33	71	66	76
Association	89.25		98.46		97.83		20.87	1.29	73.63	57.60	44.46		8.65	18.61		58.95			
Clique	10.28	93.33	1.54	68.42		94.59		93.54	24.44	32.80		24.76	76.58	77.61	89.71	25.30	77.27	87.88	84.62
Family	0.47	6.67						4.31	0.64			71.29	9.78	0.47	6.86	0.48	18.18	3.03	7.69
Economic				31.58	2.17	5.41	0.18	0.86	1.29	9.60	8.40	3.95	4.99	3.31	3.43	8.11	4.55	9.09	7.69
School							5.63									3.58			
Church							32.68				47.14					3.58			
Political							40.64												
Adult	97.31	90.00	97.26	68.42	93.48	67.57	87.46	92.67	95.18	72.80	80.73	83.80	82.22	72.56	69.12	63.72	86.36	63.64	76.93
Subadult	2.69	10.00	2.74	31.58	6.52	32.43	12.54	7.33	4.82	27.20	19.27	16.20	17.78	27.44	30.88	36.28	13.64	36.36	23.07
Male	38.92	55.56	54.19	47.37	64.78	67.57	46.04	68.53	60.77	51.20	54.39	48.77	62.94	61.67	65.69	53.98	68.18	75.76	30.76
Female	61.08	44.44	45.81	52.63	35.22	32.43	53.96	31.47	39.23	48.80	45.61	51.23	37.06	38.33	34.31	47.02	31.82	24.24	69.24
Catholic	5.54	4.44	7.18	5.26	9.13	10.81	6.73	6.47	3.54	15.20	40.65	10.01	9.13	24.60	26.47	21.00	4.55		

TABLE 1 (Continued)

Positions	26	27	28	29	30	31	32	33	34	35	36	37	38	39	40	41	42	43	44
Protestant	60.70	45.56	64.62	42.11	60.44	56.76	71.12	52.16	67.52	51.20	42.18	47.96	51.74	37.07	40.20	42.73	77.27	66.67	69.23
Jewish	0.63		0.51		1.74		0.41	1.29			0.19	0.72	0.47	2.84	0.49	3.10			
Greek					0.43		0.23					0.29	0.28	0.79		1.19			7.69
None	33.07	50.00	27.69	52.63	28.26	32.43	21.51	40.08	28.94	33.60	16.98	41.04	38.38	34.70	32.84	31.98	18.18	33.33	23.08
Native	90.35	83.33	88.38	84.21	83.91	78.38	88.10	84.91	92.61	77.60	57.25	81.74	84.29	63.09	62.25	64.20	100.00	100.00	76.93
Ethnic	9.65	16.07	11.62	15.79	16.09	21.62	11.90	15.09	7.39	22.40	42.75	18.26	15.71	36.91	37.75	35.80			23.07
Irish	8.22	16.67	9.92	15.79	11.75	18.92	9.57	13.80	6.43	22.40	41.99	15.40	14.39	31.71	36.28	29.60			7.69
French Canadian	0.32		0.68		0.87	2.70	0.82		0.32		0.19	0.94	0.38	0.63	0.49	1.67			
Jewish	0.95		0.68		2.17		0.55	1.29			0.38	1.03	0.47	3.15	0.98	3.10			
Italian			0.17				0.09		0.32			0.22		0.16					
Greek	0.16		0.17		0.43		0.73		0.32		0.19	0.54	0.47	1.10		1.43			15.38
Armenian					0.87		0.14					0.13		0.16					
Polish																			
Russian																			
Negro																			

TABLE 1 (Continued)

Positions	45	46	47	48	49	50	51	52	53	54	55	56	57	58	59	60	61	62	63	64
No. of members	507	1	18	16	171	73	4,636	461	40	170	29	1,758	1,348	1,393	1,620	37	5,673	2,513	1,464	300
Per cent of grand total	0.71	0.001	0.03	0.02	0.24	0.10	6.52	0.65	0.06	0.24	0.04	2.47	1.89	1.96	2.28	0.05	7.97	3.53	2.06	0.42
Rank order	31	81	73	75	50	56	4	32	63	51	68	14	19	18	15	64	2	7	16	42
Association	99.80				95.32		13.76	86.34		54.71		30.43	19.73	18.59	52.10		0.51	3.78	23.02	
Clique	0.20	100.00	88.89	87.50		98.63		12.58	67.50	40.00	100.00		67.95	78.25	19.14	89.19	17.96	81.09	73.90	89.00
Family				12.50				0.43	22.50				7.57	0.72	0.12	2.70	77.72	12.50	0.96	8.33
Economic			11.11		4.68	1.37	0.63	0.65	10.00	5.29		15.24	4.75	2.44	11.05	8.11	3.81	2.63	2.12	2.67
School							11.19								5.12					
Church							27.80					54.33			12.47					
Political							46.62													
Adult	94.09	100.00	55.55	50.00	85.96	75.34	79.34	94.79	72.50	73.53	31.03	75.48	76.34	71.57	64.50	89.19	75.92	60.33	58.06	47.33
Subadult	5.91		44.45	50.00	14.04	24.66	20.66	5.21	27.50	26.47	68.97	24.52	23.66	28.43	35.50	10.81	24.08	39.67	41.94	52.67
Male	67.06		27.78	50.00	50.29	71.23	49.40	66.59	62.50	48.24	41.38	50.91	54.15	50.83	51.66	86.49	51.01	51.69	51.98	62.67
Female	32.94	100.00	72.22	50.00	49.71	28.77	50.60	33.41	37.50	51.76	58.62	49.09	45.85	49.17	48.34	13.51	48.99	48.31	48.02	37.33
Catholic	12.82		11.11	25.00	11.11	27.40	12.70	8.90	15.00	30.59	6.90	54.78	17.14	27.57	27.10	5.41	15.32	25.94	28.56	18.33

TABLE 1 (Continued)

Positions	45	46	47	48	49	50	51	52	53	54	55	56	57	58	59	60	61	62	63	64
Protestant	32.74		38.89	43.75	50.30	23.29	55.41	44.25	37.50	43.53	62.07	25.48	39.84	30.37	25.86	56.75	32.17	25.87	25.27	28.67
Jewish	2.56				6.43	2.74	2.61	1.08	2.50	1.76		0.34	3.56	7.61	13.27	2.70	4.78	9.27	3.55	2.33
Greek	0.20						0.13	0.22							0.86		0.12	0.16	0.07	0.33
None	51.68	100.00	50.00	31.25	32.16	46.57	29.15	50.55	45.00	24.12	31.03	19.40	39.46	34.45	32.91	35.14	47.61	38.76	42.55	50.34
Native	72.98	100.00	72.22	56.25	75.44	53.42	71.35	87.20	72.50	55.29	31.03	39.31	69.58	48.82	42.41	86.49	63.90	44.25	42.14	52.67
Ethnic	27.02		27.78	43.75	24.56	46.58	28.65	12.80	27.50	44.71	68.97	60.69	30.42	51.18	57.59	13.51	36.10	55.75	57.86	47.33
Irish	16.56		11.11	31.25	14.05	41.10	19.16	7.16	17.50	36.47	24.14	53.48	22.93	37.54	32.64	8.11	23.11	36.41	39.69	27.67
French*	5.13		11.11	12.50	1.75	1.37	4.12	3.47	7.50	3.53	44.83	3.75	2.30	3.16	8.09		4.41	5.65	7.72	10.67
Jewish	2.96				6.44	2.74	2.85	1.30	2.50	2.35		0.40	3.86	7.82	13.40	2.70	5.47	9.67	4.17	3.66
Italian	1.38				0.58		0.86			1.18		1.76	0.82	1.87	1.36	2.70	1.41	1.51	2.25	1.33
Greek	0.20				0.58		0.39	0.22					0.07	0.07	1.05		0.48	0.52	0.20	1.33
Armenian	0.59		5.56		0.58	1.37	1.12	0.43		1.18		0.91	0.37	0.36	0.80		0.95	1.43	2.94	1.67
Polish	0.20						0.11	0.22				0.28	0.07	0.36	0.19		0.05	0.36	0.82	0.67
Russian					0.58		0.04					0.11			0.16		0.18	0.20	0.07	
Negro																	0.04			0.33

* In all tables "French" and "French Canadian" are used interchangeably.

TABLE 1 (Continued)

Positions	65	66	67	68	69	70	71	72	73	74	75	76	77	78	79
No. of members	53	59	3,915	208	36	3	2,483	972	182	2,478	54	2,832	2,122	6,275	1,287
Per cent of grand total	0.07	0.08	5.50	0.29	0.05	0.004	3.49	1.37	0.26	3.48	0.07	3.98	2.98	8.82	1.81
Rank order	60	58	5	46	65	80	8	24	49	9	59	6	12	1	20
Association	96.23		9.27	22.60			26.26	13.99		52.99		4.17	23.32	0.08	1.94
Clique		96.61		75.00	100.00	100.00		81.48	87.36	13.44	79.63	72.95	67.39	18.33	86.09
Family								1.23	7.69	0.04	1.85	20.69	1.23	79.54	11.66
Economic	3.77	3.38	0.77	2.40			9.95	3.19	4.95	13.64	18.52	2.19	0.94	2.06	0.31
School			16.27							8.56					
Church			18.75				63.79			11.34					
Political			54.94												
Adult	71.70	67.80	75.48	78.85	36.11	66.67	73.86	69.34	42.86	64.93	40.74	57.03	60.46	67.62	44.99
Subadult	28.30	32.20	24.52	21.15	63.89	33.33	26.14	30.66	57.14	35.07	59.26	42.97	39.54	32.38	55.01
Male	26.42	69.49	53.97	38.94	63.89	66.67	46.40	53.70	56.04	50.61	29.63	50.67	49.86	49.50	59.21
Female	73.58	30.51	46.03	61.06	36.11	33.33	53.60	46.30	43.96	49.39	70.37	49.33	50.14	50.50	40.79
Catholic	9.43	37.29	24.98	47.60	36.11		73.54	37.35	34.62	35.83	22.22	37.54	34.26	27.62	32.17

TABLE 1 (Continued)

Positions	65	66	67	68	69	70	71	72	73	74	75	76	77	78	79
Protestant	62.27	15.25	34.79	14.90	41.67		10.19	16.66	24.18	12.23	20.37	15.64	15.93	15.54	13.75
Jewish			1.74	0.48	2.78		0.36	3.29	5.49	7.18	1.85	5.61	0.94	2.93	1.79
Greek			0.46						2.20	2.99	3.70	0.46	0.66	1.27	5.59
None	28.30	47.46	38.03	37.02	19.44	100.00	15.91	42.70	33.51	41.77	51.86	40.75	48.21	52.64	46.70
Native	73.58	42.37	43.86	24.04	22.22	100.00	15.87	30.56	32.42	21.91	37.04	29.48	27.24	33.69	22.38
Ethnic	26.42	57.63	56.14	75.96	77.78		84.13	69.44	67.58	78.09	62.96	70.52	72.76	66.31	77.62
Irish	16.98	49.16	36.76	69.23	38.89		71.29	54.94	47.80	41.41	25.93	48.34	45.94	39.86	41.11
French	7.55	3.39	9.42	3.85	11.11		7.05	6.58	6.59	20.58	11.11	7.21	14.66	11.51	9.71
Jewish			2.48	0.48	2.78		0.44	4.73	6.59	7.79	7.41	7.31	1.51	4.14	2.80
Italian			1.46	0.96			2.82	0.93		1.57	1.85	2.68	1.89	2.31	3.73
Greek		1.69	1.72				0.24	0.51	2.75	4.32	9.26	1.20	2.26	3.71	10.02
Armenian	1.89	3.39	3.14	1.14	25.00		0.72	1.54	3.30	1.01	5.55	2.86	4.85	2.69	2.41
Polish			0.58				1.41	0.21	0.55	.89		0.67	0.99	1.15	5.28
Russian			0.58				0.16			0.52	1.85	0.21	0.66	0.94	2.56
Negro												0.04			

TABLE 1 (Continued)

Positions	80	81	82	83	84	85	86	87	88	89
No. of members	2,025	871	1,278	26	37	16	1,413	307	1,280	5,179
Per cent of grand total	2.85	1.22	1.80	0.04	0.05	0.02	1.99	0.43	1.80	7.28
Rank order	13	25	22	70	64	75	17	41	21	3
Association	7.70	15.96	35.28				31.07		6.64	0.33
Clique			11.66	88.46	70.27	75.00	67.02	87.95	82.27	15.66
Family			0.08	3.85	2.70	6.25	0.64	9.77	10.78	83.37
Economic	0.30	14.12	26.06	7.69	27.03	18.75	1.27	2.28	0.31	0.64
School	24.54		11.58							
Church	22.42	69.92	15.34							
Political	45.04									
Adult	63.80	61.31	53.76	84.64	62.16	62.50	54.92	46.91	42.58	61.69
Subadult	36.20	38.69	46.24	15.38	37.84	37.50	45.08	53.09	57.42	38.31
Male	55.51	50.75	52.58	84.62	54.05	68.75	52.30	57.33	61.72	53.20
Female	44.49	49.25	47.42	15.38	45.95	31.25	47.70	42.67	38.28	46.80
Catholic	10.62	63.04	18.08	11.54	18.92	6.25	14.51	14.98	18.98	13.69

TABLE 1 (Continued)

Positions	80	81	82	83	84	85	86	87	88	89
Protestant	36.30	16.76	9.39	30.76	16.22	12.50	13.45	28.66	12.34	12.30
Jewish	0.44		2.58			6.25	0.85	0.33	0.70	0.73
Greek	2.07	0.34	12.13	3.85	2.70	25.00	4.32	1.30	9.06	2.94
None	50.57	19.86	57.82	53.85	62.16	50.00	66.87	54.73	58.92	70.34
Native	51.01	26.41	25.90	65.38	35.13	12.50	34.32	47.56	25.08	37.21
Ethnic	48.99	73.59	74.10	34.62	64.87	87.50	65.68	52.44	74.92	62.79
Irish	14.62	25.48	14.16	7.70	10.81		18.05	16.93	14.45	11.55
French Canadian	13.53	10.45	24.26	7.69	21.63	12.50	15.36	10.10	12.03	14.44
Jewish	0.44		2.58			6.25	0.85	0.33	0.70	0.77
Italian	1.73	3.10	2.90	7.69	5.41	6.25	3.61	3.26	3.44	3.01
Greek	3.60	0.69	14.71	11.54	8.10	25.00	6.86	3.58	12.97	6.47
Armenian	3.11	1.15	1.17		8.11	12.50	3.18	0.33	1.95	1.87
Polish	7.51	27.90	10.95		8.11	6.25	14.01	11.72	22.73	19.17
Russian	1.88	1.49	2.74			6.25	3.26	3.91	5.00	3.15
Negro	2.57	3.33	0.63		2.70	12.50	0.50	2.28	1.65	2.36

position. It is necessary to know the comparative proportion of each structure's members held by a given position within the class and within the class type. This is also given for each position. When these facts are known, the behavior within a class is further defined, since, in addition to knowing the general relative membership statistics of a position in the class, we are aware of how much a class's family behavior is of this kind and not of that kind. We know, for instance, that almost none of the family behavior in the upper-middle class is in position 26 but that the vast preponderance of it is in Position 37. We immediately have a fairly exact comparative quantification of what kind of behavior is found in each structure within each class.

Our knowledge of the percentage and rank order of each structure in each position of a class type further defines the relative place of the position among the other classes and specifies the amount of each kind of social connection it has with the other five classes.

Table 1 presents a general statistical summary of the composition of each position. The vertical column at the left lists the items considered in the horizontal one at the top. The number of members for each position appears first. The per cent of the grand total and the rank order give the relative size of the position. The percentages listed for the seven structures are statements of the proportional amounts of structural members in each position. For example, there are 272 members in Position 11: 17.65 per cent belong to associations, none to clique and family, 0.74 per cent to economic institutions, 1.47 per cent to the school, 51.10 per cent to the church, and 29.04 per cent to the political organization.

The factors of age, sex, religious faith, and ethnicity are treated similarly. For example, in Position 80, there are 2,025 members: 51.01 per cent are native (Yankee), and 48.99 per cent are from all other ethnic groups. Of the 2,000-odd members, 14.62 per cent are Irish, 13.53 per cent French-Canadian, and only 0.44 per cent Jewish. The native Yankees, therefore, have a far larger membership than any other ethnic group.[3]

3. See Appendix 1 for a detailed description of one position which accounts for the interrelation of structures and characteristics. The remainder of the eighty-nine are treated in full in Volume VI, *Data Book for the Yankee City Series*.

III

THE SEVEN STRUCTURES IN THE SYSTEM

1. Membership in Each of the Seven Structures

THE previous chapter described the characteristic structural composition of each separate position and the relative proportions among the different types of membership. It did not view them, however, as a total system of interconnected statuses. The task of this chapter is to examine the amount of differentiation each of the seven structures undergoes in each of the six classes and in the whole system, and to compare them accordingly. It will also analyze the amount of status differentiation in the six classes, and give the membership by structure in each class.

In all six classes in the social system of Yankee City members participating in the family, clique, and associational structures were more numerous than those in economic, school, church, and political organizations.

The vertical column in Table 2 lists the six classes and the grand total; the horizontal column, the seven structures. The vertical rank order for each structure grades the classes according to the percentage of the structure found in each class. For instance, there are 17,415 family members in Yankee City; 247 (1.4 per cent of the total) are in the upper-upper class and give that class a rank order of sixth for family members. The horizontal percentages and rank orders show how each structure compares with the others in a given class. It will be instructive to compare the horizontal rank orders among the six classes.

Among the eighty-nine positions[1] there are thirty-five[2] which have no association members; sixteen[3] with no clique members;

1. Because of the exigencies of space and to make comparison easier, the distribution of the percentages in all positions (where a given structure was present) was divided by deciles and the results of the analysis have been placed in the Appendix.

2. Positions 4, 6–8, 10, 15, 18, 21, 23–24, 27, 29, 31, 37, 40, 42–44, 46–48, 50, 53, 55, 60, 64, 66, 69–70, 73, 75, 83–85, and 87.

3. Positions 9, 11, 16–17, 25, 30, 32, 36, 49, 51, 56, 65, 67, 71, and 80–81.

TABLE 2

The Total Membership of Each of the Seven Structures in the Six Classes

	Family	Clique	Association	Economic	School	Church	Political	Total
UU	1.4 (6) 13.3 (3) 247	3.4 (6) 40.6 (1) 757	4.8 (6) 33.5 (2) 624	0.5 (6) 0.8 (6) 14	0.02 (6) 0.2 (7) 4	1.8 (6) 7.5 (4) 139	1.3 (6) 4.2 (5) 79	2.6 (6) 1,864
LU	1.5 (5) 12.5 (3) 259	4.1 (5) 43.1 (1) 897	4.9 (5) 30.4 (2) 631	1.0 (5) 1.3 (6) 27	0.3 (5) 0.3 (7) 7	2.1 (5) 7.6 (4) 157	1.6 (5) 4.9 (5) 101	2.9 (5) 2,079
UM	10.0 (4) 18.1 (3) 1,739	12.4 (4) 28.6 (2) 2,744	21.9 (3) 29.4 (1) 2,815	10.7 (4) 3.0 (6) 287	6.1 (4) 1.4 (7) 138	12.9 (4) 10.2 (4) 976	14.1 (4) 9.3 (5) 888	13.5 (4) 9,587
LM	28.1 (2) 22.0 (2) 4,890	31.9 (2) 31.7 (1) 7,041	32.3 (1) 18.7 (3) 4,163	34.5 (1) 4.2 (6) 925	26.8 (3) 2.7 (7) 602	32.3 (2) 11.0 (4) 2,446	34.3 (1) 9.7 (5) 2,161	31.2 (2) 22,228
UL	33.2 (1) 25.2 (2) 5,781	33.2 (1) 31.9 (1) 7,333	26.1 (2) 14.6 (3) 3,356	33.2 (2) 3.9 (6) 890	37.8 (1) 3.7 (7) 849	34.3 (1) 11.3 (4) 2,599	34.2 (2) 9.4 (5) 2,151	32.3 (1) 22,959
LL	25.8 (3) 36.2 (1) 4,499	14.9 (3) 26.5 (2) 3,291	10.0 (4) 10.4 (3) 1,287	20.1 (3) 4.3 (7) 539	28.7 (2) 5.2 (6) 645	16.6 (3) 10.1 (4) 1,259	14.5 (3) 7.3 (5) 912	17.5 (3) 12,432
Total	24.5 (2) 17,415	31.0 (1) 22,063	18.1 (3) 12,876	3.8 (6) 2,682	3.2 (7) 2,245	10.6 (4) 7,576	8.8 (5) 6,292	71,149

thirty-nine[4] with no family members; twenty-one[5] which have no economic participation; seventy-nine[6] in which there is no school participation; seventy-four[7] with no church participation; and eighty-three[8] which have no political participants.

Of the total members in Yankee City, 22,063 (31.0 per cent) belonged to cliques; 17,415 (24.5 per cent) to the family structure; 12,876 (18.1 per cent) to associations; 7,576 (10.6 per cent) to the church structure; 6,292 (8.8 per cent) to political organizations; 2,682 (3.8 per cent) to economic organizations; and 2,245 (3.2 per cent) to the school structure.

The family structure ranked third highest in the two upper classes and the upper-middle; second in the lower-middle and upper-lower classes; and first in the lower-lower class.

The clique ranked first in the two upper classes, the lower-middle and upper-lower classes; second in the upper-middle and lower-lower classes.

The association held the largest percentage of members in the upper-middle class, the second largest percentage in the two upper classes, and ranked third for members of the three lower classes.

The economic structure ranked sixth for all classes but the lower-lower, in which it ranked seventh.

The school ranked seventh with all classes except the lower-lower, where it ranked sixth.

The church structure ranked fourth for all six classes, and the political structure stood fifth in all.

2. Status Differentiation by Structure and Class

The membership analysis just given does not tell how the different structures are differentiated by class, nor does it describe the further elaboration of status when structural differentiation within each position is considered. It is possible to discover how much the different structures and classes contribute to the elaboration of the status system. If each of the seven structures appeared in all the eighty-nine positions,

4. Positions 5–7, 9–11, 14–17, 22–25, 28–32, 35–36, 45–47, 49–51, 54–56, 65–71, and 80–81.

5. Positions 2–6, 8, 12–15, 23–24, 26–28, 45–46, 48, 55, and 69–70.

6. All positions except 11, 17, 32, 41, 51, 59, 67, 74, 80, and 82.

7. All positions except 11, 17, 25, 32, 36, 41, 51, 56, 59, 67, 71, 74, and 80–82.

8. All positions except 11, 17, 32, 51, 67, and 80.

TABLE 3

The Number of Times the Seven Structures Appeared in the Six Classes

	Family	Clique	Association	Economic	School	Church	Political	Total
UU	10.0 (5) 17.9 (3) 5	12.3 (5) 32.1 (1) 9	11.1 (5) 21.4 (2) 6	7.4 (5) 17.9 (3) 5	10.0 (2) 3.6 (4) 1	6.7 (3) 3.6 (4) 1	16.7 (1) 3.6 (4) 1	10.1 (5) 28
LU	12.0 (4) 15.8 (4) 6	15.1 (4) 28.9 (1) 11	16.7 (4) 23.7 (2) 9	11.8 (4) 21.1 (3) 8	10.0 (2) 2.6 (6) 1	13.3 (2) 5.3 (5) 2	16.7 (1) 2.6 (6) 1	13.8 (4) 38
UM	24.0 (1) 19.7 (2) 12	21.9 (2) 26.2 (1) 16	20.4 (2) 18.0 (3) 11	23.5 (1) 26.2 (1) 16	20.0 (1) 3.3 (5) 2	20.0 (1) 4.9 (4) 3	16.7 (1) 1.6 (6) 1	22.1 (2) 61
LM	22.0 (2) 17.7 (4) 11	23.3 (1) 27.4 (1) 17	22.2 (1) 19.4 (3) 12	23.5 (1) 25.8 (2) 16	20.0 (1) 3.2 (6) 2	20.0 (1) 4.8 (5) 3	16.7 (1) 1.6 (7) 1	22.5 (1) 62
UL	16.0 (3) 16.3 (4) 8	16.4 (3) 24.5 (2) 12	18.5 (3) 20.4 (3) 10	19.1 (2) 26.5 (1) 13	20.0 (1) 4.1 (6) 2	20.0 (1) 6.1 (5) 3	16.7 (1) 2.0 (7) 1	17.8 (3) 49
LL	16.0 (3) 21.1 (2) 8	11.0 (6) 21.1 (2) 8	11.1 (5) 15.8 (3) 6	14.7 (3) 26.3 (1) 10	20.0 (1) 5.3 (5) 2	20.0 (1) 7.9 (4) 3	16.7 (1) 2.6 (6) 1	13.8 (4) 38
Total	18.1 (4) 50	26.4 (1) 73	19.6 (3) 54	24.6 (2) 68	3.6 (6) 10	5.4 (5) 15	2.2 (7) 6	276

there would be a total of 623 statuses, whereas there are less than one half this number. This may be shown by counting the number of positions in which a given structure is present in each class and then adding the totals for all seven structures.

The seven structures appeared in the six classes in the social system of Yankee City 276 times (see Table 3). Of this total the clique, occurring 73 times, ranked first (26.4); the economic structure appeared 68 times (24.6); the association 54 times (19.6); the family 50 times (18.1); the church 15 times (5.4); the school 10 times (3.6); and the political structure 6 times (2.2).

Table 3 is set up like Table 2 and may be analyzed in the same way.[9]

9. See Appendix 2 for fuller analysis of the structural composition of positions.

IV

THE ETHNIC GROUPS IN THE STATUS SYSTEM

1. The Characteristics of Each Position

THE previous chapter described and analyzed the structural membership of the positions and provided enough information to allow the investigator to entertain certain expectancies about the kind of social behavior to be found in the structure. He may also infer something of the problems facing individual members and how they may attempt to solve them.

But such information is not sufficient. An adult woman in the upper-upper class acts differently and in a different status from an adult man. An ethnic lower-lower-class child who is a Catholic or a Jew will view his social world far differently from a Protestant Yankee of the same age and sex. A Catholic Irishman is the target of attitudes which differ from those aimed at a Catholic Pole.

The problems to be solved by the researcher here become enormously complex and of a different order. Let us first ask the questions to which we wanted answers at this point in our research. In general we asked: What are the characteristics of each position (age, sex, religion, and ethnic affiliation)? How is each characteristic distributed through the membership of the six classes? What are the interrelations of the memberships in the seven structures and the four characteristics of all the positions? Instead of having the memberships of but seven structures to account for the researcher now had to deal with two sexes, two ages, five types of religious affiliation, and ten ethnic groups.

In this chapter we shall examine first the participation of the ten ethnic groups in the social system of Yankee City. The volume in the Yankee City Series called *The Social Systems of American Ethnic Groups* is largely concerned with the study of the internal organization and changing functions of the several ethnic groups. The present chapter is not directly interested in these problems; it is concerned with questions of how, where, and why ethnic individuals are members of the whole status system of Yankee City. A mass of observable variations in social usage distinguishes ethnic groups from that part of the community which has inherited and developed Yankee customs. In some cases the observable differences are biologically as well as culturally determined. Since the individuals who compose the several ethnic groups function as interacting members of the larger society it is necessary—if one is to understand the place of ethnics in the community—to take account of them as members of the status system.

For this purpose we shall look upon "ethnicity" as one of the several characteristics which modify the social system and are modified by it. The other characteristics to be considered are age, sex, and religion. From one point of view each is a *trait* possessed by the individuals who compose the interactive units of the social aggregate. Each characteristic (by the classification and evaluation of the members of the community) separates the individual from some classes of individuals and identifies him with others.

Sex and age can be reduced to primarily biological facts which, when evaluated by the group, fit into a social context. Ethnicity may be evaluated almost entirely upon a biological basis or upon purely social characteristics. Negroes tend to be at the first extreme, since they are most physically variant of all groups in the community, and the Irish at the other extreme, since they are most like the native white stock. The Yankee City Negro's culture comes from a Yankee tradition, but the group's biological differences provide a symbol around which social differences are defined and evaluated. The Irish maintain certain social usages which differentiate them in varying degrees from the whole community. The other groups fall in between these two extremes.

2. The Members of the Ten Ethnic Groups in the Class System

TABLE 4 records the number of natives and of all ethnics in each class. Table 5 examines the ten ethnic groups to discover the percentage of each in each class. The natives outnumbered all other groups and appeared in every class. The Irish came next and were present in all but the upper-upper; the French,

Jewish, Italian, Greek, and Armenian groups had members in all classes except the two upper ones. The Poles, Russians, and Negroes had no members in the three uppermost classes.

TABLE 4

Yankees and Ethnics in the Class System

Class	Native			Ethnic			Total	
UU	5.2	10.0	1,864				2.6	1,864
LU	5.4	94.0	1,954		6.0	125	2.9	2,079
UM	21.6	81.2	7,787	0.4	18.8	1,800	13.5	9,587
LM	35.9	58.2	12,943	5.1	41.8	9,285	31.2	22,228
UL	19.3	30.4	6,970	26.4	69.6	15,989	32.3	22,959
LL	12.5	36.2	4,505	45.5	63.8	7,927	17.5	12,432
Total		50.6	36,023	22.6	49.4	35,126		71,149

Natives predominated in all classes except the upper-lower where they ranked second to the Irish. The Irish predominated in the upper-lower class and ranked second in the lower-upper and two middle classes. The Poles ranked second in the lower-lower class, and Jews ranked third in the upper-middle and lower-middle classes. The French were third in the upper-lower and lower-lower classes. The French ranked fourth in the upper-middle and the lower-middle classes, the Jews were fourth in the upper-lower, and the Irish fourth in the lower-lower class. The Greeks ranked fifth in the upper-middle, upper-lower, and lower-lower classes, with the Italians ranking fifth in the lower-middle class. The Italians were sixth in the

TABLE 5

The Members of the Ten Ethnic Groups in the Class System

Class	Native	Irish	French	Jewish	Italian	Greek	Armenian	Polish	Russian	Negro	Total
UU	5.2 100.0 1,864										2.6 1,864
LU	5.4 94.0 1,954	0.6 6.0 125									2.9 2,079
UM	21.6 81.2 7,787	7.7 16.3 1,567	1.2 0.7 66	4.2 1.0 95	0.9 0.1 10	3.2 0.6 53	0.8 0.1 9				13.5 9,587
LM	35.9 58.2 12,943	31.3 28.5 6,336	19.5 4.8 1,072	51.8 5.3 1,183	25.6 1.3 296	5.2 0.4 87	21.8 1.1 239	2.0 0.2 47	4.0 0.1 22	1.2 0.01 3	31.2 22,228
UL	19.3 30.4 6,970	51.5 45.5 10,440	45.8 11.0 2,516	39.4 3.9 900	42.1 2.1 487	38.4 2.9 640	53.6 2.6 589	11.1 1.1 263	28.0 0.7 153	0.4 0.004 1	32.3 22,959
LL	12.5 36.2 4,505	8.9 14.4 1,795	33.5 14.8 1,837	4.6 0.8 105	31.5 2.9 365	53.2 7.1 886	23.8 2.1 261	86.9 16.5 2,057	68.0 3.0 372	98.4 2.0 249	17.5 12,432
Total	50.6 36,023	28.5 20,263	7.7 5,491	3.2 2,283	1.6 1,158	2.3 1,666	1.5 1,098	3.3 2,367	0.8 547	0.4 253	71,149

upper-middle class while the Armenians were sixth in the lower-middle and upper-lower classes, and the Russians had the same ranking in the lower-lower class. The Armenians were seventh and last in the upper-middle class. The Italians were seventh in the upper-lower and lower-lower classes. The Poles ranked eighth in the lower-middle and upper-lower classes and the Armenians were eighth in the lower-lower class. The Russians were ninth in the lower-middle and upper-lower classes; the Negroes were ninth in the lower-lower class. The Negroes were tenth in the lower-middle and upper-lower classes, and the Jews were tenth in the lower-lower class.

This analysis shows that of all groups (not including the Yankees) the Irish had the largest percentage in all classes except the lower-lower, where they ranked fourth and were preceded by the French and the Polish groups. Irish membership did not concentrate in the lower-lower class as did some of the others and, while it had the largest number of the members of the upper-lower class, was also distributed in three other classes above this. This analysis also indicates that the Jews had very few members in the lower-lower group despite the fact that their total membership ranked fifth among all the ethnic groups. They ranked tenth in the lower-lower class, third in the two middle classes, and fourth in the upper-lower class. No Jewish member was found above the upper-middle class. On the other hand the French Canadians ranked third in numbers in the total system and fourth in the two middle classes. The Poles, while they ranked fourth in total numbers, came eighth in the lower-middle and upper-lower classes and second in the lower-lower class.

The largest percentage of the Irish members, a little over half (51.5), was in the upper-lower class. The second largest group was found in the lower-middle class (31.3 per cent); the third largest, in the lower-lower class (8.9 per cent); fourth, in the upper-middle class (7.7 per cent); and fifth, in the lower-upper class (0.6 per cent). In comparison with the natives the Irish were not quite as differentiated in the class system; they tended to be lower on the whole than the natives, since the largest group of Irish was in the upper-lower class and the largest group of natives in the lower-middle class. While the second largest group of Irish was in the lower-middle, the second largest group of natives was in the upper-middle class. The third largest group of Irish was found in the lower-lower class, and the third largest group of natives in the upper-lower class.

Let us now compare the other ethnic groups with the Irish. The largest number of Irish, as we have said, were in the upper-lower class. This was also true of the French, Italians, and Armenians, but the Greeks, Poles, Russians, and Negroes had their largest concentrations in the lower-lower group. The second largest number of Irish were in the lower-middle class, like the Negroes; but this constituted only 1.2 per cent (3 members) of the Negroes whereas it included 31.3 per cent or 6,336 of the Irish.

Most of the Jews, like most of the native Yankees, were in the lower-middle class. They were the only ethnic group which ranked so high. The Jews, Greeks, Poles, and Russians had their second largest concentration in the upper-lower class, and the French Canadians, Italians, and Armenians had theirs in the lower-lower class. The third largest concentration of the French Canadians, Italians, Greeks, Armenians, Poles, and Russians was in the lower-middle class; that of the Negroes in the upper-lower class; and that of the Irish and Jews in the lower-lower class.

Let us now compare the ranking of each class according to ethnic membership with the ranking of that class in the total population. The upper-lower class led (see Table 5) with 32.3 per cent of the population and the largest concentrations of Irish, French, Italians, and Armenians. The natives' and Jews' first place was above it (in the lower-middle class), and that of the Greeks, Poles, Russians, and Negroes was below it (in the lower-lower class).

The second largest membership was in the lower-middle class (31.2 per cent), which contained the second largest concentrations of Irish and Negroes. The natives' second place was above it, that of the Jews, Greeks, Poles, and Russians one class below it, and that of the French Canadians, Italians, and Armenians two classes below it.

The lower-lower class ranked third in total membership (17.5 per cent), and contained the third largest concentrations of Irish and Jews. The natives' and Negroes' third place was above it in the upper-lower class, while that of the French, Italians, Greeks, Armenians, Poles, and Russians was in the lower-middle class.

Native memberships were most numerous and most widely distributed through the class system. Then came Irish and French. Although there were more than twice as many French as there were Jews, Italians, Greeks, and Armenians, they were no more widely distributed in the class system than those groups, and had fewer members in the upper-middle class than the Jews and but little more than the Greeks. The Jews as a group tended to rank high and to have fewer members in the lower-lower class, while the Poles, Russians, and Negroes were the least differentiated groups of all, tending to be heavily concentrated in the lower-lower class.

With the completion of this analysis we are equipped with certain expectancies regarding the participation of the ten ethnic groups in each class. We may expect to find a large number of natives in each class but of course a larger number in the lower than in the upper classes. Since their distribution approximates most closely that of the natives, we shall expect to find the Irish acting more like the natives than any other group. We shall then expect to find the French, Jewish, Italian, Greek, and Armenian groups somewhat resembling the Irish, but showing fewer similarities to natives, with the Jews more like the natives and Irish than the others; and finally we will look for the Polish, Russian, and Negro groups in the three lower classes, with little participation above the lowest of the six classes.

3. The Members of the Ten Ethnic Groups in the Seven Structures

The problem which now concerns us is to determine how the ten ethnic groups participated in the seven social structures. We wish to discover what structural differences, if any, existed among the several groups, in order to learn something of the social pressures which help to determine inclusion and exclusion in the seven structures. An analysis of the ethnic membership in all the seven structures throughout the total system will indicate general structural differences in the ten ethnic groups. We can then seek to determine how the class factor affects these structural totals. Do the higher classes differ from the lower in the structural participation of the individuals in them; and is there a relationship between the differences in membership and differences in comparative rank of a class? Let us turn to an analysis of the membership of the ethnic groups in the social structures, as given in Table 6.

A higher proportion of Yankees than of any other ethnic group belonged to associations. Then came the French Canadians, Jews, Irish, Armenians, Negroes, Italians, Poles, Greeks, and Russians, in that order.

The Poles, Greeks, and Russians were all among the more recent arrivals in the community. Many of them were excluded from associations which were available to the members of the older ethnic groups and to the Yankees. The comparatively high position of the Negroes is in part due to their having their own associations and in part to the longer period of their settlement in the community. An examination of the associations to which Jews belonged indicates that they were using them for social mobility. This is also true of the Irish. The high place of the French on the list is due to their joining the several religious associations in large numbers as well as belonging to several economic and insurance organizations.

The Russians led all others in the proportion of their members who belonged to cliques. Then came the Irish, Greeks, Poles, Armenians, Jews, Italians, Yankees, French Canadians, and Negroes.

A larger proportion of the Poles were family members than of any other ethnic group. The Negroes were second, then the Italians, Russians, Greeks, French Canadians, Armenians, Yankees, Jews, and Irish.

A larger proportion of Greeks participated in the economic order than of any other ethnic group. The Italians and French tied for second place. Then came the Armenians, Yankees, Irish, Jews, Poles, Russians, and Negroes.

A higher proportion of Russians than of any other group were school members. The Poles were second, then the Greeks, French Canadians, Armenians, Jews, Italians, Negroes, Irish, and Yankees.

The Jews outranked all others in the proportion of members in the church structure. The Poles were second, then the Irish,

TABLE 6

The Ten Ethnic Groups in the Seven Structures

Total	Association	Clique	Family	Economic	School	Church	Political	Totals
Yankee	20.90 58.48 7,530	28.89 47.16 10,406	24.39 50.45 8,786	3.83 51.49 1,381	2.32 37.19 835	9.94 47.25 3,580	9.73 55.71 3,505	36,023
Irish	15.89 25.00 3,219	34.64 31.81 7,019	21.49 25.01 4,355	3.34 25.24 677	3.17 28.60 642	11.91 31.85 2,413	9.56 30.80 1,938	20,263
French	16.97 7.24 932	27.63 6.88 1,517	29.34 9.25 1,611	4.92 10.07 270	4.94 12.07 271	7.83 5.68 430	8.38 7.31 460	5,491
Jewish	16.64 2.95 380	31.84 3.30 727	22.03 2.89 503	3.33 2.83 76	3.68 3.74 84	17.08 5.15 390	5.39 1.95 123	2,283
Italian	13.90 1.25 161	30.66 1.61 355	30.40 2.02 352	4.92 2.13 57	3.63 1.87 42	9.93 1.52 115	6.56 1.21 76	1,158
Greek	10.08 1.30 168	34.03 2.57 567	29.41 2.81 490	6.18 3.84 103	6.60 4.90 110	10.86 2.39 181	2.82 0.75 47	1,666

TABLE 6 (Continued)

Total	Association	Clique	Family	Economic	School	Church	Political	Totals
Armenian	15.12 1.29 166	33.24 1.65 365	26.50 1.67 291	4.64 1.90 51	4.01 1.96 44	10.75 1.56 118	5.74 1.00 63	1,098
Polish	10.31 1.89 244	33.67 3.61 797	32.95 4.48 780	2.28 2.01 54	7.06 7.44 167	11.96 3.74 283	1.77 0.67 42	2,367
Russian	6.95 0.30 38	45.52 1.13 249	30.16 0.95 165	1.65 0.34 9	7.50 1.83 41	7.31 0.53 40	0.91 0.08 5	547
Negro	15.02 0.30 38	24.11 0.28 61	32.41 0.47 82	1.58 0.15 4	3.56 0.40 9	10.28 0.34 26	13.04 0.52 33	253
Totals	12,876	22,063	17,415	2,682	2,245	7,576	6,292	71,149

Greeks, Armenians, Negroes, Yankees, Italians, French Canadians, and Russians.

The Negroes led all others in the proportion of their members who were voters or officeholders. The Yankees were second, then the Irish, French Canadians, Italians, Armenians, Jews, Greeks, Poles, and Russians.

A brief analysis of the proportion of each ethnic group in the several structures reveals how it is participating in the social structures of Yankee City. The Negroes, for instance, had a smaller proportion of their members in the economic order than any other ethnic group, indicating in all likelihood definite exclusion of the Negro from jobs which other ethnics are able to get. Since the Poles and Russians follow them rather closely and are the most recent arrivals, meeting with the greatest prejudice, it seems highly probable that these groups too are being excluded from jobs. The Greeks may seem to contradict this, but it must be remembered that a fair proportion of the Greeks are in other enterprises than factories and that they have a reputation for being skilled workmen. The statement holds though for the Italians, Armenians, and French Canadians.

A further examination of the Negro's participation in the social structure shows that, whereas he ranked last in the economic order, he ranked first in the proportion of his members in the political system, indicating again that he attempts to use his ballot to further his own interests or to participate on a plane of equality in the one place which is open to him among the several general structures of Yankee City. This is borne out by his ranking second in the family organization where the membership is largely involuntary and not a matter of someone's else deciding who shall join. The rank order of the other ethnic groups in political organization follows very closely the period of time they have been in the community and have had opportunity to become citizens. The Yankees were second to the Negroes, followed by the Irish, French, Italians, Armenians, Jews, Greeks, and Poles; and the Russians, the last ethnic component to enter the community, had the smallest proportion of voters or officeholders.

An examination of the Russians' membership in the several structures shows that they ranked last in the political organization, last in associations, last in the church, and were eighth in the economic order. On the other hand, they were first in the clique, first in the school, and fourth in the family. What evidence there was showed that the Russians were excluded from many associations, that they were not wanted by many managers of economic enterprises, and that they had no church of their own in the community. Our investigators discovered that they banded together in small and large cliques where they found an outlet for their social interests.

The Polish story is in many respects similar to that of the Russians but with certain significant deviations. They ranked very low in the proportion of their members who were in associations and in economic and political institutions. Their exclusion from these structures is explained by the same factors which prevented the Russians from freer participation. The Catholic Church, while it had no Polish priests in the community, made a definite effort to keep the Poles in the church by having occasional missions when Polish priests were brought in from the outside to conduct the services. The evidence also showed that the Poles were stronger believers in their faith than were the Russians. The Poles, like the Russians, were high in their family, school, and clique participation.

The Armenians, who occupied a rather favorable position for ethnic members of the community, possessed an intermediate position—fifth or sixth—in the rank order of all the structures except the economic and the family where they were third and seventh.

The Greeks participated very little in the political structure and in associations. On the other hand they ranked high in the economic order, school system, the clique, and the church.

The Italians ranked comparatively low as association, clique, church, and school members, comparatively high in the family and economic order, and intermediate as political members.

The Jews ranked low in the family and in the political system, high in association and church organizations, and intermediate in all other structures.

The French Canadians ranked low in the church and clique but comparatively high in the association, economic, school, and political structures.

The Irish ranked low in the school and family organizations, and high in all institutions except the economic order where they held an intermediate position. The natives ranked high in associations, economic institutions, and in the political system of Yankee City, low in the clique, family, school, and church structures.

On the whole, when the members of an ethnic group participated in high proportions in associations, they seemed also to favor political participation; and when they were disproportionately low as political members, they were disproportionately low as members of associations.

The Yankees, Irish, French Canadians, and Negroes all participated in proportionately high numbers as voters. All except the Negroes were proportionately high as associational members. On the other hand the Italians, Greeks, Poles, and Russians had very little participation in associations and in the political system. The Armenians and Italians had an intermediate proportion of their members in political and associational structures. The Jews, however, were comparatively low as political members and comparatively high in associations, the reverse of the Negroes in these two types of structures. The Negro appears to be excluded from associations and seeks refuge in political action, while the Jew, though partially excluded, still finds ample opportunity to solve many of his social problems by becoming a member of an association. He seems to experience less need of political activity.

4. The Members of the Ten Ethnic Groups in the Class and Structure Systems

The last two analyses have told the amount of ethnic membership in each class and structure. Now what is the structural differentiation in each of the six classes and how does class affect participation by ethnic group in each structure? We shall make a sample examination of the membership in the *lower-lower* class.

A larger percentage of the Negro members belonged to associations in the lower-lower class than did any other ethnic group (see Table 7). The French Canadians were second, then the Armenians, Irish, Italians, Yankees, Poles, Greeks, Russians, and Jews.

The Russians led all other ethnic groups in proportion of

TABLE 7

Ethnic Groups in the Seven Structures of the Lower-Lower Class

LL	Association	Clique	Family	Economic	School	Church	Political	Totals
Yankee	9.77 34.19 440	22.64 30.99 1,020	38.85 38.90 1,750	5.39 45.08 243	3.86 26.98 174	9.37 33.52 422	10.12 50.00 456	4,505
Irish	11.87 16.55 213	25.91 14.13 465	32.42 12.94 582	3.62 12.06 65	4.12 11.47 74	11.20 15.97 201	10.86 21.38 195	1,795
French	12.36 17.64 227	23.08 12.88 424	38.43 15.69 706	4.74 16.14 87	6.15 17.52 113	7.02 10.25 129	8.22 16.56 151	1,837
Jewish	1.90 0.16 2	25.71 0.82 27	32.38 0.76 34	0.95 0.19 1	6.67 1.09 7	30.48 2.54 32	1.90 0.22 2	105
Italian	11.51 3.26 42	23.29 2.58 85	43.01 3.49 157	5.48 3.71 20	4.93 2.79 18	6.85 1.99 25	4.93 1.97 18	365
Greek	9.14 6.29 81	32.17 8.66 285	31.94 6.29 283	6.43 10.56 57	6.88 9.46 61	12.19 8.58 108	1.24 1.21 11	886

TABLE 7 (Continued)

LL	Association	Clique	Family	Economic	School	Church	Political	Totals
Armenian	2.41 11.88 31	1.85 23.37 61	2.07 35.63 93	2.23 4.60 12	2.48 6.13 16	3.26 15.71 41	0.77 2.68 7	261
Polish	14.69 9.19 189	20.72 33.16 682	15.76 34.47 709	8.35 2.19 45	23.10 7.24 149	19.38 11.86 244	4.28 1.90 39	2,057
Russian	1.86 6.45 24	5.59 49.46 184	2.31 27.96 104	0.93 1.34 5	3.72 6.45 24	2.46 8.33 31	— —	372
Negro	2.95 15.26 38	1.76 23.29 58	1.80 32.53 81	0.74 1.61 4	1.40 3.61 9	2.07 10.44 26	3.62 13.25 33	249
Totals	1,287	3,291	4,499	539	645	1,259	912	12,432

their members in cliques; then came the Poles, Greeks, Irish, Jews, Armenians, Negroes, Italians, French, and Yankees.

A larger proportion of the Italians than of any other ethnic group were members of the family structure, followed by the Yankees, French, Armenians, Poles, Negroes, Irish, Jews, Greeks, and Russians.

The Greeks held the highest proportion of economic members in the lower-lower class. Then came the Italians, Yankees, French, Armenians, Irish, Poles, Negroes, Russians, and Jews.

The percentage of Polish members belonging to the school structure was higher than that of any other ethnic group. The Greeks were second, then the Jews, Russians, French, Armenians, Italians, Irish, Yankees, and Negroes.

In the church structure the Jews led, followed by the Armenians, Greeks, Poles, Irish, Negroes, Yankees, Russians, French, and Italians.

The Negroes ranked highest in the proportion of their members belonging to political organizations. The Irish ranked second, then the Yankees, French, Italians, Armenians, the Poles and Jews, and the Greeks.

Let us now briefly analyze the proportion of each ethnic group in the several structures in the lower-lower class.

The Negro ranked first in proportion of members in associations and political organizations, intermediate in the family and church structures, and comparatively low in their clique, economic, and school participation.

The Russians were first in clique membership, high as school members, comparatively low in associational, family, economic, and church participation, and had no political membership in this class.

The Poles ranked low in the association, economic, and political structures, intermediate as to family members, and high in the clique, church, and school structures.

The Armenians were intermediate in all structures except the association, family, and church organizations, where they ranked comparatively high.

The Greeks held a very high position in the clique, economic, school, and church structures, but participated very little in the other structures.

The Italians were very high in the rank order of their family and economic membership, intermediate as associational and political participants, and comparatively low in the clique, school, and church structures.

As school and church members the Jews ranked very high. They were intermediate in the clique structure, and comparatively low as associational, family, economic, and political participants.

The French possessed a high ranking in the association, family, economic, and political structures, an intermediate position as members of the school system, and participated very little in cliques and church organizations.

The Irish ranked comparatively high as associational, clique, and political members, were intermediate as economic and church members, and low in the family and school structures.

The Yankees occupied a very low position in the clique, school, and church organizations, and were intermediate in associations. On the other hand, they ranked very high as family, economic, and political members.

Tables 8 to 11 provide the material for a similar analysis of each of the other classes, omitting only the upper-upper.

5. *Ethnic Status Differentiation in the Seven Structures*

The memberships in Yankee City society were classified in 276 behavioral situations, determined by counting the number of types of social situations found in each position. (See pages 69 to 71.) Some of the ten ethnic groups participated in most of the 276 places, others in only a few of them. The following questions now arise: (1) How many additional places were there because of the ten ethnic groups? (2) How many places did each group occupy? (3) What structures were used by each group and in what proportion?

The 276 places were increased to 1,095 by the ethnic factor, as can be seen in Table 12.

The natives were the most differentiated ethnic group in their participation in the seven structures, followed by the Irish, French, and Jews; and the Negroes were the least differentiated. The clique appeared in more positions than any other structure in the Positional System of Yankee City.

Let us now compare the use of each structure by each ethnic group with the general average. The clique ranked first among

TABLE 8

The Ethnic Groups in the Seven Structures of the Upper-Lower Class

UL	Association	Clique	Family	Economic	School	Church	Political	Totals
Yankee	28.04 13.50 941	27.44 28.87 2,012	35.01 29.04 2,024	33.03 4.22 294	27.56 3.36 234	27.47 10.24 714	34.91 10.77 751	6,970
Irish	47.47 15.26 1,593	48.36 33.97 3,546	39.54 21.90 2,286	36.97 3.15 329	41.70 3.39 354	49.94 12.43 1,298	48.07 9.90 1,034	10,440
French	14.06 18.76 472	9.89 28.82 725	11.16 25.64 645	15.17 5.37 135	13.19 4.45 112	7.85 8.11 204	10.37 8.86 223	2,516
Jewish	2.83 10.56 95	3.76 30.67 276	4.19 26.89 242	4.16 4.11 37	4.12 3.89 35	6.39 18.44 166	2.28 5.44 49	900
Italian	1.64 11.29 55	2.09 31.42 153	2.46 29.16 142	2.47 4.52 22	2.36 4.11 20	2.54 13.55 66	1.35 5.95 29	487
Greek	1.94 10.16 65	3.40 38.91 249	2.98 26.88 172	4.38 6.09 39	4.71 6.25 40	2.04 8.28 53	1.02 3.44 22	640

TABLE 8 (Continued)

UL	Association	Clique	Family	Economic	School	Church	Political	Totals
Armenian	13.92 82 2.44	37.52 221 3.01	25.64 151 2.61	3.90 23 2.58	3.74 22 2.59	9.17 54 2.08	6.11 36 1.67	589
Polish	16.35 43 1.28	34.60 91 1.24	25.48 67 1.16	3.04 8 0.90	6.46 17 2.00	13.31 35 1.35	0.76 2 0.09	263
Russian	6.54 10 0.30	38.56 59 0.80	33.99 52 0.90	1.96 3 0.34	9.80 15 1.77	5.88 9 0.35	3.27 5 0.23	153
Negro	—	100.00 1 0.01	—	— —	—	— —	— —	1
Totals	3,356	7,333	5,781	890	849	2,599	2,151	22,959

TABLE 9

The Ethnic Groups in the Seven Structures of the Lower-Middle Class

LM	Association	Clique	Family	Economic	School	Church	Political	Totals
Yankee	19.57 60.85 2,533	28.36 52.14 3,671	23.84 63.09 3,085	4.45 62.27 576	2.40 51.49 310	10.62 56.21 1,375	10.76 64.46 1,393	12,943
Irish	16.18 24.62 1,025	37.34 33.60 2,366	19.24 24.93 1,219	3.63 24.86 230	2.98 31.39 189	11.71 30.34 742	8.92 26.15 565	6,336
French	20.15 5.19 216	33.30 5.07 357	22.57 4.95 242	4.29 4.97 46	4.20 7.47 45	8.21 3.60 88	7.28 3.61 78	1,072
Jewish	21.22 6.03 251	33.81 5.68 400	17.75 4.29 210	2.96 3.78 35	3.38 6.64 40	15.22 7.36 180	5.66 3.10 67	1,183
Italian	20.60 1.47 61	38.17 1.60 113	17.23 1.04 51	5.07 1.62 15	1.35 0.66 4	8.11 0.98 24	9.46 1.30 28	296
Greek	13.79 0.29 12	21.84 0.27 19	28.74 0.51 25	6.90 0.65 6	5.75 0.83 5	11.49 0.41 10	11.49 0.46 10	87

TABLE 9 (Continued)

LM	Association	Clique	Family	Economic	School	Church	Political	Totals
Armenian	20.50 49 1.18	34.73 83 1.18	18.41 44 0.90	6.28 15 1.62	2.51 6 1.00	9.62 23 0.94	7.95 19 0.88	239
Polish	25.53 12 0.29	51.06 24 0.34	8.51 4 0.08	2.13 1 0.12	2.13 1 0.17	8.51 4 0.16	2.13 1 0.05	47
Russian	18.18 4 0.10	27.27 6 0.09	40.91 9 0.18	4.55 1 0.12	9.09 2 0.33	— — —	— — —	22
Negro	— —	66.67 2 0.03	33.33 1 0.02	— —	— —	— —	— —	3
Totals	4,163	7,041	4,890	925	602	2,446	2,161	22,228

TABLE 10

The Ethnic Groups in the Seven Structures of the Upper-Middle Class

UM	Association	Clique	Family	Economic	School	Church	Political	Totals
Yankee	30.65 84.80 2,387	27.07 76.82 2,108	18.44 82.58 1,436	2.93 79.44 228	1.39 78.26 108	10.09 80.53 786	9.43 82.66 734	7,787
Irish	23.10 12.86 362	37.20 21.25 583	16.15 14.55 253	3.32 18.12 52	1.47 16.67 23	10.15 16.29 159	8.62 15.20 135	1,567
French	25.76 0.60 17	16.67 0.40 11	27.27 1.04 18	3.03 0.70 2	1.52 0.72 1	13.64 0.92 9	12.12 0.90 8	66
Jewish	33.68 1.14 32	25.26 0.87 24	17.89 0.98 17	3.16 1.05 3	2.11 1.45 2	12.63 1.23 12	5.26 0.56 5	95
Italian	30.00 0.12 3	40.00 0.15 4	20.00 0.12 2	—	—	—	10.00 0.11 1	10
Greek	18.87 0.36 10	26.42 0.51 14	18.87 0.58 10	1.89 0.35 1	7.55 2.90 4	18.87 1.02 10	7.55 0.45 4	53

TABLE 10 (Continued)

UM	Association	Clique	Family	Economic	School	Church	Political	Totals
Armenian	0.14 44.44 4	—	0.17 33.33 3	0.35 11.11 1	—	—	0.11 11.11 1	9
Polish	—	—	—	—	—	—	—	—
Russian	—	—	—	—	—	—	—	—
Negro	—	—	—	—	—	—	—	—
Totals	2,815	2,744	1,739	287	138	976	888	9,587

TABLE 11

The Ethnic Groups in the Seven Structures of the Lower-Upper Class

LU	Association	Clique	Family	Economic	School	Church	Political	Total
Yankee	95.88 30.96 605	93.42 42.89 838	94.20 12.49 244	96.30 1.33 26	71.43 0.26 5	91.72 7.37 144	91.09 4.71 92	1,954
Irish	4.12 20.80 26	6.58 47.20 59	5.79 12.00 15	3.70 0.80 1	28.57 1.60 2	8.28 10.40 13	8.91 7.20 9	125
Total	631	897	259	27	7	157	101	2,079

TABLE 12

Social Differentiation by Structure of the Ten Ethnic Groups

	Native	Irish	French	Jewish	Italian	Greek	Armenian	Polish	Russian	Negro	Total Memberships
Family	(17.0) 34.1 / 45	(13.2) 19.7 / 26	(8.3) 8.3 / 11	(10.5) 7.6 / 10	(9.3) 6.1 / 8	(10.0) 6.8 / 9	(11.1) 7.6 / 10	(8.5) 4.5 / 6	(11.1) 3.8 / 5	(8.3) 1.5 / 2	(12.0) 132
Clique	(27.3) 22.5 / 72	(27.9) 17.2 / 55	(30.1) 12.5 / 40	(30.5) 9.1 / 29	(27.9) 7.5 / 24	(30.0) 8.4 / 27	(32.2) 9.1 / 29	(29.6) 6.6 / 21	(31.1) 4.4 / 14	(37.5) 2.8 / 9	(29.2) 320
Association	(20.5) 20.0 / 54	(22.8) 16.7 / 45	(24.1) 11.9 / 32	(27.4) 9.6 / 26	(29.1) 9.3 / 25	(27.8) 9.3 / 25	(27.8) 9.3 / 25	(29.6) 7.8 / 21	(24.4) 4.1 / 11	(25.0) 2.2 / 6	(24.7) 270
Economic	(25.0) 31.4 / 66	(22.3) 21.0 / 44	(21.1) 13.3 / 28	(15.8) 7.1 / 15	(16.3) 6.7 / 14	(14.4) 6.2 / 13	(15.6) 6.7 / 14	(11.3) 3.8 / 8	(11.1) 2.4 / 5	(12.5) 1.4 / 3	(19.2) 210
School	(3.4) 17.6 / 9	(4.6) 17.6 / 9	(5.3) 13.7 / 7	(4.2) 7.8 / 4	(5.8) 9.8 / 5	(5.6) 9.8 / 5	(3.3) 5.9 / 3	(7.0) 9.8 / 5	(6.7) 5.9 / 3	(4.2) 2.0 / 1	(4.7) 51
Church	(4.5) 15.8 / 12	(6.6) 17.1 / 13	(8.3) 14.5 / 11	(7.4) 9.2 / 7	(7.0) 7.9 / 6	(7.8) 9.2 / 7	(5.6) 6.6 / 5	(9.9) 9.2 / 7	(13.3) 7.9 / 6	(8.3) 2.6 / 2	(6.9) 76
Political	(2.3) 16.7 / 6	(2.5) 13.9 / 5	(3.0) 11.1 / 4	(4.2) 11.1 / 4	(4.7) 11.1 / 4	(4.4) 11.1 / 4	(4.4) 11.1 / 4	(4.2) 8.3 / 3	(2.2) 2.8 / 1	(4.2) 2.8 / 1	(3.3) 36
Total	24.1 / 264	18.0 / 197	12.1 / 133	8.7 / 95	7.9 / 86	8.2 / 90	8.2 / 90	6.5 / 71	4.1 / 45	2.2 / 24	1,095

all groups but the Italians, the Negroes using it proportionately oftener than any other ethnic group. They were followed by the Armenians, Russians, Jews, French, Irish, Italians, and last of all the native Yankees, with 27.3 per cent.

The association ranked second for the average number of places. It was used by the ten ethnic groups in the eighty-nine positions. It also ranked second for the Irish, French, Jews, Greeks, Armenians, Russians, and Negroes; tied for first place with the clique in the Polish group; ranked first among the Italians; but dropped to third place among the natives. Of the total number of places where the seven structures were used by the ten ethnic groups, the association had 24.7 per cent. The Poles used it most, then the Italians, Greeks, Armenians, Irish, French, and lastly the natives with 20.5 per cent. Let us stop a moment and attempt to ascertain what these figures mean in the actual context of the Positional System. Since the natives were less differentiated in the clique and association, and the Irish tended to be so too, it follows that the natives used associations and cliques which extended through fewer classes than those used by the other ethnic groups. Since this is counter to the more extended differentiation of the natives and Irish in the six classes, it indicates that natives and Irish, in their use of the clique and association, were probably more able to exercise their class consciousness and sense of exclusiveness than were the other groups.

In the economic organization the average participation of the ten ethnic groups was 19.2 per cent, ranking third among the seven structures. The ranking was the same for the Irish, French, Jews, Italians, Greeks, Armenians, and Negroes; fourth for the Russians; and second for the natives and the Poles.

The family ranked fourth (12.0 per cent) in the average number of places where the seven structures were used in the total system, and fourth for each of the ten ethnic groups. It was most differentiated among the natives, followed by the Irish, Armenians, and Russians. It was least differentiated in the Negro group.

The church ranked fifth in the average for the ten ethnic groups, and for the natives, Irish, Jews, Italians, Greeks, and

Armenians separately, while it was fourth for the French and Negroes, and third for the Poles and Russians.

The average ranking for the use of the school by the ten ethnic groups was sixth. The natives, Irish, Jews, Italians, and Greeks had this average; for the French, Poles, Russians, and Negroes it was fifth.

The political organization had an average ranking of seventh for the ten ethnic groups, and the same for the natives, Irish, Italians, and Greeks separately; for the French, Jews, Armenians, Poles, and Russians it ranked sixth; and for the Negroes fifth.

This whole analysis demonstrates that the natives are the most differentiated both among the seven structures and within each structure. The only exception to this is in the church, where they rank second to the Irish. The Negroes and Russians tend to be the least differentiated both among the seven structures and in each structure. Again, the amount of membership in the structures is shown to be correlated with the population: as the number of individuals increases there is a tendency for the complexity of the social structure to increase, and vice versa. However, other factors are involved since we have demonstrated earlier that the Jews, although a smaller group than some of the others, are more differentiated in class, while the Poles, although more numerous, are less differentiated than such groups as the Italians and Jews.

6. Ethnic Status Differentiation in the Six Classes

We now know how the ten ethnic groups use the seven social structures in the six classes and in the whole status system, but not how many structural places in each class they occupy. Of the 1,095 social places in the Positional System of Yankee City in which the ten ethnic groups are found, only 28 are in the upper-upper class (2.6 per cent). (See Table 13.) Sixty-two of them are in the lower-upper class (5.7 per cent); 170 are in the upper-middle class (15.5 per cent); 306 (27.9 per cent) in the lower-middle; 295 (26.9 per cent) in the upper-lower; and 234 in the lower-lower (21.4 per cent).

Again the natives are shown to be by far the most differentiated group in the class system, being found in all six classes and occupying all the places in the upper-upper class. This

TABLE 13

Social Differentiation by Class of the Ten Ethnic Groups

General Ethnic	Native	Irish	French	Jewish	Italian	Greek	Armenian	Polish	Russian	Negro	Total
UU	10.6 100.0 28										2.6 28
LU	14.4 61.3 38	12.2 38.7 24									5.7 62
UM	22.0 34.1 58	20.8 24.1 41	15.8 12.4 21	20.0 11.2 19	7.0 3.5 6	21.1 11.2 19	6.7 3.5 6				15.5 170
LM	22.3 19.3 59	26.9 17.3 53	32.3 14.1 43	35.8 11.1 34	34.9 9.8 30	22.2 6.5 20	37.8 11.1 34	31.0 7.2 22	17.8 2.6 8	12.5 1.0 3	27.9 306
UL	17.4 15.6 46	23.9 15.9 47	29.3 13.2 39	31.6 10.2 30	32.6 9.5 28	32.2 9.8 29	34.4 10.5 31	33.8 8.1 24	44.4 6.8 20	4.2 0.3 1	26.9 295
LL	13.3 15.0 35	16.2 13.7 32	22.6 12.8 30	12.6 5.1 12	25.6 9.4 22	24.4 9.4 22	21.1 8.1 19	35.2 10.7 25	37.8 7.3 17	83.3 8.5 20	21.4 234
Total	24.1 264	18.0 197	12.1 133	8.7 95	7.9 86	8.2 90	8.2 90	6.5 71	4.1 45	2.2 24	1,095

means that there are twenty-eight behavioral situations in the seven social structures which only the natives experience; all ethnic groups have only an outsider's understanding of what occurs there.

In the lower-upper class the natives share part of the positions with the Irish; but they still have a majority of over 60 per cent against less than 39 per cent for the Irish. None of the eight remaining ethnic groups participates here.

In the upper-middle class the natives still hold the majority of positions; but they share them with the French, Irish, Jews, Italians, Greeks, and Armenians, in that order. The Poles, Russians, and Negroes are still excluded.

In the lower-middle class the behavioral situation changes since, although the natives are still first with fifty-nine social places, they are closely followed by the Irish with fifty-three and by the French. The Jews' share, too, has greatly increased. In this class, for the first time as we descend the scale, the Poles, Russians, and Negroes are found to occupy social positions, though few. It might be said that, since the lower-middle class is the highest position in the class system where all ethnic groups have social places, it is the stratum which is most "democratic." This is only partly true, however, as a later examination will show. In fact, the present analysis indicates that whereas the Negroes have but three places in the lower-middle class, the Yankees have fifty-nine. This is partly due, of course, to the relative size of the two groups, but there is only 12.5 per cent of the total Negro membership in this class as against 22.3 per cent of the native whites. There are 295 positions or behavioral situations in the upper-lower class. Here for the first time the natives are not in the majority; the Irish have forty-seven places to their forty-six. The Negroes, Russians, and Poles again have the smallest amount of participation.

There are 234 behavioral positions in the lower-lower class. The natives are first with 15.0 per cent, the Irish next with 13.7 per cent, and the French follow with 12.8 per cent. Although the Jews rank fourth in the upper- and lower-middle classes, they are ninth in the lower-lower class, showing that they are a far less differentiated group in this class; and the same thing holds for them in other behavioral situations. The Poles are fourth with 10.7%, the Italians and Greeks fifth with 9.4%, and the Negroes sixth with 8.5%. The increase in the Negro ranking in the lower-lower class shows that they are more differentiated here than in the other classes. The Armenians are seventh with 8.1%, and the Russians eighth with 7.3%.

We have now described the amount of differentiation within each *class* among the ten ethnic groups. Let us examine the amount of social differentiation within each *ethnic group* among the six classes. The natives, for example, participate in 264 behavioral situations: 10.6% of these are in the upper-upper class, 14.4% in the lower-upper class, 22% in the upper-middle class, 22.3% in the lower-middle class, 17.4% in the upper-lower class, and 13.3% in the lower-lower class, 17.4% in the upper-lower class, and 13.3% in the lower-lower class. Table 13 furnishes the percentages for all the other groups.

Let us now, by examining the rank order of the number of social places which each group has in the six classes, compare the amount of participation each of the ten groups has in each class. The largest number of the natives' behavioral situations are in the lower-middle class. The same is true of the Irish, French, Jews, Italians, and Armenians, who conform to the average for all ten ethnic groups. For the Negro group this class ranks second; for the Russians, Poles, and Greeks, third.

The average ranking for the ten ethnic groups in the upper-lower class is second; and the Irish, French, Jews, Italians, Armenians, and Poles conform to this. The natives and Negroes are below it and the Russians above it. The lower-lower class comes third, the French, Italians, and Armenians conforming. The Poles and Negroes, with a rank order of one, are above it, as are the Russians and Greeks with a rank order of two. The Irish and Jews are below it with a rank order of four, as are the natives with a rank order of five.

The analysis of the behavioral situations of the ten ethnic groups in these three classes demonstrates that the Greeks participate in more social places below the average, as do the Poles, the Russians, and the Negroes. It shows that the Poles and Negroes tend to concentrate in the lower-lower class and the Russians in the upper-lower class. It demonstrates that the Irish and Jews are much less differentiated in the lower-

lower class, that they have a far smaller percentage of their total in this class than the other nine groups do, and that they conform to the average for the upper-lower class.

When we examine the upper-middle class, we discover that it averages fourth for the number of social places or behavioral situations in which the ten ethnic groups participate. This ranking below three other classes is in part due to the fact

TABLE 14

Sex Membership in the Status System

Class	Male			Female			Total	
UU	2.1	42.0	782	3.2	58.0	1,082	2.6	1,864
LU	3.0	52.7	1,095	2.9	47.3	984	2.9	2,079
UM	13.7	52.6	5,046	13.3	47.4	4,541	13.5	9,587
LM	31.3	52.0	11,551	31.2	48.0	10,677	31.2	22,228
UL	31.7	50.9	11,681	32.9	49.1	11,278	32.3	22,959
LL	18.3	54.3	6,751	16.6	45.7	5,681	17.5	12,432
Total		51.9	36,906		48.1	34,243		71,149

that three ethnic groups do not participate in this class. The rank order of the percentages for the French, Italians, Greeks, and Armenians conforms to the general average. The Jews are above it with a ranking of three, and the natives are above these two with a ranking of two.

In brief, the behavioral situations of the natives are more differentiated than those of any other ethnic group; the natives are followed by the Irish and Jews. On the other hand the behavioral situations of the Negroes, Russians, and Poles are less differentiated than those of the other groups, and the remainder fall between these two extremes.[1]

7. *Sex, Age, and Religion of the Members*

There were 36,906 male members and 34,243 female members in the social system of Yankee City. Of the total member-

TABLE 15

Age Membership in the Status System

Class	Subadult			Adult			Total	
UU	0.6	7.2	135	3.4	92.8	1,729	2.6	1,864
LU	1.0	10.0	208	3.7	90.0	1,871	2.9	2,079
UM	7.1	15.4	1,473	16.1	84.6	8,114	13.5	9,587
LM	28.8	27.0	6,006	32.2	73.0	16,222	31.2	22,228
UL	37.5	34.0	7,811	30.1	66.0	15,148	32.3	22,959
LL	25.0	41.9	5,204	14.4	58.1	7,228	17.5	12,432
Total		29.3	20,837		70.7	50,312		71,149

ship, 51.9 per cent was male and 48.1 per cent female (see Table 14).

Male members outnumbered female in all classes with the exception of the upper-upper, which possessed a higher percentage of female members.

The upper-lower class ranked first in the number of both male and female membership. The smallest percentage of male

1. Further analysis of the ethnic composition of each position is in Appendices 3, 4.

membership was found in the upper-upper class, while the lower-upper class ranked lowest for female members.

Among the eighty-nine positions there were two which had no male members.[2] Female members were found in all positions.

There were 20,837 subadult members in the social system of Yankee City (see Table 15); over twice this number (50,312) of adult. Of the total membership, 29.3 per cent was below twenty-one years of age.

Adult memberships were predominant in all six classes:[3] the lower-middle ranked first and the upper-upper class last for this age group. They seemed to be concentrated in the two middle and the upper-lower classes, while the subadult memberships were chiefly in the lower-middle and two lower classes. Adult members were in all positions; subadults were absent from four (6, 15, 16, and 46).

The following analysis, in conjunction with Table 16, tells how the 71,149 memberships in the social system of Yankee City were distributed among the six classes on the basis of religion.

Of the total number of members 29,477 (41.4 per cent) had no religious affiliation:[4] 22,377 (31.5 per cent) belonged to the Protestant faith; 16,457 (23.1 per cent) were Catholic; 1,961 (2.8 per cent) were of the Jewish faith; and 877 (1.2 per cent) belonged to the Greek Orthodox religion.

The upper-lower class had the largest number of members professing no religion; the lower-upper had the smallest number. The lower-middle class ranked highest for Protestant and Jewish membership. The upper-upper class ranked last for the former and the upper-middle class for the latter.

Catholic members were found chiefly in the upper-lower class, least in the lower-upper class. The largest percentage

2. Positions 6 and 46, in the upper-upper and lower-middle classes respectively.

3. It must be remembered that our age sample in this volume is slanted in favor of adults, but less so than that for Volume I.

4. The present analysis of the religious affiliations of the members of the status system is based on a sample. We have included only the names of those whose membership was definitely known to be formally listed in the church records. These records were incomplete and in Volume I were supplemented by us with the members of associations affiliated with particular churches. The number of those with no religion is too high but the proportions of the different religious groups in the total membership are of significance.

of the Greek Orthodox members belonged to the lower-lower class, the smallest percentage to the upper-middle class.

Protestants were found in all but two of the eighty-nine positions. They were missing only from one of the twenty lower-middle-class positions and one of the fifteen upper-lower-class positions.

TABLE 16

Religious Faiths of the Members in the Status System

Class	Protestant	Catholic	Jewish	Greek Orthodox	No Religion	Total
	73.3				26.7	
UU	1,366	—	—	—	498	1,864
	72.5	4.4			23.1	
LU	1,507	91	—	—	481	2,079
	55.3	11.8	0.8	0.3	31.8	
UM	5,304	1,132	77	26	3,048	9,587
	35.7	21.6	4.9	0.2	37.6	
LM	7,945	4,801	1,095	35	8,352	22,228
	18.1	35.7	3.0	1.2	41.9	
UL	4,160	8,206	686	277	9,630	22,959
	16.9	17.9	0.8	4.3	60.1	
LL	2,095	2,227	103	539	7,468	12,432
	31.5	23.1	2.8	1.2	41.4	
Total	22,377	16,457	1,961	877	29,477	71,149

Catholics were found in seventy-one positions, none of which belonged to the upper-upper class. They appeared in eleven out of fourteen lower-upper-class positions; seventeen out of nineteen in the upper-middle class; nineteen out of twenty in the lower-middle class; fourteen out of fifteen in the upper-lower class; and in all ten positions in the lower-lower class.

Members of the Jewish faith belonged to forty-six positions, none of which represented either of the two upper classes. They appeared in eleven positions in the upper-middle class; in sixteen lower-middle-class positions; in twelve upper-lower-class positions; and in seven of the ten positions belonging to the lower-lower class.

Members of the Greek faith belonged to only thirty-three positions, not including the two upper classes. They were found in seven upper-middle-class positions, in eight positions in the lower-middle and upper-lower classes, and in all the lower-lower-class positions.

The nonreligionists were found in all but Position 6 of the eighty-nine positions.

The upper-upper-class members were either Protestants or had no religious affiliation. Members of the lower-upper class belonged to either the Protestant or the Catholic faith or professed no religious affiliation at all. The Protestants and nonreligionists, each with fourteen positions in this class, ranked first; the Catholics second with eleven positions.[5]

5. Further analysis of the age, sex, and religious faith of each position is in Appendices 5, 6.

V

THE INTERCONNECTIONS OF EACH POSITION IN THE STATUS SYSTEM

1. *Analysis of the Interconnections of Each Class*

THE foregoing analysis of the status system has been concerned both with the structural and "characteristic" composition of each of the positions and with the comparative place of each structure and characteristic in the total system. The characteristics describe the kinds of people who are being influenced in the eighty-nine positions; the structural memberships give the form of the influence; and the interconnections the amount (by number only) of influence from other positions on a particular one. The influences are from two general sources: those emanating from the same class and those from higher and lower classes. The double-pointed arrows in Chart V symbolize these horizontal and vertical connections of the positions; but the amount of interconnection varies for each position.

By counting the number of memberships which individuals hold in each horizontal position, we were able to coördinate the remaining unconnected parts of the system in an interactive whole. For instance, at this stage of our research we knew that the four Starr members of Position 18, and others like them, had memberships in Positions 12, 13, and 19, and in other lower-upper positions. In fact we knew that all these positions were interconnected, but we did not know the number of interrelationships. To obtain an actual count, we had to use the personality card of each individual to distribute his memberships among the positions. Because of the complexity of the task, only association, clique, and family data (later referred to as ACF) were used, since they are ordinarily the most important in the lives of the individuals. After this, the number of times the members of each of the eighty-nine positions were connected with each of the other positions was counted. Mrs. Starr, for example, had one family membership in Position 18.

She had three memberships in Position 2, three in 13, one each in 14, 16, 19, 20, and 25. Similar counts were made for the other three Starr family members and for all the other lower-upper members of Position 18, and so on through all the members of the eighty-nine positions.

We were now ready to particularize further by asking (1) how many connections in equivalent relations does each position have? and (2) how many connections in superior-inferior relations? The first question needs further refinement if we are

TABLE 17

Sample Table of How Interconnection Was Counted

Individuals	Position A	Position B
T	2 memberships	2 memberships
V	2 memberships	5 memberships
W	6 memberships	4 memberships
X	0 memberships	8 memberships
Y	1 membership	0 membership
Z	0 membership	0 membership
Total memberships	11 memberships	19 memberships

to get definite answers and develop exact operations to obtain them. It breaks down into a series of questions: (1) What is the total of all the "outward" connections in relations of equivalence that each position has with *all* other positions in its class? (2) How many "outward" connections in relations of equivalence has it with *each* position in its class? (3) What is the total of *all* the "inward" connections in relations of equivalence that other positions have with it? (4) How many "inward" connections in relations of equivalence has *each* of the other positions with it?

The amount of interconnection a position has with another in its class depends on (1) what proportion of all of a position's connections are with each of the others (2) what proportion of *its own members* have membership in each of the other positions. The operation for obtaining each type of answer will now be described.

Let us suppose that the community comprises six individuals, T, V, W, X, Y, Z (see Table 17), all belonging to only two positions, A and B, in one class. T has two memberships in A and two in B. Since there are an equal number of memberships in each position, Position A is connected as much with B as B is with A.

Individual V has two memberships in A and five in B. If we disregard all other memberships, from the point of view of A that position would have five "outgoing" connections with B and B would be "inwardly" connected with A only twice. By amount of membership A would be stimulating more members in B than B would in A.

In the case of individual W, A has more memberships than B. This reverses the membership arrangement of individual V.

Individual X adds another possibility to the membership connections since he is not a member of A but has several memberships in B. Individual Y reverses this situation since he is a member only of A. If only the memberships of these two individuals were considered, Positions A and B would not be connected. Finally, individual Z has no memberships in either, but in other positions not being considered.

There are eleven memberships in A and nineteen in B; but, to reiterate, not all the members of A are connected with B and only some of the members of B are connected with A. To be exact, ten of the eleven members of A are connected with B; eleven of the nineteen members of B are connected with A. Although the larger position, B, has more members connected with the other one, the smaller one, A, has a larger percentage (ten out of eleven) of its total connected with B. This means that the percentage of members of A being influenced by B (inwardly connected) is larger than that of members of B being influenced by A.

It is now necessary to return to the actual positions.

Position 1 has a total of 1,077 outward connections and 1,439 inward connections. This total was found by counting all its outward connections with the other positions of the upper-upper class.[1] By dividing the total of all the outward and in-

1. It had 354 with Position 2, 392 with 3, 68 with 4, 138 with 5, 1 with 6, 7 with 7, 13 with 8, 46 with 9, 10 with 10, and 48 with 11. (See left-hand column of the first page of Table 18).

ward connections of Position 1 by its connections with each position, the proportion of its connections of equivalence is obtained. For example, 32.87 per cent of its outward connections and 23.84 per cent of its inward connections were with Position 2.

These answers offer a measurement of the total amount of interaction Position 1 has with each of the other upper-upper positions. We know Positions 2 and 3 have, both inwardly and outwardly, more connections with Position 1 than with any other position, and that Positions 6 and 7 have the least connection. Such knowledge indicates that the members of Position 1 are likely to be more influenced by the status behavior in the first two connected positions than with the latter two.

Such an analysis of mutual influencing (social interaction) within a class is very helpful in obtaining an estimate of the probable amount of pressure given and taken by members of a position. There are limitations, however, in the use of this system in determining social interaction, for it must be remembered that the positions have unequal membership. Position 1 has 516 members; Position 2 has 361; and Position 7 has only 9 members. To discover how much each of these positions is connected with Position 1, other operations are necessary. Since Position 2 has 361 members, 354 of whom are also members of Position 1, this means that 98.06 per cent of the members in Position 2 are members of Position 1. On the other hand 343 members of Position 1 are members of Position 2, which means that 66.47 per cent of the members in Position 1 are also in Position 2. Position 1 has 31.59 per cent more members of Position 2 than Position 2 has of the members of Position 1. The number of members of 2 directly influenced by the status position of 1 is appreciably larger than the number of members of 1 who are influenced by 2.

Let us examine the connections with Position 6, the smallest of the upper-upper positions. Position 1 is connected but once with the one member of Position 6, constituting only 0.09 per cent of the total outward connections of Position 1. The one member of Position 6 has seven connections with Position 1, which is 0.49 per cent of the total inward connections of 1. However, the one outward connection Position 1 has with 6 represents 100 per cent of the total membership of 6 and the seven connections 6 has with 1 comprise only 1.36 per cent of the membership of 1. There is, therefore, an enormous difference in the amount of influence the two positions have on each other.

Each of the operations in the analysis just described was applied to all the eighty-nine positions, and detailed answers concerning the amount of inner and outer connections in relations of equivalence were obtained for all of them. These will be presented later.

In the horizontal relations one individual can occupy several statuses; in the vertical order he can hold only one position, for he belongs to but one class in a given moment of his lifetime. The connections in the vertical relations therefore were of a different order and had to be computed by different methods from those just described.

Position 1 has no positions above or below it (see Chart V), so we shall turn for our example to Position 3 which is connected with Positions 13 and 26. There are 399 members in Position 3; 395 in 13; and 632 in 26. Position 3 has four more members than 13 and therefore has a greater numerical influence on 13 than the latter has on it. On the other hand, 26 has 233 more members than 3, with a similar result. If the total number of members of 3 and 13 is divided into the difference between them, the percentage of difference is obtained; and when this is done for all positions it is possible to compare the amount of numerical influence they have on each other.

These vertical computations are of less significance and are less reliable than are those for the relations of equivalence. But they are useful for rapid calculation of the proportionate amount of relation between two or more positions.

2. Computation Table for the Interconnections of the Eighty-nine Positions

Space will not permit accounting in detail in this volume for all the interconnections among all the positions; furthermore, since the investigator must be aware of all the variables which are influencing individual or group behavior if he is to understand the events which he is trying to analyze, such information is only useful if all of it is available at one time. A detailed analysis of concrete behavior will be given in the volume on symbolic behavior. Our purpose here is simply to provide a complete description of all the parts of the system and their interconnections.

With this in mind a computation table (18) has been devised to reckon the interconnections of all positions. Under "Horizontal" connections, the column at the extreme left gives the position ("Position 1"); its total association, clique, and family members (516); and its total outward (1,077) and inward (1,439) connections with all other positions in the same class. The columns below these figures give the number of outward and inward connections Position 1 has with each of the other ten positions in the class, and what percentage they are of its total connections. This percentage was obtained for outgoing connections by dividing 1,077 into 354 for Position 2, 392 for Position 3, etc.; for incoming by dividing 1,439 into 343 for Position 2, 390 for Position 3, etc. The percentage of members in each position who have membership in another position is indicated in the central column for Position 1 by "(1) 98.06 $\longleftrightarrow$ (2) 66.47 = + 31.59," which shows that Position 1 is interconnected outwardly with 2 more than 2 is inwardly connected with 1. Careful perusal of the table will supply the reader with information on the horizontal interconnections of all positions.

The right-hand or "Vertical" column tabulates the amount of direct and internal connection between a position and others above or below it. Position 1 has no direct vertical connections. Position 2, however, is connected with Position 12 in the class below it. The 361 (ACF) individuals who have membership in Position 2 and the 364 in Position 12 are connected by virtue of belonging to the same associations, cliques, and families. The word "internal" refers to this fact (see Chapter I). It is therefore reckoned that 0.41 per cent more were influenced than influencing. The — mark indicates this, just as a + mark indicates a position has greater influence.

3. Limitations of the Positional System for Analyzing Social Behavior

The computation table provides an analytical device by which (1) all the variables (the positions and relations involved) may be considered within a complex social situation; (2) a given individual's whole position in the society may be examined to

TABLE 18

Computation Table for the Interconnections of the Eighty-nine Positions

Horizontal								Vertical
Direct and external connections which each position has with all others in its class								Connections which are direct and internal
Per cent of *total* outgoing and incoming connections for each position				Per cent of totals between a position and totals of one other position				
POSITION 1 Total ACF: 516 Total Out: 1,077 Total In: 1,439								
	Outgoing		Incoming	Outgoing		Incoming	Difference	
P2	354 (32.87)	⟷	343 (23.84)	(1) 98.06	⟷	(2) 66.47:	+31.59	
P3	392 (36.40)	⟷	390 (27.10)	(1) 98.25	⟷	(3) 75.58:	+22.67	0
P4	68 (6.31)	⟷	135 (9.38)	(1) 93.15	⟷	(4) 26.16:	+66.99	
P5	138 (12.81)	⟷	233 (16.19)	(1) 98.57	⟷	(5) 45.16:	+53.41	
P6	1 (0.09)	⟷	7 (0.49)	(1) 100.00	⟷	(6) 1.36:	+98.64	
P7	7 (0.65)	⟷	35 (2.43)	(1) 77.78	⟷	(7) 6.78:	+71.00	
P8	13 (1.21)	⟷	45 (3.13)	(1) 59.09	⟷	(8) 8.72:	+50.37	
P9	46 (4.27)	⟷	122 (8.48)	(1) 97.87	⟷	(9) 23.64:	+74.23	
P10	10 (0.93)	⟷	13 (0.90)	(1) 83.33	⟷	(10) 2.52:	+80.81	
P11	48 (4.46)	⟷	116 (8.06)	(1) 100.00	⟷	(11) 22.48:	+77.52	

TABLE 18 (Continued)

	Horizontal				Vertical
	Direct and external connections which each position has with all others in its class				Connections which are direct and internal
	Per cent of *total* outgoing and incoming connections for each position		Per cent of totals between a position and totals of one other position		
Position 2 Total ACF: 361 Total Out: 887 Total In: 1,287					
	Outgoing	Incoming	Outgoing ⟷ Incoming	Difference	
P1	343 (38.67) ⟷	354 (27.51)	(2) 66.47 ⟷ (1) 98.06:	−31.59	(2) ⟷ (12): −0.41
P3	289 (32.58) ⟷	308 (23.93)	(2) 72.43 ⟷ (3) 85.32:	−12.89	
P4	49 (5.52) ⟷	121 (9.40)	(2) 67.12 ⟷ (4) 33.52:	+33.60	
P5	107 (12.06) ⟷	197 (15.31)	(2) 76.43 ⟷ (5) 54.57:	+21.86	
P6	1 (0.11) ⟷	11 (0.85)	(2) 100.00 ⟷ (6) 3.05:	+96.95	
P7	6 (0.68) ⟷	32 (2.49)	(2) 66.67 ⟷ (7) 8.86:	+57.81	
P8	10 (1.13) ⟷	38 (2.95)	(2) 45.45 ⟷ (8) 10.53:	+34.92	
P9	36 (4.06) ⟷	107 (8.31)	(2) 76.60 ⟷ (9) 29.64:	+46.96	
P10	8 (0.90) ⟷	20 (1.55)	(2) 66.67 ⟷ (10) 5.54:	+61.13	
P11	38 (4.28) ⟷	99 (7.69)	(2) 79.17 ⟷ (11) 27.42:	+51.75	
Position 3 Total ACF: 399 Total Out: 996 Total In: 1,389					
	Outgoing	Incoming	Outgoing ⟷ Incoming	Difference	
P1	390 (39.16) ⟷	392 (28.22)	(3) 75.58 ⟷ (1) 98.25:	−22.67	(3) ⟷ (13): +0.50
P2	308 (30.92) ⟷	289 (20.81)	(3) 85.32 ⟷ (2) 72.43:	+12.89	(3) ⟷ (26): −22.60

TABLE 18 (Continued)

Horizontal								Vertical
Direct and external connections which each position has with all others in its class								Connections which are direct and internal
Per cent of *total* outgoing and incoming connections for each position			Per cent of totals between a position and totals of one other position					
	Outgoing	Incoming	Outgoing		Incoming		Difference	
P4	62 (6.22) ⟷	125 (9.00)	(3) 84.93 ⟷		(4) 31.33:		+53.60	
P5	125 (12.55) ⟷	239 (17.21)	(3) 89.29 ⟷		(5) 59.90:		+22.39	
P6	1 (0.10) ⟷	7 (0.50)	(3) 100.00 ⟷		(6) 1.75:		+98.25	
P7	6 (0.60) ⟷	28 (2.02)	(3) 66.67 ⟷		(7) 7.02:		+59.65	
P8	10 (1.00) ⟷	30 (2.16)	(3) 45.45 ⟷		(8) 7.52:		+37.93	
P9	43 (4.32) ⟷	148 (10.66)	(3) 91.49 ⟷		(9) 37.09:		+54.40	
P10	8 (0.80) ⟷	19 (1.37)	(3) 66.67 ⟷		(10) 4.76:		+61.91	
P11	43 (4.32) ⟷	112 (8.06)	(3) 89.58 ⟷		(11) 28.07:		+61.51	
POSITION 4 Total ACF: 73 Total Out: 490 Total In: 320								
	Outgoing	Incoming	Outgoing		Incoming		Difference	
P1	135 (27.55) ⟷	68 (21.25)	(4) 26.16 ⟷		(1) 93.15:		−66.99	
P2	121 (24.69) ⟷	49 (15.31)	(4) 33.52 ⟷		(2) 67.12:		−33.60	(4) ⟷ (27): −10.43
P3	125 (25.51) ⟷	62 (19.38)	(4) 31.33 ⟷		(3) 84.93:		−53.60	
P5	51 (10.41) ⟷	48 (15.00)	(4) 36.43 ⟷		(5) 65.75:		−29.32	
P6			(4) 00.00 ⟷		(6) 00.00:		0.00	

TABLE 18 (Continued)

	Horizontal: Direct and external connections which each position has with all others in its class								Vertical
	Per cent of *total* outgoing and incoming connections for each position			Per cent of totals between a position and totals of one other position					Connections which are direct and internal
	Outgoing		Incoming	Outgoing		Incoming		Difference	
P7	5 (1.02)	⟷	11 (3.44)	(4) 55.56	⟷	(7) 15.07:		+40.49	
P8	10 (2.04)	⟷	9 (2.81)	(4) 45.45	⟷	(8) 12.33:		+33.12	
P9	17 (3.47)	⟷	30 (9.38)	(4) 36.17	⟷	(9) 41.10:		−4.93	
P10	6 (1.22)	⟷	9 (2.81)	(4) 50.00	⟷	(10) 12.33:		+37.67	
P11	20 (4.08)	⟷	34 (10.63)	(4) 41.67	⟷	(11) 46.58:		−4.91	
POSITION 5 Total ACF: 140 Total Out: 792 Total In: 566									
	Outgoing		Incoming	Outgoing		Incoming		Difference	
P1	233 (29.42)	⟷	138 (24.38)	(5) 45.16	⟷	(1) 98.57:		−53.41	(5) ⟷ (14): −7.28
P2	197 (24.87)	⟷	107 (18.90)	(5) 54.57	⟷	(2) 76.43:		−21.86	(5) ⟷ (28): −61.38
P3	239 (30.18)	⟷	125 (22.08)	(5) 59.90	⟷	(3) 89.29:		−29.39	(5) ⟷ (45): −56.72
P4	48 (6.06)	⟷	51 (9.01)	(5) 65.75	⟷	(4) 36.43:		+29.32	
P6				(5) 00.00	⟷	(6) 00.00:		0.00	
P7	4 (0.51)	⟷	14 (2.47)	(5) 44.44	⟷	(7) 9.10:		+35.34	
P8	5 (0.63)	⟷	14 (2.47)	(5) 22.73	⟷	(8) 9.10:		+13.63	
P9	33 (4.17)	⟷	57 (10.07)	(5) 70.21	⟷	(9) 40.71:		+29.50	
P10	4 (0.51)	⟷	10 (1.77)	(5) 33.33	⟷	(10) 7.14:		+26.19	
P11	29 (3.66)	⟷	50 (8.83)	(5) 60.42	⟷	(11) 35.71:		+24.71	

TABLE 18 (Continued)

Horizontal						Vertical	
Direct and external connections which each position has with all others in its class						Connections which are direct and internal	
Per cent of *total* outgoing and incoming connections for each position			Per cent of totals between a position and totals of one other position				
Position 6							
Total ACF: 1							
Total Out: 27			Outgoing	Incoming	Difference		
Total In: 5			(6) 1.36 ⟷	(1) 100.00:	−98.64		
	Outgoing	Incoming	(6) 3.05 ⟷	(2) 100.00:	−96.95		
P1	7 (25.93) ⟷	1 (20.00)	(6) 1.75 ⟷	(3) 100.00:	−98.25	(6) ⟷ (15):	−60.00
P2	11 (40.74) ⟷	1 (20.00)	(6) 0.00 ⟷	(4) 00.00:	0.00	(6) ⟷ (46):	0.00
P3	7 (25.93) ⟷	1 (20.00)	(6) 0.00 ⟷	(5) 00.00:	0.00		
P4			(6) 11.11 ⟷	(7) 100.00:	−88.89		
P5			(6) 0.00 ⟷	(8) 00.00:	0.00		
P7	1 (3.70) ⟷	1 (20.00)	(6) 2.13 ⟷	(9) 100.00:	−97.87		
P8			(6) 0.00 ⟷	(10) 00.00:	0.00		
P9	1 (3.70) ⟷	1 (20.00)	(6) 0.00 ⟷	(11) 00.00:	0.00		
P10							
P11							
Position 7							
Total ACF: 9							
Total Out: 138							
Total In: 40							
	Outgoing	Incoming	Outgoing	Incoming	Difference		
P1	35 (25.36) ⟷	7 (17.50)	(7) 6.78 ⟷	(1) 77.78:	−71.00	(7) ⟷ (29):	−31.03
P2	32 (23.19) ⟷	6 (15.00)	(7) 8.86 ⟷	(2) 66.67:	−57.81	(7) ⟷ (47):	−28.57

TABLE 18 (Continued)

	Horizontal								Vertical
	Direct and external connections which each position has with all others in its class								Connections which are direct and internal
	Per cent of *total* outgoing and incoming connections for each position			Per cent of totals between a position and totals of one other position					
	Outgoing		Incoming	Outgoing		Incoming		Difference	
P3	28 (20.29)	⟷	6 (15.00)	(7) 7.02	⟷	(3) 66.67:		−59.65	
P4	11 (7.97)	⟷	5 (12.50)	(7) 15.07	⟷	(4) 55.56:		−40.49	
P5	14 (10.14)	⟷	4 (10.00)	(7) 9.10	⟷	(5) 44.44:		−35.34	
P6	1 (0.72)	⟷	1 (2.50)	(7) 100.00	⟷	(6) 11.11:		+88.89	
P8	5 (3.62)	⟷	3 (7.50)	(7) 22.73	⟷	(8) 33.33:		−10.60	
P9	6 (4.35)	⟷	5 (12.50)	(7) 12.77	⟷	(9) 55.56:		−42.79	
P10	2 (1.45)	⟷	1 (2.50)	(7) 16.67	⟷	(10) 11.11:		+5.56	
P11	4 (2.90)	⟷	2 (5.00)	(7) 8.33	⟷	(11) 22.22:		−13.89	
POSITION 8 Total ACF: 22 Total Out: 147 Total In: 68									
	Outgoing		Incoming	Outgoing		Incoming		Difference	
P1	45 (30.61)	⟷	13 (19.12)	(8) 8.72	⟷	(1) 59.09:		−50.37	(8) ⟷ (48): +15.79
P2	38 (25.85)	⟷	10 (14.71)	(8) 10.53	⟷	(2) 45.45:		−34.92	
P3	30 (20.41)	⟷	10 (14.71)	(8) 7.52	⟷	(3) 45.45:		−37.93	
P4	9 (6.12)	⟷	10 (14.71)	(8) 12.33	⟷	(4) 45.45:		−33.12	

TABLE 18 (Continued)

	Horizontal						Vertical	
	Direct and external connections which each position has with all others in its class						Connections which are direct and internal	
	Per cent of *total* outgoing and incoming connections for each position			Per cent of totals between a position and totals of one other position				
	Outgoing		Incoming	Outgoing	Incoming	Difference		
P5	14 (9.52)	⟷	5 (7.35)	(8) 9.10 ⟷	(5) 22.73:	−13.63		
P6				(8) 0.00 ⟷	(6) 0.00:	0.00		
P7	3 (2.04)	⟷	5 (7.35)	(8) 33.33 ⟷	(7) 22.73:	+10.60		
P9	4 (2.72)	⟷	6 (8.82)	(8) 8.51 ⟷	(9) 22.27:	−13.76		
P10	2 (1.36)	⟷	4 (5.88)	(8) 16.67 ⟷	(10) 18.18:	−1.51		
P11	2 (1.36)	⟷	5 (7.35)	(8) 4.17 ⟷	(11) 22.73:	−18.56		
POSITION 9								
Total ACF: 47								
Total Out: 496								
Total In: 204								
	Outgoing		Incoming	Outgoing	Incoming	Difference		
P1	122 (24.60)	⟷	46 (22.55)	(9) 23.64 ⟷	(1) 97.87:	−74.23	(9) ⟷ (16):	+8.51
P2	107 (21.57)	⟷	36 (17.65)	(9) 29.64 ⟷	(2) 76.60:	−46.96	(9) ⟷ (30):	−63.70
P3	148 (29.84)	⟷	43 (21.08)	(9) 37.09 ⟷	(3) 91.49:	−54.40	(9) ⟷ (49):	−54.50
P4	30 (6.05)	⟷	17 (8.33)	(9) 41.10 ⟷	(4) 36.17:	+4.93	(9) ⟷ (65):	−1.92
P5	57 (11.49)	⟷	33 (16.18)	(9) 40.71 ⟷	(5) 70.21:	−29.50		
P6	1 (0.20)	⟷	1 (0.49)	(9) 100.00 ⟷	(6) 2.13:	+97.87		
P7	5 (1.01)	⟷	6 (2.94)	(9) 55.56 ⟷	(7) 12.77:	+42.79		
P8	6 (1.21)	⟷	4 (1.96)	(9) 22.27 ⟷	(8) 8.51:	+13.76		
P10	2 (0.40)	⟷	1 (0.49)	(9) 16.67 ⟷	(10) 2.13:	+14.54		
P11	18 (3.63)	⟷	17 (8.33)	(9) 37.50 ⟷	(11) 36.17:	+1.33		

TABLE 18 (Continued)

	Horizontal					Vertical	
	Direct and external connections which each position has with all others in its class					Connections which are direct and internal	
	Per cent of *total* outgoing and incoming connections for each position		Per cent of totals between a position and totals of one other position				
Position 10 Total ACF: 12 Total Out: 82 Total In: 49							
	Outgoing	Incoming	Outgoing	Incoming	Difference		
P1	13 (15.85) ⟷	10 (20.41)	(10) 2.52 ⟷	(1) 83.33:	−80.81	(10) ⟷ (31):	−48.00
P2	20 (24.39) ⟷	8 (16.33)	(10) 5.54 ⟷	(2) 66.67:	−61.13	(10) ⟷ (50):	−69.77
P3	19 (23.17) ⟷	8 (16.33)	(10) 4.76 ⟷	(3) 66.67:	−61.91	(10) ⟷ (66):	−63.89
P4	9 (10.98) ⟷	6 (12.24)	(10) 12.33 ⟷	(4) 50.00:	−37.67		
P5	10 (12.20) ⟷	4 (8.16)	(10) 7.14 ⟷	(5) 33.33:	−26.19		
P6			(10) 0.00 ⟷	(6) 0.00:	0.00		
P7	1 (1.22) ⟷	2 (4.08)	(10) 11.11 ⟷	(7) 16.67:	−5.56		
P8	4 (4.88) ⟷	2 (4.08)	(10) 18.18 ⟷	(8) 16.67:	+1.51		
P9	1 (1.22) ⟷	2 (4.08)	(10) 2.13 ⟷	(9) 16.67:	−14.54		
P11	5 (6.10) ⟷	7 (14.29)	(10) 10.42 ⟷	(11) 58.33:	−47.91		
Position 11 Total ACF: 48 Total Out: 442 Total In: 207							
	Outgoing	Incoming	Outgoing	Incoming	Difference		
P1	116 (26.24) ⟷	48 (23.19)	(11) 22.48 ⟷	(1) 100.00:	−77.52	(11) ⟷ (17):	−6.53
P2	99 (22.40) ⟷	38 (18.36)	(11) 27.42 ⟷	(2) 79.17:	−51.75	(11) ⟷ (32):	−77.86

TABLE 18 (Continued)

	Horizontal					Vertical
	Direct and external connections which each position has with all others in its class					Connections which are direct and internal
	Per cent of *total* outgoing and incoming connections for each position		Per cent of totals between a position and totals of one other position			
	Outgoing	Incoming	Outgoing	Incoming	Difference	
P3	112 (25.34) ⟷	43 (20.77)	(11) 28.07 ⟷	(3) 89.58:	−61.51	(11) ⟷ (51): −88.92
P4	34 (7.69) ⟷	20 (9.66)	(11) 46.58 ⟷	(4) 41.67:	+4.91	(11) ⟷ (67): −87.01
P5	50 (11.31) ⟷	29 (14.01)	(11) 35.71 ⟷	(5) 60.42:	−24.71	(11) ⟷ (80): −76.32
P6			(11) 0.00 ⟷	(6) 0.00:	0.00	
P7	2 (0.45) ⟷	4 (1.93)	(11) 22.22 ⟷	(7) 8.33:	+13.89	
P8	5 (1.13) ⟷	2 (0.97)	(11) 22.73 ⟷	(8) 4.17:	+18.56	
P9	17 (3.85) ⟷	18 (8.70)	(11) 36.17 ⟷	(9) 37.50:	−1.33	
P10	7 (1.58) ⟷	5 (2.42)	(11) 58.33 ⟷	(10) 10.42:	+47.91	
Position 18 Total ACF: 412 Total Out: 1,262 Total In: 1,255						
	Outgoing	Incoming	Outgoing	Incoming	Difference	
P12	353 (27.97) ⟷	270 (21.51)	(18) 96.98 ⟷	(12) 65.53:	+31.45	0
P13	378 (29.95) ⟷	306 (24.38)	(18) 95.70 ⟷	(13) 74.27:	+21.43	
P14	154 (12.20) ⟷	174 (13.86)	(18) 95.06 ⟷	(14) 42.23:	+52.83	
P15	4 (0.32) ⟷	5 (0.40)	(18) 100.00 ⟷	(15) 1.21:	+98.79	
P16	39 (3.09) ⟷	80 (6.37)	(18) 97.50 ⟷	(16) 19.42:	+78.08	

TABLE 18 (Continued)

	Horizontal							Vertical
	Direct and external connections which each position has with all others in its class							Connections which are direct and internal
	Per cent of *total* outgoing and incoming connections for each position			Per cent of totals between a position and totals of one other position				
	Outgoing		Incoming	Outgoing		Incoming	Difference	
P17	52 (4.12)	⟷	94 (7.49)	(18) 89.66	⟷	(17) 22.82:	+66.84	
P19	157 (12.44)	⟷	175 (13.94)	(18) 83.51	⟷	(19) 42.48:	+41.03	
P20	40 (3.17)	⟷	64 (5.10)	(18) 80.00	⟷	(20) 15.53:	+64.47	
P21	18 (1.43)	⟷	27 (2.15)	(18) 64.29	⟷	(21) 6.55:	+57.74	
P22	22 (1.74)	⟷	33 (2.63)	(18) 88.00	⟷	(22) 8.01:	+79.99	
P23	14 (1.11)	⟷	14 (1.12)	(18) 82.35	⟷	(23) 3.40:	+78.95	
P24	5 (0.40)	⟷	7 (0.56)	(18) 100.00	⟷	(24) 1.70:	+98.30	
P25	26 (2.06)	⟷	6 (0.48)	(18) 66.67	⟷	(25) 14.56:	+52.11	
POSITION 12								
Total ACF: 364								
Total Out: 943								
Total In: 1,481								
	Outgoing		Incoming	Outgoing		Incoming	Difference	
P13	287 (30.43)	⟷	323 (21.81)	(12) 72.66	⟷	(13) 88.74:	−16.08	(12) ⟷ (2): +0.41
P14	114 (12.09)	⟷	227 (15.33)	(12) 70.37	⟷	(14) 62.36:	+8.01	
P15	3 (0.32)	⟷	9 (0.61)	(12) 75.00	⟷	(15) 2.47:	+72.53	
P16	34 (3.61)	⟷	115 (7.77)	(12) 85.00	⟷	(16) 31.59:	+53.41	
P17	38 (4.03)	⟷	89 (6.01)	(12) 65.52	⟷	(17) 24.45:	+41.07	

TABLE 18 (Continued)

	Horizontal					Vertical
	Direct and external connections which each position has with all others in its class					Connections which are direct and internal
	Per cent of *total* outgoing and incoming connections for each position		Per cent of totals between a position and totals of one other position			
	Outgoing	Incoming	Outgoing	Incoming	Difference	
P18	270 (28.63) ⟷	353 (23.84)	(12) 65.53 ⟷	(18) 96.98:	−31.45	
P19	124 (13.15) ⟷	200 (13.50)	(12) 65.96 ⟷	(19) 54.95:	+11.01	
P20	22 (2.33) ⟷	43 (2.90)	(12) 44.00 ⟷	(20) 11.81:	+32.19	
P21	12 (1.27) ⟷	26 (1.76)	(12) 42.86 ⟷	(21) 7.14:	+35.72	
P22	10 (1.06) ⟷	26 (1.76)	(12) 40.00 ⟷	(22) 7.14:	+32.86	
P23	8 (0.85) ⟷	7 (0.47)	(12) 47.06 ⟷	(23) 1.92:	+45.14	
P24	1 (0.11) ⟷	1 (0.07)	(12) 20.00 ⟷	(24) 0.27:	+19.73	
P25	20 (2.12) ⟷	62 (4.19)	(12) 51.28 ⟷	(25) 17.03:	+34.25	
POSITION 13 Total ACF: 395 Total Out: 1,122 Total In: 1,567						
	Outgoing	Incoming	Outgoing	Incoming	Difference	
P12	323 (28.79) ⟷	287 (18.32)	(13) 88.74 ⟷	(12) 72.66:	+16.08	(13) ⟷ (3): −0.50
P14	148 (13.19) ⟷	251 (16.02)	(13) 91.36 ⟷	(14) 63.54:	+27.82	(13) ⟷ (26): −23.08
P15	4 (0.36) ⟷	8 (0.51)	(13) 100.00 ⟷	(15) 2.03:	+97.97	
P16	37 (3.30) ⟷	121 (7.72)	(13) 92.50 ⟷	(16) 30.63:	+61.87	
P17	48 (4.28) ⟷	113 (7.21)	(13) 82.76 ⟷	(17) 28.61:	+54.15	

TABLE 18 (Continued)

	Horizontal								Vertical
	Direct and external connections which each position has with all others in its class								Connections which are direct and internal
	Per cent of *total* outgoing and incoming connections for each position			Per cent of totals between a position and totals of one other position					
	Outgoing		Incoming	Outgoing			Incoming	Difference	
P18	306 (27.27)	⟷	378 (24.12)	(13) 74.27	⟷	(18)	95.70:	−21.43	
P19	151 (13.46)	⟷	194 (12.38)	(13) 80.32	⟷	(19)	49.11:	+31.21	
P20	41 (3.65)	⟷	71 (4.53)	(13) 82.00	⟷	(20)	17.97:	+64.03	
P21	16 (1.43)	⟷	29 (1.85)	(13) 57.14	⟷	(21)	7.34:	+49.80	
P22	16 (1.43)	⟷	39 (2.49)	(13) 64.00	⟷	(22)	9.87:	+54.13	
P23	6 (0.53)	⟷	12 (0.77)	(13) 35.29	⟷	(23)	3.04:	+32.25	
P24	1 (0.09)	⟷	1 (0.06)	(13) 20.00	⟷	(24)	0.25:	+19.75	
P25	25 (2.23)	⟷	63 (4.02)	(13) 64.10	⟷	(25)	15.95:	+48.15	
Position 14 Total ACF: 162 Total Out: 908 Total In: 747									
	Outgoing		Incoming	Outgoing			Incoming	Difference	
P12	227 (25.00)	⟷	114 (15.26)	(14) 62.36	⟷	(12)	70.37:	−8.01	(14) ⟷ (5): +7.28
P13	251 (27.64)	⟷	148 (19.81)	(14) 63.54	⟷	(13)	91.36:	−27.82	(14) ⟷ (28): −56.63
P15	1 (0.11)	⟷	1 (0.13)	(14) 25.00	⟷	(15)	0.62:	+24.38	(14) ⟷ (45): −51.57
P16	31 (3.41)	⟷	53 (7.10)	(14) 77.50	⟷	(16)	32.72:	+44.78	
P17	42 (4.63)	⟷	68 (9.10)	(14) 72.41	⟷	(17)	41.98:	+30.43	

TABLE 18 (Continued)

	Horizontal: Direct and external connections which each position has with all others in its class — Per cent of *total* outgoing and incoming connections for each position			Horizontal: Per cent of totals between a position and totals of one other position			Vertical: Connections which are direct and internal
	Outgoing		Incoming	Outgoing	Incoming	Difference	
P18	174 (19.16)	⟷	154 (20.62)	(14) 42.23 ⟷	(18) 95.06:	−52.83	
P19	102 (11.23)	⟷	92 (12.32)	(14) 54.26 ⟷	(19) 56.79:	−2.53	
P20	32 (3.52)	⟷	45 (6.02)	(14) 64.00 ⟷	(20) 27.78:	+36.22	
P21	12 (1.32)	⟷	18 (2.41)	(14) 42.86 ⟷	(21) 11.11:	+31.75	
P22	12 (1.32)	⟷	16 (2.14)	(14) 48.00 ⟷	(22) 9.88:	+38.12	
P23	3 (0.33)	⟷	5 (0.67)	(14) 17.65 ⟷	(23) 3.09:	+14.56	
P24				(14) 0.00 ⟷	(24) 0.00:	0.00	
P25	21 (2.31)	⟷	33 (4.42)	(14) 53.85 ⟷	(25) 20.37:	+33.48	
Position 15 Total ACF: 4 Total Out: 30 Total In: 18							
	Outgoing		Incoming	Outgoing	Incoming	Difference	
P12	9 (30.00)	⟷	3 (16.67)	(15) 2.47 ⟷	(12) 75.00:	−72.53	(15) ⟷ (6): +60.00
P13	8 (26.67)	⟷	4 (22.22)	(15) 2.03 ⟷	(13) 100.00:	−97.97	(15) ⟷ (46): +60.00
P14	1 (3.33)	⟷	1 (5.56)	(15) 0.62 ⟷	(14) 25.00:	−24.38	
P16	1 (3.33)	⟷	1 (5.56)	(15) 2.50 ⟷	(16) 25.00:	−22.50	
P17	1 (3.33)	⟷	1 (5.56)	(15) 1.72 ⟷	(17) 25.00:	−23.28	

TABLE 18 (Continued)

	Horizontal							Vertical
	Direct and external connections which each position has with all others in its class							Connections which are direct and internal
	Per cent of *total* outgoing and incoming connections for each position			Per cent of totals between a position and totals of one other position				
	Outgoing		Incoming	Outgoing		Incoming	Difference	
P18	5 (16.67)	⟷	4 (22.22)	(15) 1.21	⟷	(18) 100.00:	−98.79	
P19	5 (16.67)	⟷	4 (22.22)	(15) 2.66	⟷	(19) 100.00:	−97.34	
P20				(15) 0.00	⟷	(20) 0.00:	0.00	
P21				(15) 0.00	⟷	(21) 0.00:	0.00	
P22				(15) 0.00	⟷	(22) 0.00:	0.00	
P23				(15) 0.00	⟷	(23) 0.00:	0.00	
P24				(15) 0.00	⟷	(24) 0.00:	0.00	
P25				(15) 0.00	⟷	(25) 0.00:	0.00	
Position 16 Total ACF: 40 Total Out: 458 Total In: 214								
	Outgoing		Incoming	Outgoing		Incoming	Difference	
P12	115 (25.11)	⟷	34 (15.89)	(16) 31.59	⟷	(12) 85.00:	−53.41	(16) ⟷ (9): −8.51
P13	121 (26.42)	⟷	37 (17.29)	(16) 30.63	⟷	(13) 92.50:	−61.87	(16) ⟷ (30): −68.50
P14	53 (11.57)	⟷	31 (14.49)	(16) 32.72	⟷	(14) 77.50:	−44.78	(16) ⟷ (49): −59.81
P15	1 (0.22)	⟷	1 (0.47)	(16) 25.00	⟷	(15) 2.50:	+22.50	(16) ⟷ (65): −10.42
P17	20 (4.37)	⟷	21 (9.81)	(16) 34.48	⟷	(17) 52.50:	−18.02	

TABLE 18 (Continued)

	Horizontal					Vertical	
	Direct and external connections which each position has with all others in its class					Connections which are direct and internal	
	Per cent of *total* outgoing and incoming connections for each position		Per cent of totals between a position and totals of one other position				
	Outgoing	Incoming	Outgoing	Incoming	Difference		
P18	80 (17.47) ⟷	39 (18.22)	(16) 19.42 ⟷	(18) 97.50:	−78.08		
P19	44 (9.61) ⟷	22 (10.28)	(16) 23.40 ⟷	(19) 55.00:	−31.60		
P20	11 (2.40) ⟷	12 (5.61)	(16) 22.00 ⟷	(20) 30.00:	−8.00		
P21	2 (0.44) ⟷	4 (1.87)	(16) 7.14 ⟷	(21) 10.00:	−2.86		
P22	2 (0.44) ⟷	4 (1.87)	(16) 8.00 ⟷	(22) 10.00:	−2.00		
P23			(16) 0.00 ⟷	(23) 0.00:	0.00		
P24	1 (0.22) ⟷	1 (0.47)	(16) 20.00 ⟷	(24) 2.50:	+17.50		
P25	8 (1.75) ⟷	8 (3.74)	(16) 20.51 ⟷	(25) 20.00:	+0.51		
Position 17 Total ACF: 58 Total Out: 519 Total In: 294							
	Outgoing	Incoming	Outgoing	Incoming	Difference		
P12	89 (17.15) ⟷	38 (12.93)	(17) 24.45 ⟷	(12) 65.52:	−41.07	(17) ⟷ (11):	+6.53
P13	113 (21.77) ⟷	48 (16.33)	(17) 28.61 ⟷	(13) 82.76:	−54.15	(17) ⟷ (32):	−75.15
P14	68 (13.10) ⟷	42 (14.29)	(17) 41.98 ⟷	(14) 72.41:	−30.43	(17) ⟷ (51):	−87.46
P15	1 (0.19) ⟷	1 (0.34)	(17) 25.00 ⟷	(15) 1.72:	+23.28	(17) ⟷ (67):	−85.33
P16	21 (4.05) ⟷	20 (6.80)	(17) 52.50 ⟷	(16) 34.48:	+18.02	(17) ⟷ (80):	−73.45

TABLE 18 (Continued)

Horizontal							Vertical
Direct and external connections which each position has with all others in its class							Connections which are direct and internal
	Per cent of *total* outgoing and incoming connections for each position			Per cent of totals between a position and totals of one other position			
	Outgoing		Incoming	Outgoing	Incoming	Difference	
P18	94 (18.11)	⟷	52 (17.69)	(17) 22.82 ⟷	(18) 89.66:	−66.84	
P19	77 (14.84)	⟷	36 (12.24)	(17) 40.96 ⟷	(19) 62.07:	−21.11	
P20	23 (4.43)	⟷	20 (6.80)	(17) 46.00 ⟷	(20) 34.48:	+11.52	
P21	7 (1.35)	⟷	11 (3.74)	(17) 25.00 ⟷	(21) 18.97:	+6.03	
P22	9 (1.73)	⟷	9 (3.06)	(17) 36.00 ⟷	(22) 15.52:	+20.48	
P23	3 (0.58)	⟷	3 (1.02)	(17) 17.65 ⟷	(23) 5.17:	+12.48	
P24	1 (0.19)	⟷	1 (0.34)	(17) 20.00 ⟷	(24) 1.72:	+18.28	
P25	13 (2.50)	⟷	13 (4.42)	(17) 33.33 ⟷	(25) 22.41:	+10.92	
POSITION 19 Total ACF: 188 Total Out: 840 Total In: 861							
	Outgoing		Incoming	Outgoing	Incoming	Difference	
P12	200 (23.81)	⟷	124 (14.40)	(19) 54.95 ⟷	(12) 65.96:	−11.01	(19) ⟷ (33): −10.21
P13	194 (23.10)	⟷	151 (17.54)	(19) 49.11 ⟷	(13) 80.32:	−31.21	
P14	92 (10.95)	⟷	102 (11.85)	(19) 56.79 ⟷	(14) 54.26:	+2.53	
P15	4 (0.48)	⟷	5 (0.58)	(19) 100.00 ⟷	(15) 2.66:	+97.34	
P16	22 (2.62)	⟷	44 (5.11)	(19) 55.00 ⟷	(16) 23.40:	+31.60	

TABLE 18 (Continued)

	Horizontal								Vertical	
	Direct and external connections which each position has with all others in its class								Connections which are direct and internal	
	Per cent of *total* outgoing and incoming connections for each position			Per cent of totals between a position and totals of one other position						
	Outgoing		Incoming	Outgoing		Incoming		Difference		
P17	36 (4.29)	⟷	77 (8.94)	(19) 62.07	⟷	(17) 40.96:		+21.11		
P18	175 (20.83)	⟷	157 (18.23)	(19) 42.48	⟷	(18) 83.51:		−41.03		
P20	37 (4.40)	⟷	58 (6.74)	(19) 74.00	⟷	(20) 30.85:		+43.15		
P21	20 (2.38)	⟷	38 (4.41)	(19) 71.43	⟷	(21) 20.21:		+51.22		
P22	15 (1.79)	⟷	34 (3.95)	(19) 60.00	⟷	(22) 18.09:		+41.91		
P23	13 (1.55)	⟷	16 (1.86)	(19) 76.47	⟷	(23) 8.51:		+67.96		
P24	1 (0.12)	⟷	1 (0.12)	(19) 20.00	⟷	(24) 0.53:		+19.47		
P25	31 (3.69)	⟷	54 (6.27)	(19) 79.49	⟷	(25) 28.72:		+50.77		
Position 20 Total ACF: 50 Total Out: 362 Total In: 275										
	Outgoing		Incoming	Outgoing		Incoming		Difference		
P12	43 (11.88)	⟷	22 (8.00)	(20) 11.81	⟷	(12) 44.00:		−32.19	(20) ⟷ (34):	−70.88
P13	71 (19.61)	⟷	41 (14.91)	(20) 17.97	⟷	(13) 82.00:		−64.03	(20) ⟷ (52):	−79.38
P14	45 (12.43)	⟷	32 (11.64)	(20) 27.78	⟷	(14) 64.00:		−36.22		
P15				(20) 0.00	⟷	(15) 0.00:		0.00		

TABLE 18 (Continued)

	Horizontal							Vertical
	Direct and external connections which each position has with all others in its class							Connections which are direct and internal
	Per cent of *total* outgoing and incoming connections for each position			Per cent of totals between a position and totals of one other position				
	Outgoing		Incoming	Outgoing		Incoming	Difference	
P16	12 (3.31)	⟷	11 (4.00)	(20) 30.00	⟷	(16) 22.00:	+8.00	
P17	20 (5.52)	⟷	23 (8.36)	(20) 34.48	⟷	(17) 46.00:	−11.52	
P18	64 (17.68)	⟷	40 (14.55)	(20) 15.53	⟷	(18) 80.00:	−64.47	
P19	58 (16.02)	⟷	37 (13.45)	(20) 30.85	⟷	(19) 74.00:	−43.15	
P21	13 (3.59)	⟷	18 (6.55)	(20) 46.43	⟷	(21) 36.00:	+10.43	
P22	12 (3.31)	⟷	18 (6.55)	(20) 48.00	⟷	(22) 36.00:	+12.00	
P23	3 (0.83)	⟷	7 (2.55)	(20) 17.65	⟷	(23) 14.00:	+3.65	
P24				(20) 0.00	⟷	(24) 0.00:	0.00	
P25	21 (5.80)	⟷	26 (9.45)	(20) 53.85	⟷	(25) 52.00:	+1.85	
Position 21 Total ACF: 28 Total Out: 190 Total In: 125								
	Outgoing		Incoming	Outgoing		Incoming	Difference	
P12	26 (13.68)	⟷	12 (9.60)	(21) 7.14	⟷	(12) 42.86:	−42.72	(21) ⟷ (53): −14.29
P13	29 (15.26)	⟷	16 (12.80)	(21) 7.34	⟷	(13) 57.14:	−49.80	
P14	18 (9.47)	⟷	12 (9.60)	(21) 11.11	⟷	(14) 42.86:	−31.75	
P15				(21) 0.00	⟷	(15) 0.00:	0.00	

TABLE 18 (Continued)

	Horizontal							Vertical	
	Direct and external connections which each position has with all others in its class							Connections which are direct and internal	
	Per cent of *total* outgoing and incoming connections for each position			Per cent of totals between a position and totals of one other position					
	Outgoing		Incoming	Outgoing		Incoming	Difference		
P16	4 (2.11)	⟷	2 (1.60)	(21) 10.00	⟷	(16) 7.14:	+2.86		
P17	11 (5.79)	⟷	7 (5.60)	(21) 18.97	⟷	(17) 25.00:	−6.03		
P18	27 (14.21)	⟷	18 (14.40)	(21) 6.55	⟷	(18) 64.29:	−57.74		
P19	38 (20.00)	⟷	20 (16.00)	(21) 20.21	⟷	(19) 71.43:	−51.22		
P20	18 (9.47)	⟷	13 (10.40)	(21) 36.00	⟷	(20) 46.43:	−10.43		
P22	8 (4.21)	⟷	12 (9.60)	(21) 32.00	⟷	(22) 42.86:	−10.86		
P23	2 (1.05)	⟷	2 (1.60)	(21) 11.76	⟷	(23) 7.14:	+4.62		
P24				(21) 0.00	⟷	(24) 0.00:	0.00		
P25	9 (4.74)	⟷	11 (8.80)	(21) 23.08	⟷	(25) 39.29:	−16.21		
POSITION 22									
Total ACF: 25									
Total Out: 205									
Total In: 121									
	Outgoing		Incoming	Outgoing		Incoming	Difference		
P12	26 (12.68)	⟷	10 (8.26)	(22) 7.14	⟷	(12) 40.00:	−32.86	(22) ⟷ (35):	−64.47
P13	39 (19.02)	⟷	16 (13.22)	(22) 9.87	⟷	(13) 64.00:	−54.13	(22) ⟷ (54):	−72.59
P14	16 (7.80)	⟷	12 (9.92)	(22) 9.88	⟷	(14) 48.00:	−38.12	(22) ⟷ (68):	−77.02
P15				(22) 0.00	⟷	(15) 0.00:	0.00		

TABLE 18 (Continued)

	Horizontal							Vertical
	Direct and external connections which each position has with all others in its class							Connections which are direct and internal
	Per cent of *total* outgoing and incoming connections for each position			Per cent of totals between a position and totals of one other position				
	Outgoing		Incoming	Outgoing		Incoming	Difference	
P16	4 (1.95)	⟷	2 (1.65)	(22) 10.00	⟷	(16) 8.00:	+2.00	
P17	9 (4.39)	⟷	9 (7.44)	(22) 15.52	⟷	(17) 36.00:	−20.48	
P18	33 (16.10)	⟷	22 (18.18)	(22) 8.01	⟷	(18) 88.00:	−79.99	
P19	34 (16.59)	⟷	15 (12.40)	(22) 18.09	⟷	(19) 60.00:	−41.91	
P20	18 (8.78)	⟷	12 (9.92)	(22) 36.00	⟷	(20) 48.00:	−12.00	
P21	12 (5.85)	⟷	8 (6.61)	(22) 42.86	⟷	(21) 32.00:	+10.86	
P23	4 (1.95)	⟷	5 (4.13)	(22) 23.53	⟷	(23) 20.00:	+3.53	
P24	1 (0.49)	⟷	1 (0.83)	(22) 20.00	⟷	(24) 4.00:	+16.00	
P25	9 (4.39)	⟷	9 (7.44)	(22) 23.08	⟷	(25) 36.00:	−12.92	
Position 23 Total ACF: 17 Total Out: 81 Total In: 66								
	Outgoing		Incoming	Outgoing		Incoming	Difference	
P12	7 (8.64)	⟷	8 (12.12)	(23) 1.92	⟷	(12) 47.06:	−45.14	(23) ⟷ (55): −26.09
P13	12 (14.81)	⟷	6 (9.09)	(23) 3.04	⟷	(13) 35.29:	−32.25	(23) ⟷ (69): −35.85
P14	5 (6.17)	⟷	3 (4.55)	(23) 3.09	⟷	(14) 17.65:	−14.56	
P15				(23) 0.00	⟷	(15) 0.00:	0.00	

TABLE 18 (Continued)

	Horizontal					Vertical
	Direct and external connections which each position has with all others in its class					Connections which are direct and internal
	Per cent of *total* outgoing and incoming connections for each position		Per cent of totals between a position and totals of one other position			
	Outgoing	Incoming	Outgoing	Incoming	Difference	
P16			(23) 0.00 ⟷	(16) 0.00:	0.00	
P17	3 (3.70) ⟷	3 (4.55)	(23) 5.17 ⟷	(17) 17.65:	−12.48	
P18	14 (17.28) ⟷	14 (21.21)	(23) 3.40 ⟷	(18) 82.35:	−78.95	
P19	16 (19.75) ⟷	13 (19.70)	(23) 8.51 ⟷	(19) 76.47:	−67.96	
P20	7 (8.64) ⟷	3 (4.55)	(23) 14.00 ⟷	(20) 17.65:	−3.65	
P21	2 (2.47) ⟷	2 (3.03)	(23) 7.14 ⟷	(21) 11.76:	−4.62	
P22	5 (6.17) ⟷	4 (6.06)	(23) 20.00 ⟷	(22) 23.53:	−3.53	
P24	1 (1.23) ⟷	1 (1.52)	(23) 20.00 ⟷	(24) 5.88:	+14.12	
P25	9 (11.11) ⟷	9 (13.64)	(23) 23.08 ⟷	(25) 52.94:	−29.86	
POSITION 24						
Total ACF: 5						
Total Out: 15						
Total In: 13						
	Outgoing	Incoming	Outgoing	Incoming	Difference	(24) ⟷ (70): +25.00
P12	1 (6.67) ⟷	1 (7.69)	(24) 0.27 ⟷	(12) 20.00:	−19.73	
P13	1 (6.67) ⟷	1 (7.69)	(24) 0.25 ⟷	(13) 20.00:	−19.75	
P14			(24) 0.00 ⟷	(14) 0.00:	0.00	
P15			(24) 0.00 ⟷	(15) 0.00:	0.00	

TABLE 18 (Continued)

	Horizontal					Vertical
	Direct and external connections which each position has with all others in its class					Connections which are direct and internal
	Per cent of *total* outgoing and incoming connections for each position		Per cent of totals between a position and totals of one other position			
	Outgoing	Incoming	Outgoing	Incoming	Difference	
P16	1 (6.67) ⟷	1 (7.69)	(24) 2.50 ⟷	(16) 20.00:	−17.50	
P17	1 (6.67) ⟷	1 (7.69)	(24) 1.72 ⟷	(17) 20.00:	−18.28	
P18	7 (46.67) ⟷	5 (38.46)	(24) 1.70 ⟷	(18) 100.00:	−98.30	
P19	1 (6.67) ⟷	1 (7.69)	(24) 0.53 ⟷	(19) 20.00:	−19.47	
P20			(24) 0.00 ⟷	(20) 0.00:	0.00	
P21			(24) 0.00 ⟷	(21) 0.00:	0.00	
P22	1 (6.67) ⟷	1 (7.69)	(24) 4.00 ⟷	(22) 20.00:	−16.00	
P23	1 (6.67) ⟷	1 (7.69)	(24) 5.88 ⟷	(23) 20.00:	−14.12	
P25	1 (6.67) ⟷	1 (7.69)	(24) 2.56 ⟷	(25) 20.00:	−17.44	
POSITION 25 Total ACF: 39 Total Out: 295 Total In: 193						
	Outgoing	Incoming	Outgoing	Incoming	Difference	
P12	62 (17.77) ⟷	20 (10.36)	(25) 17.03 ⟷	(12) 51.28:	−34.25	(25) ⟷ (36): −78.53
P13	63 (18.05) ⟷	25 (12.95)	(25) 15.95 ⟷	(13) 64.10:	−48.15	(25) ⟷ (56): −93.08
P14	33 (9.46) ⟷	21 (10.88)	(25) 20.37 ⟷	(14) 53.85:	−33.48	(25) ⟷ (71): −95.05
P15			(25) 0.00 ⟷	(15) 0.00:	0.00	(25) ⟷ (81): −86.51

TABLE 18 (Continued)

	Horizontal					Vertical
	Direct and external connections which each position has with all others in its class					Connections which are direct and internal
	Per cent of *total* outgoing and incoming connections for each position		Per cent of totals between a position and totals of one other position			
	Outgoing	Incoming	Outgoing	Incoming	Difference	
P16	8 (2.29) ⟷	8 (4.15)	(25) 20.00 ⟷	(16) 20.51:	−0.51	
P17	13 (3.72) ⟷	13 (6.74)	(25) 22.41 ⟷	(17) 33.33:	−10.92	
P18	6 (17.19) ⟷	26 (13.47)	(25) 14.56 ⟷	(18) 66.67:	−52.11	
P19	54 (15.47) ⟷	31 (16.06)	(25) 28.72 ⟷	(19) 79.49:	−50.77	
P20	26 (7.45) ⟷	21 (10.88)	(25) 52.00 ⟷	(20) 53.85:	−1.85	
P21	11 (3.15) ⟷	9 (4.66)	(25) 39.29 ⟷	(21) 23.08:	+16.21	
P22	9 (2.58) ⟷	9 (4.66)	(25) 36.00 ⟷	(22) 23.08:	+12.92	
P23	9 (2.58) ⟷	9 (4.66)	(25) 52.94 ⟷	(23) 23.08:	+29.86	
P24	1 (0.29) ⟷	1 (0.52)	(25) 20.00 ⟷	(24) 2.56:	+17.44	
POSITION 37 Total ACF: 2,141 Total Out: 4,744 Total In: 5,588						
	Outgoing	Incoming	Outgoing	Incoming	Difference	
P26	593 (12.50) ⟷	635 (11.36)	(37) 93.83 ⟷	(26) 29.66:	+64.17	0
P27	83 (1.75) ⟷	155 (2.77)	(37) 92.22 ⟷	(27) 7.24:	+84.98	
P28	546 (11.51) ⟷	632 (11.31)	(37) 93.33 ⟷	(28) 29.52:	+63.81	
P29	11 (0.23) ⟷	15 (0.27)	(37) 84.62 ⟷	(29) 0.70:	+83.92	

TABLE 18 (Continued)

	Horizontal: Direct and external connections which each position has with all others in its class — Per cent of *total* outgoing and incoming connections for each position	Horizontal: Per cent of totals between a position and totals of one other position	Vertical: Connections which are direct and internal
P30	210 (4.43) ⟷ 302 (5.40)	(37) 93.33 ⟷ (30) 14.11: +79.22	
P31	34 (0.72) ⟷ 52 (0.93)	(37) 97.14 ⟷ (31) 2.43: +94.71	
P32	416 (8.77) ⟷ 569 (10.18)	(37) 91.23 ⟷ (32) 26.58: +64.65	
P33	212 (4.47) ⟷ 288 (5.15)	(37) 92.17 ⟷ (33) 13.45: +78.72	
P34	294 (6.20) ⟷ 414 (7.41)	(37) 95.77 ⟷ (34) 19.34: +76.43	
P35	102 (2.15) ⟷ 158 (2.83)	(37) 90.27 ⟷ (35) 7.38: +82.89	
P36	224 (4.72) ⟷ 348 (6.23)	(37) 96.14 ⟷ (36) 16.25: +79.89	
P38	891 (18.78) ⟷ 746 (13.35)	(37) 88.22 ⟷ (38) 34.84: +53.38	
P39	576 (12.14) ⟷ 535 (9.57)	(37) 93.96 ⟷ (39) 24.99: +68.97	
P40	177 (3.73) ⟷ 267 (4.78)	(37) 89.85 ⟷ (40) 12.47: +77.38	
P41	320 (6.75) ⟷ 407 (7.28)	(37) 90.14 ⟷ (41) 19.01: +71.13	
P42	18 (0.38) ⟷ 17 (0.30)	(37) 85.71 ⟷ (42) 0.79: +84.92	
P43	27 (0.57) ⟷ 32 (0.57)	(37) 90.00 ⟷ (43) 1.49: +88.51	
P44	10 (0.21) ⟷ 16 (0.29)	(37) 83.33 ⟷ (44) 0.75: +82.58	
POSITION 26 Total ACF: 632 Total Out: 2,355 Total In: 2,427			
	Outgoing ⟷ Incoming	Outgoing ⟷ Incoming: Difference	
P27	55 (2.34) ⟷ 67 (2.76)	(26) 61.11 ⟷ (27) 10.60: −50.51	(26) ⟷ (3): +22.60
P28	319 (13.55) ⟷ 319 (13.14)	(26) 54.53 ⟷ (28) 50.47: +4.06	(26) ⟷ (13): +23.08
P29	5 (0.21) ⟷ 5 (0.21)	(26) 38.46 ⟷ (29) 0.79: +37.67	
P30	109 (4.63) ⟷ 155 (6.39)	(26) 48.44 ⟷ (30) 24.53: +23.91	

TABLE 18 (Continued)

	Horizontal							Vertical
	Direct and external connections which each position has with all others in its class							Connections which are direct and internal
	Per cent of *total* outgoing and incoming connections for each position			Per cent of totals between a position and totals of one other position				
	Outgoing		Incoming	Outgoing		Incoming	Difference	
P31	16 (0.68)	⟷	23 (0.95)	(26) 45.71	⟷	(31) 3.64:	+42.07	
P32	204 (8.66)	⟷	233 (9.60)	(26) 44.74	⟷	(32) 36.87:	+7.87	
P33	146 (6.20)	⟷	204 (8.41)	(26) 63.48	⟷	(33) 32.28:	+31.20	
P34	217 (9.21)	⟷	154 (6.35)	(26) 70.68	⟷	(34) 24.37:	+46.31	
P35	39 (1.66)	⟷	62 (2.55)	(26) 34.51	⟷	(35) 9.81:	+24.70	
P36	77 (3.27)	⟷	108 (4.45)	(26) 33.05	⟷	(36) 17.09:	+15.96	
P37	635 (26.96)	⟷	593 (24.43)	(26) 29.66	⟷	(37) 93.83:	−64.17	
P38	287 (12.19)	⟷	233 (9.60)	(26) 28.42	⟷	(38) 36.87:	−8.45	
P39	124 (5.27)	⟷	137 (5.64)	(26) 20.23	⟷	(39) 21.68:	−1.45	
P40	43 (1.83)	⟷	44 (1.81)	(26) 21.83	⟷	(40) 6.96:	+14.87	
P41	68 (2.89)	⟷	78 (3.21)	(26) 19.15	⟷	(41) 12.34	+6.81	
P42	5 (0.21)	⟷	6 (0.25)	(26) 23.81	⟷	(42) 0.95:	+22.86	
P43	4 (0.17)	⟷	4 (0.16)	(26) 13.33	⟷	(43) 0.63:	+12.70	
P44	2 (0.08)	⟷	2 (0.08)	(26) 16.67	⟷	(44) 0.32:	+16.35	
POSITION 27 Total ACF: 90 Total Out: 599 Total In: 437								
	Outgoing		Incoming	Outgoing		Incoming	Difference	
P26	67 (11.19)	⟷	55 (12.59)	(27) 10.60	⟷	(26) 61.11:	−50.51	(27) ⟷ (4) +10.43
P28	56 (9.35)	⟷	41 (9.38)	(27) 9.57	⟷	(28) 45.56:	−35.99	

TABLE 18 (Continued)

	Horizontal: Direct and external connections which each position has with all others in its class — Per cent of *total* outgoing and incoming connections for each position		Horizontal: Per cent of totals between a position and totals of one other position			Vertical: Connections which are direct and internal
	Outgoing	Incoming	Outgoing	Incoming	Difference	
P29	2 (0.33) ⟷	4 (0.92)	(27) 15.38 ⟷	(29) 4.44:	+10.94	
P30	21 (3.51) ⟷	22 (5.03)	(27) 9.33 ⟷	(30) 24.44:	−15.11	
P31	8 (1.34) ⟷	7 (1.60)	(27) 22.86 ⟷	(31) 7.78:	+15.08	
P32	38 (6.34) ⟷	34 (7.78)	(27) 8.33 ⟷	(32) 37.78:	−29.45	
P33	49 (8.18) ⟷	33 (7.55)	(27) 21.30 ⟷	(33) 36.67:	−15.37	
P34	22 (3.67) ⟷	27 (6.18)	(27) 7.17 ⟷	(34) 30.00:	−22.83	
P35	7 (1.17) ⟷	8 (1.83)	(27) 6.19 ⟷	(35) 8.89:	−2.70	
P36	20 (3.34) ⟷	14 (3.20)	(27) 8.58 ⟷	(36) 15.56:	−6.98	
P37	155 (25.88) ⟷	83 (18.99)	(27) 7.24 ⟷	(37) 92.22:	−84.98	
P38	58 (9.68) ⟷	32 (7.32)	(27) 5.74 ⟷	(38) 35.56:	−29.82	
P39	43 (7.18) ⟷	32 (7.32)	(27) 7.01 ⟷	(39) 35.56:	−28.55	
P40	28 (4.67) ⟷	22 (5.03)	(27) 14.21 ⟷	(40) 24.44:	−10.23	
P41	21 (3.51) ⟷	19 (4.35)	(27) 5.92 ⟷	(41) 21.11:	−15.19	
P42			(27) 0.00 ⟷	(42) 0.00	0.00	
P43	2 (0.33) ⟷	2 (0.46)	(27) 6.67 ⟷	(43) 2.22:	+4.45	
P44	2 (0.33) ⟷	2 (0.46)	(27) 16.67 ⟷	(44) 2.22:	+14.45	
Position 28 Total ACF: 585 Total Out: 2,348 Total In: 2,500						
	Outgoing	Incoming	Outgoing	Incoming	Difference	
P26	319 (13.59) ⟷	319 (12.76)	(28) 50.47 ⟷	(26) 54.53:	−4.06	(28) ⟷ (5): +61.38
P27	41 (1.75) ⟷	56 (2.24)	(28) 45.56 ⟷	(27) 9.57:	+35.99	(28) ⟷ (14): +56.63

TABLE 18 (Continued)

	Horizontal									Vertical
	Direct and external connections which each position has with all others in its class									Connections which are direct and internal
	Per cent of *total* outgoing and incoming connections for each position				Per cent of totals between a position and totals of one other position					
	Outgoing			Incoming	Outgoing			Incoming	Difference	
P29	2 (0.09)	⟷		3 (0.12)	(28) 15.38	⟷		(29) 0.51:	+14.87	(28) ⟷ (45): +7.14
P30	117 (4.98)	⟷		176 (7.04)	(28) 52.00	⟷		(30) 30.09:	+21.91	
P31	18 (0.77)	⟷		30 (1.20)	(28) 51.43	⟷		(31) 5.13:	+46.30	
P32	210 (8.94)	⟷		259 (10.36)	(28) 46.05	⟷		(32) 44.27:	+1.78	
P33	113 (4.81)	⟷		111 (4.44)	(28) 49.13	⟷		(33) 18.97:	+30.16	
P34	131 (5.58)	⟷		204 (8.16)	(28) 42.67	⟷		(34) 34.87:	+7.80	
P35	47 (2.00)	⟷		65 (2.60)	(28) 41.59	⟷		(35) 11.11:	+30.48	
P36	83 (3.53)	⟷		112 (4.48)	(28) 35.62	⟷		(36) 19.15:	+16.47	
P37	632 (26.92)	⟷		546 (21.84)	(28) 29.52	⟷		(37) 93.33:	−63.81	
P38	320 (13.63)	⟷		280 (11.20)	(28) 31.68	⟷		(38) 47.86:	−16.18	
P39	179 (7.62)	⟷		171 (6.84)	(28) 29.20	⟷		(39) 29.23:	−0.03	
P40	44 (1.87)	⟷		58 (2.32)	(28) 22.34	⟷		(40) 9.91:	+12.43	
P41	78 (3.32)	⟷		92 (3.68)	(28) 21.97	⟷		(41) 15.73:	+6.24	
P42	8 (0.34)	⟷		11 (0.44)	(28) 38.10	⟷		(42) 1.88:	+36.22	
P43	5 (0.21)	⟷		5 (0.20)	(28) 16.67	⟷		(43) 0.85:	+15.82	
P44	1 (0.04)	⟷		2 (0.08)	(28) 8.33	⟷		(44) 0.34:	+7.99	

TABLE 18 (Continued)

	Horizontal					Vertical
	Direct and external connections which each position has with all others in its class					Connections which are direct and internal
	Per cent of *total* outgoing and incoming connections for each position		Per cent of totals between a position and totals of one other position			
Position 29 Total ACF: 13 Total Out: 74 Total In: 59	Outgoing	Incoming	Outgoing	Incoming	Difference	
P26	5 (6.76) ⟷	5 (8.47)	(29) 0.79 ⟷	(26) 38.46:	−37.67	(29) ⟷ (7): +31.03
P27	4 (5.41) ⟷	2 (3.39)	(29) 4.44 ⟷	(27) 15.38:	−10.94	(29) ⟷ (47): +2.70
P28	3 (4.05) ⟷	2 (3.39)	(29) 0.51 ⟷	(28) 15.38:	−14.87	
P30	4 (5.41) ⟷	3 (5.08)	(29) 1.78 ⟷	(30) 23.08:	−21.30	
P31	1 (1.35) ⟷	1 (1.69)	(29) 2.86 ⟷	(31) 7.69:	−4.83	
P32	4 (5.41) ⟷	3 (5.08)	(29) 0.88 ⟷	(32) 23.08:	−22.20	
P33	7 (9.46) ⟷	4 (6.78)	(29) 3.04 ⟷	(33) 30.77:	−27.73	
P34	2 (2.70) ⟷	2 (3.39)	(29) 0.65 ⟷	(34) 15.38:	−14.73	
P35	4 (5.41) ⟷	4 (6.78)	(29) 3.54 ⟷	(35) 30.77:	−27.23	
P36	6 (8.11) ⟷	4 (6.78)	(29) 2.58 ⟷	(36) 30.77:	−28.19	
P37	15 (20.27) ⟷	11 (18.64)	(29) 0.70 ⟷	(37) 84.62:	−83.92	
P38	8 (10.81) ⟷	11 (18.64)	(29) 0.79 ⟷	(38) 84.62:	−83.83	
P39	4 (5.41) ⟷	3 (5.08)	(29) 0.65 ⟷	(39) 23.08:	−22.43	
P40	3 (4.05) ⟷	1 (1.69)	(29) 1.52 ⟷	(40) 7.69:	−6.17	
P41	3 (4.05) ⟷	2 (3.39)	(29) 0.85 ⟷	(41) 15.38:	−14.53	
P42	1 (1.35) ⟷	1 (1.69)	(29) 4.70 ⟷	(42) 7.69:	−2.99	
P43			(29) 0.00 ⟷	(43) 0.00:	0.00	
P44			(29) 0.00 ⟷	(44) 0.00:	0.00	

TABLE 18 (Continued)

	Horizontal						Vertical
	Direct and external connections which each position has with all others in its class						Connections which are direct and internal
	Per cent of *total* outgoing and incoming connections for each position			Per cent of totals between a position and totals of one other position			
Position 30 Total ACF: 225 Total Out: 1,446 Total In: 1,037							
	Outgoing		Incoming	Outgoing	Incoming	Difference	
P26	155 (10.72)	⟷	109 (10.51)	(30) 24.53 ⟷	(26) 48.44:	−23.91	(30) ⟷ (9): +63.70
P27	22 (1.52)	⟷	21 (2.03)	(30) 24.44 ⟷	(27) 9.33:	+15.11	(30) ⟷ (16): +68.50
P28	176 (12.17)	⟷	117 (11.28)	(30) 30.09 ⟷	(28) 52.00:	−21.91	(30) ⟷ (49): +14.71
P29	3 (0.21)	⟷	4 (0.39)	(30) 23.08 ⟷	(29) 1.78:	+21.30	(30) ⟷ (65): +62.54
P31	14 (0.97)	⟷	11 (1.06)	(30) 40.00 ⟷	(31) 4.89:	+35.11	
P32	142 (9.82)	⟷	123 (11.86)	(30) 31.14 ⟷	(32) 54.67:	−23.53	
P33	61 (4.22)	⟷	36 (3.47)	(30) 26.52 ⟷	(33) 16.00:	+10.52	
P34	80 (5.53)	⟷	75 (7.23)	(30) 26.06 ⟷	(34) 33.33:	−7.27	
P35	36 (2.49)	⟷	24 (2.31)	(30) 31.86 ⟷	(35) 10.67:	+21.19	
P36	50 (3.46)	⟷	47 (4.53)	(30) 21.46 ⟷	(36) 20.89:	+0.57	
P37	302 (20.89)	⟷	210 (20.25)	(30) 14.11 ⟷	(37) 93.33:	−79.22	
P38	211 (14.59)	⟷	114 (10.99)	(30) 20.89 ⟷	(38) 50.67:	−29.78	
P39	104 (7.19)	⟷	72 (6.94)	(30) 16.97 ⟷	(39) 32.00:	−15.03	
P40	32 (2.21)	⟷	25 (2.41)	(30) 16.24 ⟷	(40) 11.11:	+5.13	
P41	51 (3.53)	⟷	43 (4.15)	(30) 14.37 ⟷	(41) 19.11:	−4.74	
P42	4 (0.28)	⟷	3 (0.29)	(30) 19.05 ⟷	(42) 1.33:	+17.72	
P43	2 (0.14)	⟷	2 (0.19)	(30) 6.67 ⟷	(43) 0.89:	+5.78	
P44	1 (0.07)	⟷	1 (0.10)	(30) 8.33 ⟷	(44) 0.44:	+7.89	

TABLE 18 (Continued)

	Horizontal											Vertical	
	Direct and external connections which each position has with all others in its class											Connections which are direct and internal	
	Per cent of *total* outgoing and incoming connections for each position				Per cent of totals between a position and totals of one other position								
Position 31 Total ACF: 35 Total Out: 332 Total In: 226	Outgoing		Incoming		Outgoing			Incoming			Difference		
P26	23	(6.93) ⟷	16	(7.08)	(31)	3.64 ⟷		(26)	45.71:		−42.07	(31) ⟷ (10):	+48.00
P27	7	(2.11) ⟷	8	(3.54)	(31)	7.78 ⟷		(27)	22.86:		−15.08	(31) ⟷ (50):	−32.73
P28	30	(9.04) ⟷	18	(7.96)	(31)	5.13 ⟷		(28)	51.43:		−46.30	(31) ⟷ (66):	−22.92
P29	1	(0.30) ⟷	1	(0.44)	(31)	7.69 ⟷		(29)	2.86:		+4.83		
P30	11	(3.31) ⟷	14	(6.19)	(31)	4.89 ⟷		(30)	40.00:		−35.11		
P32	21	(6.33) ⟷	18	(7.96)	(31)	4.61 ⟷		(32)	51.43:		−46.82		
P33	23	(6.93) ⟷	11	(4.81)	(31)	10.00 ⟷		(33)	31.43:		−21.43		
P34	13	(3.92) ⟷	10	(4.42)	(31)	4.23 ⟷		(34)	28.57:		−24.34		
P35	3	(0.90) ⟷	4	(1.77)	(31)	2.65 ⟷		(35)	11.43:		−8.78		
P36	12	(3.61) ⟷	15	(6.64)	(31)	5.15 ⟷		(36)	42.86:		−37.71		
P37	52	(15.66) ⟷	34	(15.04)	(31)	2.43 ⟷		(37)	97.14:		−94.71		
P38	61	(18.37) ⟷	24	(10.62)	(31)	6.04 ⟷		(38)	68.57:		−62.53		
P39	40	(12.05) ⟷	25	(11.06)	(31)	6.53 ⟷		(39)	71.43:		−64.90		
P40	14	(4.22) ⟷	11	(4.87)	(31)	7.11 ⟷		(40)	31.43:		−24.32		
P41	17	(5.12) ⟷	13	(5.75)	(31)	4.79 ⟷		(41)	37.14:		−32.35		
P42	1	(0.30) ⟷	1	(0.44)	(31)	4.76 ⟷		(42)	2.86:		+1.90		
P43	2	(0.60) ⟷	2	(0.88)	(31)	6.67 ⟷		(43)	5.71:		+0.96		
P44	1	(0.30) ⟷	1	(0.44)	(31)	8.33 ⟷		(44)	2.86:		+5.47		

TABLE 18 (Continued)

	Horizontal					Vertical	
	Direct and external connections which each position has with all others in its class					Connections which are direct and internal	
	Per cent of *total* outgoing and incoming connections for each position		Per cent of totals between a position and totals of one other position				
POSITION 32 Total ACF: 456 Total Out: 2,393 Total In: 2,072							
	Outgoing	Incoming	Outgoing	Incoming	Difference		
P26	233 (9.74) ⟷	204 (9.85)	(32) 36.87 ⟷	(26) 44.74:	−7.87	(32) ⟷ (11):	+77.86
P27	34 (1.42) ⟷	38 (1.83)	(32) 37.78 ⟷	(27) 8.33:	+29.45	(32) ⟷ (17):	+75.15
P28	259 (10.82) ⟷	210 (10.14)	(32) 44.27 ⟷	(28) 46.05:	−1.78	(32) ⟷ (51):	−35.93
P29	3 (0.13) ⟷	4 (0.19)	(32) 23.08 ⟷	(29) 0.88:	+22.20	(32) ⟷ (67):	−28.36
P30	123 (5.14) ⟷	142 (6.85)	(32) 54.67 ⟷	(30) 31.14:	+23.53	(32) ⟷ (80):	+3.80
P31	18 (0.75) ⟷	21 (1.01)	(32) 51.43 ⟷	(31) 4.61:	+46.82		
P33	101 (4.22) ⟷	73 (3.52)	(32) 43.91 ⟷	(33) 16.01:	+27.90		
P34	116 (4.85) ⟷	225 (10.86)	(32) 37.78 ⟷	(34) 49.34:	−11.56		
P35	41 (1.71) ⟷	57 (2.75)	(32) 36.28 ⟷	(35) 12.50:	+23.78		
P36	100 (4.18) ⟷	108 (5.21)	(32) 42.92 ⟷	(36) 23.68:	+19.24		
P37	569 (23.78) ⟷	416 (20.08)	(32) 26.58 ⟷	(37) 91.23:	−64.65		
P38	402 (16.80) ⟷	242 (11.68)	(32) 39.80 ⟷	(38) 53.07:	−13.27		
P39	207 (8.65) ⟷	151 (7.29)	(32) 33.77 ⟷	(39) 33.11:	+0.66		
P40	72 (3.01) ⟷	63 (3.04)	(32) 36.55 ⟷	(40) 13.82:	+22.73		
P41	101 (4.22) ⟷	103 (4.97)	(32) 28.45 ⟷	(41) 22.59:	+5.86		
P42	8 (0.33) ⟷	8 (0.39)	(32) 38.10 ⟷	(42) 1.75:	+36.35		
P43	4 (0.17) ⟷	5 (0.24)	(32) 13.13 ⟷	(43) 1.10:	+12.03		
P44	2 (0.08) ⟷	2 (0.10)	(32) 16.67 ⟷	(44) 0.44:	+16.23		

TABLE 18 (Continued)

Horizontal											Vertical
Direct and external connections which each position has with all others in its class											Connections which are direct and internal
Per cent of *total* outgoing and incoming connections for each position					Per cent of totals between a position and totals of one other position						
POSITION 33 Total ACF: 230 Total Out: 1,283 Total In: 1,122											
	Outgoing			Incoming	Outgoing			Incoming		Difference	
P26	204 (15.90)	⟷		146 (13.01)	(33)	32.28	⟷	(26)	63.48:	−31.20	(33) ⟷ (19): +10.21
P27	33 (2.57)	⟷		49 (4.37)	(33)	36.67	⟷	(27)	21.30:	+15.37	
P28	111 (8.65)	⟷		113 (10.07)	(33)	18.97	⟷	(28)	49.13:	−30.16	
P29	4 (0.31)	⟷		7 (0.62)	(33)	30.77	⟷	(29)	3.04:	+27.73	
P30	36 (2.81)	⟷		61 (5.44)	(33)	16.00	⟷	(30)	26.52:	−10.52	
P31	11 (0.86)	⟷		23 (2.05)	(33)	31.43	⟷	(31)	10.00:	+21.43	
P32	73 (5.69)	⟷		101 (9.00)	(33)	16.01	⟷	(32)	43.91:	−27.90	
P34	39 (3.04)	⟷		74 (6.60)	(33)	12.70	⟷	(34)	32.17:	−19.47	
P35	20 (1.56)	⟷		34 (3.03)	(33)	17.70	⟷	(35)	14.78:	+2.92	
P36	33 (2.57)	⟷		54 (4.81)	(33)	14.16	⟷	(36)	23.48:	−9.32	
P37	288 (22.45)	⟷		212 (18.89)	(33)	13.45	⟷	(37)	92.17:	−78.72	
P38	130 (10.13)	⟷		109 (9.71)	(33)	12.87	⟷	(38)	47.39:	−34.52	
P39	59 (4.60)	⟷		61 (5.44)	(33)	9.62	⟷	(39)	26.52:	−16.90	
P40	22 (1.71)	⟷		35 (3.12)	(33)	11.17	⟷	(40)	15.22:	−4.05	
P41	215 (16.76)	⟷		39 (3.48)	(33)	60.56	⟷	(41)	16.96:	+43.60	
P42	4 (0.31)	⟷		3 (0.27)	(33)	19.05	⟷	(42)	1.30:	+17.75	
P43					(33)	0.00	⟷	(43)	0.00:	0.00	
P44	1 (0.08)	⟷		1 (0.09)	(33)	8.33	⟷	(44)	0.43:	+7.90	

TABLE 18 (Continued)

	Horizontal							Vertical	
	Direct and external connections which each position has with all others in its class							Connections which are direct and internal	
	Per cent of *total* outgoing and incoming connections for each position			Per cent of totals between a position and totals of one other position					
Position 34 Total ACF: 307 Total Out: 1,755 Total In: 1,359									
	Outgoing		Incoming	Outgoing		Incoming	Difference		
P26	154 (8.77)	⟷	217 (15.97)	(34) 24.37	⟷	(26) 70.68:	−46.31	(34) ⟷ (20):	+70.88
P27	27 (1.54)	⟷	22 (1.62)	(34) 30.00	⟷	(27) 7.17:	+22.83	(34) ⟷ (52):	−19.43
P28	204 (11.62)	⟷	131 (9.64)	(34) 34.87	⟷	(28) 42.67:	−7.80		
P29	2 (0.11)	⟷	2 (0.15)	(34) 15.38	⟷	(29) 0.65:	+14.73		
P30	75 (4.27)	⟷	80 (5.89)	(34) 33.33	⟷	(30) 26.06:	+7.27		
P31	10 (0.57)	⟷	13 (0.96)	(34) 28.57	⟷	(31) 4.23:	+24.34		
P32	225 (12.82)	⟷	116 (8.54)	(34) 49.34	⟷	(32) 37.78:	+11.56		
P33	74 (4.22)	⟷	39 (2.87)	(34) 32.17	⟷	(33) 12.70:	+19.47		
P35	37 (2.11)	⟷	44 (3.24)	(34) 32.74	⟷	(35) 14.33:	+18.41		
P36	58 (3.30)	⟷	70 (5.15)	(34) 24.89	⟷	(36) 22.80:	+2.09		
P37	414 (23.59)	⟷	294 (21.63)	(34) 19.34	⟷	(37) 95.77:	−76.43		
P38	274 (15.61)	⟷	151 (11.11)	(34) 27.13	⟷	(38) 49.19:	−22.06		
P39	89 (5.07)	⟷	78 (5.74)	(34) 14.52	⟷	(39) 25.41:	−10.89		
P40	29 (1.65)	⟷	24 (1.77)	(34) 14.72	⟷	(40) 7.82:	+6.90		
P41	79 (4.50)	⟷	74 (5.45)	(34) 22.25	⟷	(41) 24.10:	−1.85		
P42	1 (0.06)	⟷	1 (0.07)	(34) 4.76	⟷	(42) 0.33:	+4.43		
P43	2 (0.11)	⟷	2 (0.15)	(34) 6.67	⟷	(43) 0.65:	+6.02		
P44	1 (0.06)	⟷	1 (0.07)	(34) 8.33	⟷	(44) 0.33:	+8.00		

TABLE 18 (Continued)

	Horizontal								Vertical	
	Direct and external connections which each position has with all others in its class								Connections which are direct and internal	
	Per cent of *total* outgoing and incoming connections for each position		Per cent of totals between a position and totals of one other position							
Position 35 Total ACF: 113 Total Out: 782 Total In: 539										
	Outgoing	Incoming	Outgoing		Incoming		Difference			
P26	62 (7.93) ⟷	39 (7.24)	(35)	9.81 ⟷	(26)	34.51:	−24.70		(35) ⟷ (62)	+64.47
P27	8 (1.02) ⟷	7 (1.30)	(35)	8.89 ⟷	(27)	6.19:	+2.70		(35) ⟷ (54)	−15.25
P28	65 (8.31) ⟷	47 (8.72)	(35)	11.11 ⟷	(28)	41.59:	−30.48		(35) ⟷ (68)	−24.92
P29	4 (0.51) ⟷	4 (0.74)	(35)	30.77 ⟷	(29)	3.54:	+27.23			
P30	24 (3.07) ⟷	36 (6.68)	(35)	10.67 ⟷	(30)	31.86:	−21.19			
P31	4 (0.51) ⟷	3 (0.56)	(35)	11.43 ⟷	(31)	2.65:	+8.78			
P32	57 (7.29) ⟷	41 (7.61)	(35)	12.50 ⟷	(32)	36.28:	−23.78			
P33	34 (4.35) ⟷	20 (3.71)	(35)	14.78 ⟷	(33)	17.70:	−2.92			
P34	44 (5.63) ⟷	37 (6.86)	(35)	14.33 ⟷	(34)	32.74:	−18.41			
P36	43 (5.50) ⟷	38 (7.05)	(35)	18.45 ⟷	(36)	33.63:	−15.18			
P37	158 (20.20) ⟷	102 (18.92)	(35)	7.38 ⟷	(37)	90.27:	−82.89			
P38	125 (15.98) ⟷	65 (12.06)	(35)	12.38 ⟷	(38)	57.52:	−45.14			
P39	83 (10.61) ⟷	46 (8.53)	(35)	13.54 ⟷	(39)	40.71:	−27.17			
P40	26 (3.32) ⟷	13 (2.41)	(35)	13.20 ⟷	(40)	11.50:	+1.70			
P41	41 (5.24) ⟷	35 (6.49)	(35)	11.55 ⟷	(41)	30.97:	−19.42			
P42	2 (0.26) ⟷	3 (0.56)	(35)	9.52 ⟷	(42)	2.65:	+6.87			
P43	1 (0.13) ⟷	2 (0.37)	(35)	3.33 ⟷	(43)	1.77:	+1.56			
P44	1 (0.13) ⟷	1 (0.19)	(35)	8.33 ⟷	(44)	0.88:	+7.45			

TABLE 18 (Continued)

	Horizontal							Vertical	
	Direct and external connections which each position has with all others in its class							Connections which are direct and internal	
	Per cent of *total* outgoing and incoming connections for each position			Per cent of totals between a position and totals of one other position					
POSITION 36 Total ACF: 233 Total Out: 1,572 Total In: 1,078									
	Outgoing		Incoming	Outgoing		Incoming	Difference		
P26	108 (6.87)	⟷	77 (7.14)	(36) 17.09	⟷	(26) 33.05:	−15.96	(36) ⟷ (25)	+78.53
P27	14 (0.89)	⟷	20 (1.86)	(36) 15.56	⟷	(27) 8.58:	+6.98	(36) ⟷ (56)	−54.08
P28	112 (7.12)	⟷	83 (7.70)	(36) 19.15	⟷	(28) 35.62:	−16.47	(36) ⟷ (71)	−65.15
P29	4 (0.25)	⟷	6 (0.56)	(36) 30.77	⟷	(29) 2.58:	+28.19	(36) ⟷ (81)	−24.87
P30	47 (2.99)	⟷	50 (4.64)	(36) 20.89	⟷	(30) 21.46:	−0.57		
P31	15 (0.95)	⟷	12 (1.11)	(36) 42.86	⟷	(31) 5.15:	+37.71		
P32	108 (6.87)	⟷	100 (9.28)	(36) 23.68	⟷	(32) 42.92:	−19.24		
P33	54 (3.44)	⟷	33 (3.06)	(36) 23.48	⟷	(33) 14.16:	+9.32		
P34	70 (4.45)	⟷	58 (5.38)	(36) 22.80	⟷	(34) 24.89:	−2.09		
P35	38 (2.42)	⟷	43 (3.99)	(36) 33.63	⟷	(35) 18.45:	+15.18		
P37	348 (22.14)	⟷	224 (20.78)	(36) 16.25	⟷	(37) 96.14:	−79.89		
P38	285 (18.13)	⟷	124 (11.50)	(36) 28.22	⟷	(38) 53.22:	−25.00		
P39	183 (11.64)	⟷	106 (9.83)	(36) 29.85	⟷	(39) 45.49:	−15.64		
P40	68 (4.33)	⟷	45 (4.17)	(36) 34.52	⟷	(40) 19.31:	+15.21		
P41	108 (6.87)	⟷	87 (8.07)	(36) 30.42	⟷	(41) 37.34:	−6.92		
P42	6 (0.38)	⟷	6 (0.56)	(36) 28.57	⟷	(42) 2.58:	+25.99		
P43	2 (0.13)	⟷	2 (0.19)	(36) 6.67	⟷	(43) 0.86:	+5.81		
P44	2 (0.13)	⟷	2 (0.19)	(36) 16.67	⟷	(44) 0.86:	+15.81		

TABLE 18 (Continued)

	Horizontal								Vertical	
	Direct and external connections which each position has with all others in its class								Connections which are direct and internal	
	Per cent of *total* outgoing and incoming connections for each position				Per cent of totals between a position and totals of one other position					
Position 38 Total ACF: 1,010 Total Out: 2,825 Total In: 4,170										
	Outgoing		Incoming		Outgoing		Incoming	Difference		
P26	233	(8.25) ⟷	287	(6.88)	(38) 36.87 ⟷	(26)	28.42:	+8.45	(38) ⟷ (57)	−11.82
P27	32	(1.13) ⟷	58	(1.39)	(38) 35.56 ⟷	(27)	5.74:	+29.82		
P28	280	(9.91) ⟷	320	(7.67)	(38) 47.86 ⟷	(28)	31.68:	+16.18		
P29	11	(0.39) ⟷	8	(0.19)	(38) 84.62 ⟷	(29)	0.79:	+83.83		
P30	114	(4.04) ⟷	211	(5.06)	(38) 50.67 ⟷	(30)	20.89:	+29.78		
P31	24	(0.85) ⟷	61	(1.46)	(38) 68.57 ⟷	(31)	6.04:	+62.53		
P32	242	(8.57) ⟷	402	(9.64)	(38) 53.07 ⟷	(32)	39.80:	+13.27		
P33	109	(3.80) ⟷	130	(3.12)	(38) 47.39 ⟷	(33)	12.87:	+34.52		
P34	151	(5.35) ⟷	274	(6.57)	(38) 49.19 ⟷	(34)	27.13:	+22.06		
P35	65	(2.30) ⟷	125	(3.00)	(38) 57.52 ⟷	(35)	12.38:	+45.14		
P36	124	(4.39) ⟷	285	(6.83)	(38) 53.22 ⟷	(36)	28.22:	+25.00		
P37	746	(26.41) ⟷	891	(21.37)	(38) 34.84 ⟷	(37)	88.22:	−53.38		
P39	357	(12.64) ⟷	519	(12.45)	(38) 58.24 ⟷	(39)	57.39:	+0.85		
P40	113	(4.00) ⟷	217	(5.20)	(38) 57.36 ⟷	(40)	21.49:	+35.87		
P41	203	(7.19) ⟷	342	(8.20)	(38) 57.18 ⟷	(41)	33.86:	+23.32		
P42	4	(0.14) ⟷	7	(0.17)	(38) 19.05 ⟷	(42)	0.69:	+18.36		
P43	14	(0.50) ⟷	24	(0.58)	(38) 46.67 ⟷	(43)	2.38:	+44.29		
P44	3	(0.11) ⟷	9	(0.22)	(38) 25.00 ⟷	(44)	0.89:	+24.11		

TABLE 18 (Continued)

	Horizontal				Vertical
	Direct and external connections which each position has with all others in its class				Connections which are direct and internal
	Per cent of *total* outgoing and incoming connections for each position		Per cent of totals between a position and totals of one other position		
Position 39 Total ACF: 613 Total Out: 2,236 Total In: 2,609					
	Outgoing ⟷ Incoming	Outgoing ⟷ Incoming		Difference	
P26	137 (6.13) ⟷ 124 (4.75)	(39) 21.68 ⟷ (26) 20.23:		+1.45	(39) ⟷ (58) −37.44
P27	32 (1.43) ⟷ 43 (1.65)	(39) 35.56 ⟷ (27) 7.01:		+28.55	(39) ⟷ (72) −21.05
P28	171 (7.65) ⟷ 179 (6.86)	(39) 29.23 ⟷ (28) 29.20:		+0.03	
P29	3 (0.13) ⟷ 4 (0.15)	(39) 23.08 ⟷ (29) 0.65:		+22.43	
P30	72 (3.22) ⟷ 104 (3.99)	(39) 32.00 ⟷ (30) 16.97:		+15.03	
P31	25 (1.12) ⟷ 40 (1.53)	(39) 71.43 ⟷ (31) 6.53:		+64.90	
P32	151 (6.75) ⟷ 207 (7.93)	(39) 33.11 ⟷ (32) 33.77:		−0.66	
P33	61 (2.73) ⟷ 59 (2.26)	(39) 26.52 ⟷ (33) 9.62:		+16.90	
P34	78 (3.49) ⟷ 89 (3.41)	(39) 25.41 ⟷ (34) 14.52:		+10.89	
P35	46 (2.06) ⟷ 83 (3.18)	(39) 40.71 ⟷ (35) 13.54:		+27.17	
P36	106 (4.74) ⟷ 183 (7.01)	(39) 45.49 ⟷ (36) 29.85:		+15.64	
P37	535 (23.93) ⟷ 576 (22.08)	(39) 24.99 ⟷ (37) 93.96:		−68.97	
P38	519 (23.21) ⟷ 357 (13.68)	(39) 51.39 ⟷ (38) 58.24:		−6.85	
P40	120 (5.37) ⟷ 287 (11.00)	(39) 60.91 ⟷ (40) 46.82:		+14.09	
P41	166 (7.42) ⟷ 236 (9.05)	(39) 46.76 ⟷ (41) 38.50:		+8.26	
P42	4 (0.18) ⟷ 12 (0.46)	(39) 19.05 ⟷ (42) 1.96:		+17.09	
P43	6 (0.27) ⟷ 15 (0.57)	(39) 20.00 ⟷ (43) 2.45:		+17.55	
P44	4 (0.18) ⟷ 11 (0.42)	(39) 33.33 ⟷ (44) 1.79:		+31.54	

TABLE 18 (Continued)

	Horizontal					Vertical
	Direct and external connections which each position has with all others in its class					Connections which are direct and internal
	Per cent of *total* outgoing and incoming connections for each position		Per cent of totals between a position and totals of one other position			
Position 40 Total ACF: 197 Total Out: 1,203 Total In: 897						
	Outgoing	Incoming	Outgoing	Incoming	Difference	
P26	44 (3.66) ⟷	43 (4.79)	(40) 6.96 ⟷	(26) 21.83:	−14.87	(40) ⟷ (73) +5.70
P27	22 (1.83) ⟷	28 (3.12)	(40) 24.44 ⟷	(27) 14.21:	+10.23	
P28	58 (4.82) ⟷	44 (4.91)	(40) 9.91 ⟷	(28) 22.34:	−12.43	
P29	1 (0.08) ⟷	3 (0.33)	(40) 7.69 ⟷	(29) 1.52:	+6.17	
P30	25 (2.08) ⟷	32 (3.57)	(40) 11.11 ⟷	(30) 16.24:	−5.13	
P31	11 (0.91) ⟷	14 (1.56)	(40) 31.43 ⟷	(31) 7.11:	+24.32	
P32	63 (5.24) ⟷	72 (8.03)	(40) 13.82 ⟷	(32) 36.55:	−22.73	
P33	35 (2.91) ⟷	22 (2.45)	(40) 15.22 ⟷	(33) 11.17:	+4.05	
P34	24 (2.00) ⟷	29 (3.23)	(40) 7.82 ⟷	(34) 14.72:	−6.90	
P35	13 (1.08) ⟷	26 (2.90)	(40) 11.50 ⟷	(35) 13.20:	−1.70	
P36	45 (3.74) ⟷	68 (7.58)	(40) 19.31 ⟷	(36) 34.52:	−15.21	
P37	267 (22.19) ⟷	177 (19.73)	(40) 12.47 ⟷	(37) 89.85:	−77.38	
P38	217 (18.04) ⟷	113 (12.60)	(40) 21.49 ⟷	(38) 57.36:	−35.87	
P39	287 (23.86) ⟷	120 (13.38)	(40) 46.82 ⟷	(39) 60.91:	−14.09	
P41	82 (6.82) ⟷	88 (9.81)	(40) 23.10 ⟷	(41) 44.67:	−21.57	
P42			(40) 0.00 ⟷	(42) 0.00:	0.00	
P43	8 (0.67) ⟷	16 (1.78)	(40) 26.67 ⟷	(43) 8.12:	+18.55	
P44	1 (0.08) ⟷	2 (0.22)	(40) 8.33 ⟷	(44) 1.02:	+7.31	

TABLE 18 (Continued)

	Horizontal					Vertical	
	Direct and external connections which each position has with all others in its class					Connections which are direct and internal	
	Per cent of *total* outgoing and incoming connections for each position		Per cent of totals between a position and totals of one other position				
Position 41 Total ACF: 355 Total Out: 1,676 Total In: 1,583							
	Outgoing	Incoming	Outgoing	Incoming	Difference		
P26	78 (4.65) ⟷	68 (4.30)	(41) 12.34 ⟷	(26) 19.15:	−6.81	(41) ⟷ (59)	−58.90
P27	19 (1.13) ⟷	21 (1.33)	(41) 21.11 ⟷	(27) 5.92:	+15.19	(41) ⟷ (74)	−71.07
P28	92 (5.49) ⟷	78 (4.93)	(41) 15.73 ⟷	(28) 21.97:	−6.24	(41) ⟷ (82)	−50.62
P29	2 (0.12) ⟷	3 (0.19)	(41) 15.38 ⟷	(29) 0.85:	+14.53		
P30	43 (2.57) ⟷	51 (3.22)	(41) 19.11 ⟷	(30) 14.37:	+4.74		
P31	13 (0.78) ⟷	17 (1.07)	(41) 37.14 ⟷	(31) 4.79:	+32.35		
P32	103 (6.15) ⟷	101 (6.38)	(41) 22.59 ⟷	(32) 28.45:	−5.86		
P33	39 (2.33) ⟷	215 (13.58)	(41) 16.96 ⟷	(33) 60.56:	−43.60		
P34	74 (4.42) ⟷	79 (4.99)	(41) 24.10 ⟷	(34) 22.25:	+1.85		
P35	35 (2.09) ⟷	41 (2.59)	(41) 30.97 ⟷	(35) 11.55:	+19.42		
P36	87 (5.19) ⟷	108 (6.82)	(41) 37.34 ⟷	(36) 30.42:	+6.92		
P37	407 (24.28) ⟷	320 (20.21)	(41) 19.01 ⟷	(37) 90.14:	−71.13		
P38	342 (20.41) ⟷	203 (12.82)	(41) 33.86 ⟷	(38) 57.18:	−23.32		
P39	236 (14.08) ⟷	166 (10.49)	(41) 38.50 ⟷	(39) 46.76:	−8.26		
P40	88 (5.25) ⟷	82 (5.18)	(41) 44.67 ⟷	(40) 23.10:	+21.57		
P42	5 (0.30) ⟷	7 (0.44)	(41) 23.81 ⟷	(42) 1.97:	+21.84		
P43	10 (0.60) ⟷	18 (1.14)	(41) 33.33 ⟷	(43) 5.07:	+28.26		
P44	3 (0.18) ⟷	5 (0.32)	(41) 25.00 ⟷	(44) 1.41:	+23.59		

TABLE 18 (Continued)

	Horizontal								Vertical	
	Direct and external connections which each position has with all others in its class								Connections which are direct and internal	
	Per cent of *total* outgoing and incoming connections for each position			Per cent of totals between a position and totals of one other position						
Position 42 Total ACF: 21 Total Out: 87 Total In: 72										
	Outgoing		Incoming	Outgoing		Incoming		Difference		
P26	6 (6.90)	⟷	5 (6.94)	(42) 0.95	⟷	(26) 23.81:		−22.86	(42) ⟷ (60)	−25.42
P27				(42) 0.00	⟷	(27) 0.00:		0.00	(42) ⟷ (83)	−8.33
P28	11 (12.64)	⟷	8 (11.11)	(42) 1.88	⟷	(28) 38.10:		−36.22		
P29	1 (1.15)	⟷	1 (1.39)	(42) 7.69	⟷	(29) 4.76:		+2.93		
P30	3 (3.45)	⟷	4 (5.56)	(42) 1.33	⟷	(30) 19.05:		−17.72		
P31	1 (1.15)	⟷	1 (1.39)	(42) 2.86	⟷	(31) 4.76:		−1.90		
P32	8 (9.20)	⟷	8 (11.11)	(42) 1.75	⟷	(32) 38.10:		−36.35		
P33	3 (3.45)	⟷	4 (5.56)	(42) 1.30	⟷	(33) 19.05:		−17.75		
P34	1 (1.15)	⟷	1 (1.39)	(42) 0.33	⟷	(34) 4.76:		−4.43		
P35	3 (3.45)	⟷	2 (2.78)	(42) 2.65	⟷	(35) 9.52:		−6.87		
P36	6 (6.90)	⟷	6 (8.33)	(42) 2.58	⟷	(36) 28.57:		−25.99		
P37	17 (19.54)	⟷	18 (25.00)	(42) 0.79	⟷	(37) 85.71:		−84.92		
P38	7 (8.05)	⟷	4 (5.56)	(42) 0.69	⟷	(38) 19.05:		−18.36		
P39	12 (13.79)	⟷	4 (5.56)	(42) 1.96	⟷	(39) 19.05:		−17.09		
P40				(42) 0.00	⟷	(40) 0.00:		0.00		
P41	7 (8.05)	⟷	5 (6.94)	(42) 1.97	⟷	(41) 23.81:		−21.84		
P43				(42) 0.00	⟷	(43) 0.00:		0.00		
P44	1 (1.15)	⟷	1 (1.39)	(42) 8.33	⟷	(44) 4.76:		+3.57		

TABLE 18 (Continued)

	Horizontal									Vertical	
	Direct and external connections which each position has with all others in its class									Connections which are direct and internal	
	Per cent of *total* outgoing and incoming connections for each position			Per cent of totals between a position and totals of one other position							
Position 43 Total ACF: 30 Total Out: 131 Total In: 89	Outgoing		Incoming	Outgoing			Incoming		Difference		
P26	4 (3.05)	⟷	4 (4.49)	(43)	0.63	⟷	(26)	13.33:	−12.70	(43) ⟷ (75)	−24.14
P27	2 (1.53)	⟷	2 (2.25)	(43)	2.22	⟷	(27)	6.67:	−4.45	(43) ⟷ (84)	−5.71
P28	5 (3.82)	⟷	5 (5.62)	(43)	0.85	⟷	(28)	16.67:	−15.82		
P29				(43)	0.00	⟷	(29)	0.00:	0.00		
P30	2 (1.53)	⟷	2 (2.25)	(43)	0.89	⟷	(30)	6.67:	−5.78		
P31	2 (1.53)	⟷	2 (2.25)	(43)	5.71	⟷	(31)	6.67:	−0.96		
P32	5 (3.82)	⟷	4 (4.49)	(43)	1.10	⟷	(32)	13.33:	−12.23		
P33				(43)	0.00	⟷	(33)	0.00:	0.00		
P34	2 (1.53)	⟷	2 (2.25)	(43)	0.65	⟷	(34)	6.67:	−6.02		
P35	2 (1.53)	⟷	1 (1.12)	(43)	1.77	⟷	(35)	3.33:	−1.56		
P36	2 (1.53)	⟷	2 (2.25)	(43)	0.86	⟷	(36)	6.67:	−5.81		
P37	32 (24.43)	⟷	27 (30.34)	(43)	1.49	⟷	(37)	90.00:	−88.51		
P38	24 (18.32)	⟷	14 (15.73)	(43)	2.38	⟷	(38)	46.67:	−44.29		
P39	15 (11.45)	⟷	6 (6.74)	(43)	2.45	⟷	(39)	20.00:	−17.55		
P40	16 (12.21)	⟷	8 (8.99)	(43)	8.12	⟷	(40)	26.67:	−18.55		
P41	18 (13.74)	⟷	10 (11.24)	(43)	5.07	⟷	(41)	33.33:	−28.26		
P42				(43)	0.00	⟷	(42)	0.00:	0.00		
P44				(43)	0.00	⟷	(44)	0.00:	0.00		

TABLE 18 (Continued)

	Horizontal									Vertical	
	Direct and external connections which each position has with all others in its class									Connections which are direct and internal	
	Per cent of *total* outgoing and incoming connections for each position			Per cent of totals between a position and totals of one other position							
POSITION 44 Total ACF: 12 Total Out: 59 Total In: 36											
	Outgoing		Incoming	Outgoing			Incoming		Difference		
P26	2 (3.39)	⟷	2 (5.56)	(44)	0.32	⟷	(26)	16.67:	−16.35	(44) ⟷ (85)	−10.34
P27	2 (3.39)	⟷	2 (5.56)	(44)	2.22	⟷	(27)	16.67:	−14.45		
P28	2 (3.39)	⟷	1 (2.78)	(44)	0.34	⟷	(28)	8.33:	−7.99		
P29				(44)	0.00	⟷	(29)	0.00:	0.00		
P30	1 (1.69)	⟷	1 (2.78)	(44)	0.44	⟷	(30)	8.33:	−7.89		
P31	1 (1.69)	⟷	1 (2.78)	(44)	2.86	⟷	(31)	8.33:	−5.47		
P32	2 (3.39)	⟷	2 (5.56)	(44)	0.44	⟷	(32)	16.67:	−16.23		
P33	1 (1.69)	⟷	1 (2.78)	(44)	0.43	⟷	(33)	8.33:	−7.90		
P34	1 (1.69)	⟷	1 (2.78)	(44)	0.33	⟷	(34)	8.33:	−8.00		
P35	1 (1.69)	⟷	1 (2.78)	(44)	0.88	⟷	(35)	8.33:	−7.45		
P36	2 (3.39)	⟷	2 (5.56)	(44)	0.86	⟷	(36)	16.67:	−15.81		
P37	16 (27.12)	⟷	10 (27.78)	(44)	0.75	⟷	(37)	83.33:	−82.58		
P38	9 (15.25)	⟷	3 (8.33)	(44)	0.89	⟷	(38)	25.00:	−24.11		
P39	11 (18.64)	⟷	4 (11.11)	(44)	1.79	⟷	(39)	33.33:	−31.54		
P40	2 (3.39)	⟷	1 (2.78)	(44)	1.02	⟷	(40)	8.33:	−7.31		
P41	5 (8.47)	⟷	3 (8.33)	(44)	1.41	⟷	(41)	25.00:	−23.59		
P42	1 (1.69)	⟷	1 (2.78)	(44)	4.76	⟷	(42)	8.33:	−3.57		
P43				(44)	0.00	⟷	(43)	0.00:	0.00		

TABLE 18 (Continued)

Horizontal								Vertical
Direct and external connections which each position has with all others in its class								Connections which are direct and internal
Per cent of *total* outgoing and incoming connections for each position				Per cent of totals between a position and totals of one other position				
POSITION 61								
Total ACF: 5,457								
Total Out: 9,241								
Total In: 9,172								
	Outgoing		Incoming	Outgoing		Incoming	Difference	
P45	456 (4.93)	⟷	536 (5.84)	(61) 89.94	⟷	(45) 9.82:	+80.12	0
P46	1 (0.01)	⟷	1 (0.01)	(61) 100.00	⟷	(46) 0.02:	+99.98	
P47	15 (0.16)	⟷	18 (0.20)	(61) 93.75	⟷	(47) 0.33:	+93.42	
P48	15 (0.16)	⟷	23 (0.25)	(61) 93.75	⟷	(48) 0.42:	+93.33	
P49	153 (1.66)	⟷	175 (1.91)	(61) 93.87	⟷	(49) 3.21:	+90.66	
P50	68 (0.74)	⟷	91 (0.99)	(61) 94.44	⟷	(50) 1.67:	+92.77	
P51	599 (6.48)	⟷	724 (7.89)	(61) 93.89	⟷	(51) 13.27:	+80.62	
P52	431 (4.66)	⟷	485 (5.29)	(61) 94.10	⟷	(52) 8.89:	+85.21	
P53	26 (0.28)	⟷	28 (0.31)	(61) 72.22	⟷	(53) 0.51:	+71.71	
P54	143 (1.55)	⟷	225 (2.45)	(61) 88.82	⟷	(54) 4.12:	+84.70	
P55	26 (0.28)	⟷	27 (0.29)	(61) 89.66	⟷	(55) 0.49:	+89.17	
P56	478 (5.17)	⟷	625 (6.81)	(61) 89.35	⟷	(56) 11.45:	+77.90	
P57	1,102 (11.93)	⟷	1,060 (11.56)	(61) 85.83	⟷	(57) 19.42:	+66.41	
P58	1,170 (12.66)	⟷	1,097 (11.96)	(61) 86.09	⟷	(58) 20.10:	+65.99	
P59	1,025 (11.09)	⟷	1,125 (12.27)	(61) 88.67	⟷	(59) 20.62:	+68.05	
P60	33 (0.36)	⟷	38 (0.41)	(61) 97.06	⟷	(60) 0.70:	+96.36	
P62	1,990 (21.54)	⟷	1,542 (16.81)	(61) 81.32	⟷	(62) 28.26:	+53.06	
P63	1,257 (13.60)	⟷	1,064 (11.60)	(61) 87.72	⟷	(63) 19.50:	+68.22	
P64	253 (2.74)	⟷	288 (3.14)	(61) 86.64	⟷	(64) 5.28:	+81.36	

TABLE 18 (Continued)

Position 45
Total ACF: 507
Total Out: 1,884
Total In: 1,431

	Horizontal					Vertical	
	Direct and external connections which each position has with all others in its class					Connections which are direct and internal	
	Per cent of *total* outgoing and incoming connections for each position		Per cent of totals between a position and totals of one other position				
	Outgoing	Incoming	Outgoing	Incoming	Difference		
P46			(45) 0.00 ⟷	(46) 0.00:	0.00	(45) ⟷ (5)	+56.72
P47	4 (0.21) ⟷	5 (0.35)	(45) 25.00 ⟷	(47) 0.99:	+24.01	(45) ⟷ (14)	+51.57
P48	2 (0.11) ⟷	2 (0.14)	(45) 12.50 ⟷	(48) 0.39:	+12.11	(45) ⟷ (28)	−7.14
P49	42 (2.23) ⟷	45 (3.14)	(45) 25.77 ⟷	(49) 8.88:	+16.89		
P50	14 (0.74) ⟷	13 (0.91)	(45) 19.44 ⟷	(50) 2.56:	+16.88		
P51	110 (5.84) ⟷	104 (7.27)	(45) 17.24 ⟷	(51) 20.51:	−3.27		
P52	75 (3.98) ⟷	67 (4.68)	(45) 16.38 ⟷	(52) 13.21:	+3.17		
P53	2 (0.11) ⟷	2 (0.14)	(45) 5.56 ⟷	(53) 0.39:	+5.17		
P54	26 (1.38) ⟷	24 (1.68)	(45) 16.15 ⟷	(54) 4.73:	+11.42		
P55	3 (0.16) ⟷	3 (0.21)	(45) 10.34 ⟷	(55) 0.59:	+9.75		
P56	71 (3.77) ⟷	70 (4.89)	(45) 13.27 ⟷	(56) 13.81:	−0.54		
P57	223 (11.84) ⟷	156 (10.90)	(45) 17.37 ⟷	(57) 30.77:	−13.40		
P58	174 (9.24) ⟷	113 (7.90)	(45) 12.80 ⟷	(58) 22.29:	−9.49		
P59	134 (7.11) ⟷	106 (7.41)	(45) 11.59 ⟷	(59) 20.91:	−9.32		
P60	4 (0.21) ⟷	4 (0.28)	(45) 11.76 ⟷	(60) 0.79:	+10.97		
P61	536 (28.45) ⟷	456 (31.87)	(45) 9.82 ⟷	(61) 89.94:	−80.12		
P62	294 (15.60) ⟷	154 (10.76)	(45) 12.01 ⟷	(62) 30.37:	−18.36		
P63	144 (7.64) ⟷	85 (5.94)	(45) 10.05 ⟷	(63) 16.77:	−6.72		
P64	26 (1.38) ⟷	22 (1.54)	(45) 8.90 ⟷	(64) 4.34:	+4.56		

TABLE 18 (Continued)

	Horizontal					Vertical	
	Direct and external connections which each position has with all others in its class					Connections which are direct and internal	
	Per cent of *total* outgoing and incoming connections for each position		Per cent of totals between a position and totals of one other position				
Position 46 Total ACF: 1 Total Out: 2 Total In: 2							
	Outgoing	Incoming	Outgoing	Incoming	Difference		
P45			(46) 0.00 ⟷	(45) 0.00:	0.00	(46) ⟷ (6)	0.00
P47			(46) 0.00 ⟷	(47) 0.00:	0.00	(46) ⟷ (15)	−60.00
P48			(46) 0.00 ⟷	(48) 0.00:	0.00		
P49			(46) 0.00 ⟷	(49) 0.00:	0.00		
P50			(46) 0.00 ⟷	(50) 0.00:	0.00		
P51	1 (50.00) ⟷	1 (50.00)	(46) 0.16 ⟷	(51) 100.00:	−99.84		
P52			(46) 0.00 ⟷	(52) 0.00:	0.00		
P53			(46) 0.00 ⟷	(53) 0.00:	0.00		
P54			(46) 0.00 ⟷	(54) 0.00:	0.00		
P55			(46) 0.00 ⟷	(55) 0.00:	0.00		
P56			(46) 0.00 ⟷	(56) 0.00:	0.00		
P57			(46) 0.00 ⟷	(57) 0.00:	0.00		
P58			(46) 0.00 ⟷	(58) 0.00:	0.00		
P59			(46) 0.00 ⟷	(59) 0.00:	0.00		
P60			(46) 0.00 ⟷	(60) 0.00:	0.00		
P61	1 (50.00) ⟷	1 (50.00)	(46) 0.02 ⟷	(61) 100.00:	−99.98		
P62			(46) 0.00 ⟷	(62) 0.00:	0.00		
P63			(46) 0.00 ⟷	(63) 0.00:	0.00		
P64			(46) 0.00 ⟷	(64) 0.00:	0.00		

TABLE 18 (Continued)

	Horizontal								Vertical		
	Direct and external connections which each position has with all others in its class								Connections which are direct and internal		
	Per cent of *total* outgoing and incoming connections for each position			Per cent of totals between a position and totals of one other position							
Position 47 Total ACF: 16 Total Out: 61 Total In: 52											
	Outgoing		Incoming	Outgoing		Incoming		Difference			
P45	5 (8.20)	⟷	4 (7.69)	(47) 0.99	⟷	(45) 25.00:		−24.01	(47) ⟷ (7)		+28.57
P46				(47) 0.00	⟷	(46) 0.00:		0.00	(47) ⟷ (29)		−2.70
P48	6 (9.83)	⟷	5 (9.62)	(47) 37.50	⟷	(48) 31.25:		+6.25			
P49	1 (1.64)	⟷	1 (1.92)	(47) 0.61	⟷	(49) 6.25:		−5.64			
P50				(47) 0.00	⟷	(50) 0.00:		0.00			
P51	3 (4.92)	⟷	3 (5.77)	(47) 0.47	⟷	(51) 18.75:		−18.28			
P52	2 (3.28)	⟷	2 (3.85)	(47) 0.44	⟷	(52) 12.50:		−12.06			
P53				(47) 0.00	⟷	(53) 0.00:		0.00			
P54				(47) 0.00	⟷	(54) 0.00:		0.00			
P55				(47) 0.00	⟷	(55) 0.00:		0.00			
P56	3 (4.92)	⟷	2 (3.85)	(47) 0.56	⟷	(56) 12.50:		−11.94			
P57	9 (14.75)	⟷	9 (17.31)	(47) 0.70	⟷	(57) 56.25:		−55.55			
P58	5 (8.80)	⟷	2 (3.85)	(47) 0.37	⟷	(58) 12.50:		−12.13			
P59	2 (3.28)	⟷	1 (1.92)	(47) 0.17	⟷	(59) 6.25:		−6.08			
P60				(47) 0.00	⟷	(60) 0.00:		0.00			
P61	18 (29.51)	⟷	15 (28.85)	(47) 0.33	⟷	(61) 93.75:		−93.42			
P62	6 (9.83)	⟷	7 (13.46)	(47) 0.25	⟷	(62) 43.75:		−43.50			
P63	1 (1.64)	⟷	1 (1.92)	(47) 0.07	⟷	(63) 6.25:		−6.18			
P64				(47) 0.00	⟷	(64) 0.00:		0.00			

TABLE 18 (Continued)

	Horizontal						Vertical
	Direct and external connections which each position has with all others in its class						Connections which are direct and internal
	Per cent of *total* outgoing and incoming connections for each position			Per cent of totals between a position and totals of one other position			
Position 48 Total ACF: 16 Total Out: 108 Total In: 67							
	Outgoing		Incoming	Outgoing	Incoming	Difference	
P45	2 (1.85)	⟷	2 (2.99)	(48) 0.39 ⟷	(45) 12.50:	−12.11	(48) ⟷ (8) −15.79
P46				(48) 0.00 ⟷	(46) 0.00:	0.00	
P47	5 (4.63)	⟷	6 (8.96)	(48) 31.25 ⟷	(47) 37.50:	−6.25	
P49				(48) 0.00 ⟷	(49) 0.00:	0.00	
P50	3 (2.78)	⟷	2 (2.99)	(48) 4.17 ⟷	(50) 12.50:	−8.33	
P51	3 (2.78)	⟷	2 (2.99)	(48) 0.47 ⟷	(51) 12.50:	−12.03	
P52	4 (3.70)	⟷	3 (4.48)	(48) 0.87 ⟷	(52) 18.75:	−17.88	
P53				(48) 0.00 ⟷	(53) 0.00:	0.00	
P54				(48) 0.00 ⟷	(54) 0.00:	0.00	
P55				(48) 0.00 ⟷	(55) 0.00:	0.00	
P56	6 (5.56)	⟷	4 (5.97)	(48) 1.12 ⟷	(56) 25.00:	−23.88	
P57	19 (17.59)	⟷	6 (8.96)	(48) 1.48 ⟷	(57) 37.50:	−36.02	
P58	11 (10.19)	⟷	4 (5.97)	(48) 0.81 ⟷	(58) 25.00:	−24.19	
P59	7 (6.48)	⟷	6 (8.96)	(48) 0.61 ⟷	(59) 37.50:	−36.89	
P60				(48) 0.00 ⟷	(60) 0.00:	0.00	
P61	23 (21.30)	⟷	15 (22.39)	(48) 0.42 ⟷	(61) 93.75:	−93.33	
P62	14 (12.96)	⟷	10 (14.93)	(48) 0.57 ⟷	(62) 62.50:	−61.93	
P63	9 (8.33)	⟷	6 (8.96)	(48) 0.63 ⟷	(63) 37.50:	−36.87	
P64	2 (1.85)	⟷	1 (1.49)	(48) 0.68 ⟷	(64) 6.25:	−5.57	

TABLE 18 (Continued)

	Horizontal						Vertical	
	Direct and external connections which each position has with all others in its class						Connections which are direct and internal	
	Per cent of *total* outgoing and incoming connections for each position		Per cent of totals between a position and totals of one other position					
Position 49 Total ACF: 163 Total Out: 683 Total In: 548								
	Outgoing	Incoming	Outgoing	Incoming		Difference		
P45	45 (6.59)	42 (7.66)	(49) 8.88	(45) 25.77:		−16.89	(49) ⟷ (9)	+54.50
P46			(49) 0.00	(46) 0.00:		0,00	(49) ⟷ (16)	+59.81
P47	1 (0.15)	1 (0.18)	(49) 6.25	(47) 0.61:		+5.64	(49) ⟷ (30)	−14.71
P48			(49) 0.00	(48) 0.00:		0.00	(49) ⟷ (65)	+52.68
P50	6 (0.88)	6 (1.10)	(49) 8.33	(50) 3.68:		+4.65		
P51	52 (7.61)	48 (8.76)	(49) 8.15	(51) 29.45:		−21.30		
P52	23 (3.37)	21 (3.83)	(49) 5.02	(52) 12.88:		−7.86		
P53	4 (0.59)	3 (0.55)	(49) 11.11	(53) 1.84:		+9.27		
P54	9 (1.32)	13 (2.37)	(49) 5.59	(54) 7.98:		−2.39		
P55			(49) 0.00	(55) 0.00:		0.00		
P56	18 (2.64)	26 (4.74)	(49) 3.36	(56) 15.95:		−12.59		
P57	101 (14.78)	61 (11.13)	(49) 7.87	(57) 37.42:		−29.55		
P58	74 (10.83)	56 (10.22)	(49) 5.45	(58) 34.36:		−28.91		
P59	49 (7.17)	32 (5.84)	(49) 4.24	(59) 19.63:		−15.39		
P60	4 (0.59)	5 (0.91)	(49) 11.76	(60) 3.07:		+8.69		
P61	175 (25.62)	153 (27.92)	(49) 3.21	(61) 93.87:		−90.66		
P62	73 (10.69)	44 (8.03)	(49) 2.98	(62) 26.99:		−24.01		
P63	42 (6.15)	31 (5.66)	(49) 2.93	(63) 19.02:		−16.09		
P64	7 (1.02)	6 (1.10)	(49) 2.40	(64) 3.68:		−1.28		

TABLE 18 (Continued)

	Horizontal					Vertical	
	Direct and external connections which each position has with all others in its class					Connections which are direct and internal	
	Per cent of *total* outgoing and incoming connections for each position		Per cent of totals between a position and totals of one other position				
Position 50 Total ACF: 72 Total Out: 376 Total In: 275	Outgoing	Incoming	Outgoing	Incoming	Difference		
P45	13 (3.46) ⟷	14 (5.09)	(50) 2.56 ⟷	(45) 19.44:	−16.88	(50) ⟷ (10)	+69.77
P46			(50) 0.00 ⟷	(46) 0.00:	0.00	(50) ⟷ (31)	+32.73
P47			(50) 0.00 ⟷	(47) 0.00:	0.00	(50) ⟷ (66)	+10.61
P48	2 (0.53) ⟷	3 (1.09)	(50) 12.50 ⟷	(48) 4.17:	+8.33		
P49	6 (1.60) ⟷	6 (2.18)	(50) 3.68 ⟷	(49) 8.33:	−4.65		
P51	13 (3.46) ⟷	14 (5.09)	(50) 2.04 ⟷	(51) 19.44:	−17.40		
P52	12 (3.19) ⟷	12 (4.36)	(50) 2.62 ⟷	(52) 16.67:	−14.05		
P53	1 (0.26) ⟷	1 (0.36)	(50) 2.78 ⟷	(53) 1.39:	+1.39		
P54	11 (2.93) ⟷	6 (2.18)	(50) 6.83 ⟷	(54) 8.33:	−1.50		
P55			(50) 0.00 ⟷	(55) 0.00:	0.00		
P56	15 (3.99) ⟷	15 (5.45)	(50) 2.80 ⟷	(56) 20.83:	−18.03		
P57	54 (14.36) ⟷	28 (10.18)	(50) 4.21 ⟷	(57) 38.89:	−34.68		
P58	48 (12.76) ⟷	31 (11.27)	(50) 3.53 ⟷	(58) 43.06:	−39.53		
P59	17 (4.52) ⟷	17 (6.18)	(50) 1.47 ⟷	(59) 23.61:	−22.14		
P60			(50) 0.00 ⟷	(60) 0.00:	0.00		
P61	91 (24.20) ⟷	68 (24.73)	(50) 1.67 ⟷	(61) 94.44:	−92.77		
P62	41 (10.90) ⟷	34 (12.36)	(50) 1.68 ⟷	(62) 47.22:	−45.54		
P63	47 (12.50) ⟷	21 (7.64)	(50) 3.28 ⟷	(63) 29.17:	−25.89		
P64	5 (1.34) ⟷	5 (1.82)	(50) 1.71 ⟷	(64) 6.94:	−5.23		

TABLE 18 (Continued)

	Horizontal													Vertical			
	Direct and external connections which each position has with all others in its class													Connections which are direct and internal			
	Per cent of *total* outgoing and incoming connections for each position					Per cent of totals between a position and totals of one other position											
Position 51 Total ACF: 638 Total Out: 2,675 Total In: 2,065	Outgoing			Incoming		Outgoing			Incoming		Difference						
P45	104	(3.89)	⟷	110	(5.33)	(51)	20.51	⟷	(45)	17.24:	+3.27			(51)	⟷	(11)	+88.92
P46	1	(0.04)	⟷	1	(0.05)	(51)	100.00	⟷	(46)	0.16:	+99.84			(51)	⟷	(17)	+87.46
P47	3	(0.11)	⟷	3	(0.15)	(51)	18.75	⟷	(47)	0.47:	+18.28			(51)	⟷	(32)	+35.93
P48	2	(0.07)	⟷	3	(0.15)	(51)	12.50	⟷	(48)	0.47:	+12.03			(51)	⟷	(67)	+8.43
P49	48	(1.79)	⟷	52	(2.52)	(51)	29.45	⟷	(49)	8.15:	+21.30			(51)	⟷	(80)	+39.20
P50	14	(0.52)	⟷	13	(0.63)	(51)	19.44	⟷	(50)	2.04:	+17.40						
P52	102	(3.81)	⟷	109	(5.28)	(51)	22.27	⟷	(52)	17.08:	+5.19						
P53	6	(0.22)	⟷	5	(0.24)	(51)	16.67	⟷	(53)	0.78:	+15.89						
P54	39	(1.46)	⟷	42	(2.03)	(51)	24.22	⟷	(54)	6.58:	+17.64						
P55	6	(0.22)	⟷	6	(0.29)	(51)	20.69	⟷	(55)	0.94:	+19.75						
P56	138	(5.16)	⟷	115	(5.57)	(51)	25.79	⟷	(56)	18.03:	+7.76						
P57	290	(10.84)	⟷	201	(9.73)	(51)	22.59	⟷	(57)	31.50:	−8.91						
P58	264	(9.87)	⟷	192	(9.30)	(51)	19.43	⟷	(58)	30.09:	−10.66						
P59	199	(7.44)	⟷	174	(8.43)	(51)	17.21	⟷	(59)	27.27:	−10.06						
P60	13	(0.49)	⟷	12	(0.58)	(51)	38.24	⟷	(60)	1.88:	+36.36						
P61	724	(27.07)	⟷	599	(29.01)	(51)	13.27	⟷	(61)	93.89:	−80.62						
P62	410	(15.33)	⟷	216	(10.46)	(51)	16.76	⟷	(62)	33.86:	−17.10						
P63	261	(9.76)	⟷	171	(8.28)	(51)	18.21	⟷	(63)	26.80:	−8.59						
P64	51	(1.91)	⟷	41	(1.99)	(51)	17.47	⟷	(64)	6.43:	+11.04						

TABLE 18 (Continued)

	Horizontal					Vertical	
	Direct and external connections which each position has with all others in its class					Connections which are direct and internal	
	Per cent of *total* outgoing and incoming connections for each position		Per cent of totals between a position and totals of one other position				
Position 52 Total ACF: 458 Total Out: 1,506 Total In: 1,273							
	Outgoing	Incoming	Outgoing	Incoming	Difference		
P45	67 (4.45) ⟷	75 (5.89)	(52) 13.21 ⟷	(45) 16.38:	−3.17	(52) ⟷ (20)	+79.38
P46			(52) 0.00 ⟷	(46) 0.00:	0.00	(52) ⟷ (34)	+19.43
P47	2 (0.13) ⟷	2 (0.16)	(52) 12.50 ⟷	(47) 0.44:	+12.06		
P48	3 (0.20) ⟷	4 (0.31)	(52) 18.75 ⟷	(48) 0.87:	+17.88		
P49	21 (1.39) ⟷	23 (1.81)	(52) 12.88 ⟷	(49) 5.02:	+7.86		
P50	12 (0.80) ⟷	12 (0.94)	(52) 16.67 ⟷	(50) 2.62:	+14.05		
P51	109 (7.24) ⟷	102 (8.01)	(52) 17.08 ⟷	(51) 22.27:	−5.19		
P53	7 (0.46) ⟷	9 (0.71)	(52) 19.44 ⟷	(53) 1.97:	+17.47		
P54	24 (1.59) ⟷	21 (1.65)	(52) 14.91 ⟷	(54) 4.59:	+10.32		
P55			(52) 0.00 ⟷	(55) 0.00:	0.00		
P56	57 (3.79) ⟷	58 (4.56)	(52) 10.65 ⟷	(56) 12.66:	−2.01		
P57	229 (15.21) ⟷	166 (13.04)	(52) 17.83 ⟷	(57) 36.24:	−18.41		
P58	111 (7.37) ⟷	95 (7.46)	(52) 8.17 ⟷	(58) 20.74:	−12.57		
P59	102 (6.77) ⟷	83 (6.52)	(52) 8.82 ⟷	(59) 18.12:	−9.30		
P60	6 (0.40) ⟷	6 (0.47)	(52) 17.65 ⟷	(60) 1.31:	+16.34		
P61	485 (32.21) ⟷	431 (33.86)	(52) 8.89 ⟷	(61) 94.10:	−85.21		
P62	150 (9.96) ⟷	100 (7.86)	(52) 6.13 ⟷	(62) 21.83:	−15.70		
P63	102 (6.77) ⟷	70 (5.50)	(52) 7.12 ⟷	(63) 15.28:	−8.16		
P64	19 (1.26) ⟷	16 (1.26)	(52) 6.51 ⟷	(64) 3.49:	+3.02		

TABLE 18 (Continued)

Horizontal							Vertical
Direct and external connections which each position has with all others in its class							Connections which are direct and internal
Per cent of *total* outgoing and incoming connections for each position			Per cent of totals between a position and totals of one other position				
POSITION 53 Total ACF: 36 Total Out: 108 Total In: 86							
	Outgoing	Incoming	Outgoing		Incoming	Difference	
P45	2 (1.85) ⟷	2 (2.33)	(53)	0.39 ⟷	(45) 5.56:	−5.17	(53) ⟷ (21) +14.29
P46			(53)	0.00 ⟷	(46) 0.00:	0.00	
P47			(53)	0.00 ⟷	(47) 0.00:	0.00	
P48			(53)	0.00 ⟷	(48) 0.00:	0.00	
P49	3 (2.78) ⟷	4 (4.65)	(53)	1.84 ⟷	(49) 11.11:	−9.27	
P50	1 (0.93) ⟷	1 (1.16)	(53)	1.39 ⟷	(50) 2.78:	−1.39	
P51	5 (4.63) ⟷	6 (6.98)	(53)	0.78 ⟷	(51) 16.67:	−15.89	
P52	9 (8.33) ⟷	7 (8.14)	(53)	1.97 ⟷	(52) 19.44:	−17.47	
P54	3 (2.78) ⟷	2 (2.23)	(53)	1.86 ⟷	(54) 5.56:	−3.70	
P55			(53)	0.00 ⟷	(55) 0.00:	0.00	
P56	5 (4.63) ⟷	6 (6.98)	(53)	0.93 ⟷	(56) 16.67:	−15.74	
P57	14 (12.96) ⟷	9 (10.47)	(53)	1.09 ⟷	(57) 25.00:	−23.91	
P58	17 (15.74) ⟷	7 (8.14)	(53)	1.25 ⟷	(58) 19.44:	−18.19	
P59	9 (8.33) ⟷	7 (8.14)	(53)	0.78 ⟷	(59) 19.44:	−18.66	
P60			(53)	0.00 ⟷	(60) 0.00:	0.00	
P61	28 (25.93) ⟷	26 (30.23)	(53)	0.51 ⟷	(61) 72.22:	−71.71	
P62	5 (4.63) ⟷	5 (5.81)	(53)	0.20 ⟷	(62) 13.89:	−13.69	
P63	7 (6.48) ⟷	4 (4.65)	(53)	0.49 ⟷	(63) 11.11:	−10.62	
P64			(53)	0.00 ⟷	(64) 0.00:	0.00	

TABLE 18 (Continued)

	Horizontal					Vertical	
	Direct and external connections which each position has with all others in its class					Connections which are direct and internal	
	Per cent of *total* outgoing and incoming connections for each position		Per cent of totals between a position and totals of one other position				
Position 54 Total ACF: 161 Total Out: 839 Total In: 619	Outgoing	Incoming	Outgoing	Incoming	Difference		
P45	24 (2.86) ⟷	26 (4.20)	(54) 4.73 ⟷	(45) 16.15:	−11.42	(54) ⟷ (22)	+72.59
P46			(54) 0.00 ⟷	(46) 0.00:	0.00	(54) ⟷ (35)	+15.25
P47			(54) 0.00 ⟷	(47) 0.00:	0.00	(54) ⟷ (68)	−10.05
P48			(54) 0.00 ⟷	(48) 0.00:	0.00		
P49	13 (1.55) ⟷	9 (1.45)	(54) 7.98 ⟷	(49) 5.59:	+2.39		
P50	6 (0.72) ⟷	11 (1.78)	(54) 8.33 ⟷	(50) 6.83:	+1.50		
P51	42 (5.01) ⟷	39 (6.30)	(54) 6.58 ⟷	(51) 24.22:	−17.64		
P52	21 (2.50) ⟷	24 (3.88)	(54) 4.59 ⟷	(52) 14.91:	−10.32		
P53	2 (0.24) ⟷	3 (0.48)	(54) 5.56 ⟷	(53) 1.86:	+3.70		
P55	1 (0.12) ⟷	1 (0.16)	(54) 3.45 ⟷	(55) 0.62:	+2.83		
P56	43 (5.13) ⟷	40 (6.46)	(54) 8.04 ⟷	(56) 24.84:	−16.80		
P57	82 (9.77) ⟷	53 (8.56)	(54) 6.39 ⟷	(57) 32.92:	−26.53		
P58	82 (9.77) ⟷	63 (10.18)	(54) 6.03 ⟷	(58) 39.13:	−33.10		
P59	71 (3.46) ⟷	61 (9.85)	(54) 6.14 ⟷	(59) 37.89:	−31.75		
P60	2 (0.24) ⟷	2 (0.32)	(54) 5.88 ⟷	(60) 1.24:	+4.64		
P61	225 (26.82) ⟷	143 (23.10)	(54) 4.12 ⟷	(61) 88.82:	−84.70		
P62	144 (17.16) ⟷	81 (13.09)	(54) 5.88 ⟷	(62) 50.31:	−44.43		
P63	70 (8.34) ⟷	55 (8.89)	(54) 4.88 ⟷	(63) 34.16:	−29.28		
P64	11 (1.31) ⟷	8 (1.29)	(54) 3.77 ⟷	(64) 4.97:	−1.20		

TABLE 18 (Continued)

	Horizontal										Vertical			
	Direct and external connections which each position has with all others in its class										Connections which are direct and internal			
	Per cent of *total* outgoing and incoming connections for each position				Per cent of totals between a position and totals of one other position									
Position 55 Total ACF: 29 Total Out: 131 Total In: 101														
	Outgoing		Incoming		Outgoing			Incoming		Difference				
P45	3 (2.29)	⟷	3 (2.97)		(55)	0.59	⟷	(45)	10.34:	−9.75	(55)	⟷	(23)	+26.09
P46					(55)	0.00	⟷	(46)	0.00:	0.00	(55)	⟷	(69)	−10.77
P47					(55)	0.00	⟷	(47)	0.00:	0.00				
P48					(55)	0.00	⟷	(48)	0.00:	0.00				
P49					(55)	0.00	⟷	(49)	0.00:	0.00				
P50					(55)	0.00	⟷	(50)	0.00:	0.00				
P51	6 (4.58)	⟷	6 (5.94)		(55)	0.94	⟷	(51)	20.69:	−19.75				
P52					(55)	0.00	⟷	(52)	0.00:	0.00				
P53					(55)	0.00	⟷	(53)	0.00:	0.00				
P54	1 (0.76)	⟷	1 (0.99)		(55)	0.62	⟷	(54)	3.45:	−2.83				
P56	9 (6.87)	⟷	7 (6.93)		(55)	1.68	⟷	(56)	24.14:	−22.46				
P57	9 (6.87)	⟷	4 (3.96)		(55)	0.70	⟷	(57)	13.79:	−13.09				
P58	9 (6.87)	⟷	12 (11.88)		(55)	0.66	⟷	(58)	41.38:	−40.72				
P59	9 (6.87)	⟷	8 (7.92)		(55)	0.78	⟷	(59)	27.59:	−26.81				
P60					(55)	0.00	⟷	(60)	0.00:	0.00				
P61	27 (20.61)	⟷	26 (25.74)		(55)	0.49	⟷	(61)	89.66:	−89.17				
P62	35 (26.72)	⟷	17 (16.83)		(55)	1.43	⟷	(62)	58.62:	−57.19				
P63	19 (14.51)	⟷	11 (10.89)		(55)	1.33	⟷	(63)	37.93:	−36.60				
P64	4 (3.05)	⟷	6 (5.94)		(55)	1.37	⟷	(64)	20.69:	−19.32				

TABLE 18 (Continued)

	Horizontal					Vertical	
	Direct and external connections which each position has with all others in its class					Connections which are direct and internal	
	Per cent of *total* outgoing and incoming connections for each position		Per cent of totals between a position and totals of one other position				
Position 56 Total ACF: 535 Total Out: 2,576 Total In: 1,865	Outgoing	Incoming	Outgoing	Incoming	Difference		
P45	70 (2.72) ⟷	71 (3.81)	(56) 13.81 ⟷	(45) 13.27:	+0.54	(56) ⟷ (25)	+93.08
P46			(56) 0.00 ⟷	(46) 0.00:	0.00	(56) ⟷ (36)	+54.08
P47	2 (0.08) ⟷	3 (0.16)	(56) 12.50 ⟷	(47) 0.56:	+11.94	(56) ⟷ (71)	−17.10
P48	4 (0.16) ⟷	6 (0.32)	(56) 25.00 ⟷	(48) 1.12:	+23.88	(56) ⟷ (81)	+33.74
P49	26 (1.01) ⟷	18 (0.97)	(56) 15.95 ⟷	(49) 3.36:	+12.59		
P50	15 (0.58) ⟷	15 (0.80)	(56) 20.83 ⟷	(50) 2.80:	+18.03		
P51	115 (4.47) ⟷	138 (7.40)	(56) 18.03 ⟷	(51) 25.79:	−7.76		
P52	58 (2.25) ⟷	57 (3.06)	(56) 12.66 ⟷	(52) 10.65:	+2.01		
P53	6 (0.23) ⟷	5 (0.27)	(56) 16.67 ⟷	(53) 0.93:	+15.74		
P54	40 (1.55) ⟷	43 (2.31)	(56) 24.84 ⟷	(54) 8.04:	+16.80		
P55	7 (0.27) ⟷	9 (0.48)	(56) 24.14 ⟷	(55) 1.68:	+22.46		
P57	270 (10.48) ⟷	167 (8.95)	(56) 21.03 ⟷	(57) 31.21:	−10.18		
P58	278 (10.79) ⟷	171 (9.17)	(56) 20.46 ⟷	(58) 31.96:	−11.50		
P59	250 (9.71) ⟷	216 (11.58)	(56) 21.63 ⟷	(59) 40.37:	−18.74		
P60	5 (0.19) ⟷	5 (0.27)	(56) 14.71 ⟷	(60) 0.93:	+13.78		
P61	625 (24.26) ⟷	478 (25.63)	(56) 11.45 ⟷	(61) 89.35:	−77.90		
P62	515 (19.99) ⟷	262 (14.05)	(56) 21.05 ⟷	(62) 48.97:	−27.92		
P63	257 (9.98) ⟷	164 (8.79)	(56) 17.93 ⟷	(63) 30.65:	−12.72		
P64	33 (1.28) ⟷	37 (1.98)	(56) 11.30 ⟷	(64) 6.92:	+4.38		

TABLE 18 (Continued)

	Horizontal: Direct and external connections which each position has with all others in its class — Per cent of *total* outgoing and incoming connections for each position			Horizontal: Per cent of totals between a position and totals of one other position			Vertical: Connections which are direct and internal	
Position 57 Total ACF: 1,284 Total Out: 3,553 Total In: 4,017								
	Outgoing		Incoming	Outgoing	Incoming	Difference		
P45	156 (4.39)	⟷	223 (5.55)	(57) 30.77 ⟷	(45) 17.37:	+13.40	(57) ⟷ (38)	+11.82
P46				(57) 0.00 ⟷	(46) 0.00:	0.00		
P47	9 (0.25)	⟷	9 (0.22)	(57) 56.25 ⟷	(47) 0.70:	+55.55		
P48	6 (0.17)	⟷	19 (0.47)	(57) 37.50 ⟷	(48) 1.48:	+36.02		
P49	61 (1.72)	⟷	101 (2.51)	(57) 37.42 ⟷	(49) 7.87:	+29.55		
P50	28 (0.79)	⟷	54 (1.34)	(57) 38.89 ⟷	(50) 4.21:	+34.68		
P51	201 (5.66)	⟷	290 (7.22)	(57) 31.50 ⟷	(51) 22.59:	+8.91		
P52	166 (4.67)	⟷	229 (5.70)	(57) 36.24 ⟷	(52) 17.83:	+18.41		
P53	9 (0.25)	⟷	14 (0.35)	(57) 25.00 ⟷	(53) 1.09:	+23.91		
P54	53 (1.49)	⟷	82 (2.04)	(57) 32.92 ⟷	(54) 6.39:	+26.53		
P55	4 (0.11)	⟷	9 (0.22)	(57) 13.79 ⟷	(55) 0.70:	+13.09		
P56	167 (4.70)	⟷	270 (6.72)	(57) 31.21 ⟷	(56) 21.03:	+10.18		
P58	403 (11.34)	⟷	417 (10.38)	(57) 29.65 ⟷	(58) 32.48:	−2.83		
P59	306 (8.61)	⟷	365 (9.09)	(57) 26.47 ⟷	(59) 28.43:	−1.96		
P60	12 (0.34)	⟷	16 (0.40)	(57) 35.29 ⟷	(60) 1.25:	+34.04		
P61	1,060 (29.84)	⟷	102 (27.43)	(57) 19.42 ⟷	(61) 85.83:	−66.41		
P62	549 (15.45)	⟷	479 (11.92)	(57) 22.44 ⟷	(62) 37.31:	−14.87		
P63	311 (8.76)	⟷	273 (6.80)	(57) 21.70 ⟷	(63) 21.26:	+0.44		
P64	52 (1.46)	⟷	65 (1.62)	(57) 17.81 ⟷	(64) 5.06:	+12.75		

TABLE 18 (Continued)

	Horizontal: Direct and external connections which each position has with all others in its class — Per cent of *total* outgoing and incoming connections for each position		Horizontal: Per cent of totals between a position and totals of one other position			Vertical: Connections which are direct and internal	
Position 58 Total ACF: 1,359 Total Out: 3,899 Total In: 4,241							
	Outgoing	Incoming	Outgoing	Incoming	Difference		
P45	113 (2.90) ⟷	174 (4.10)	(58) 22.29 ⟷	(45) 12.80:	+9.49	(58) ⟷ (39)	+37.44
P46			(58) 0.00 ⟷	(46) 0.00:	0.00	(58) ⟷ (72)	+17.80
P47	2 (0.05) ⟷	5 (0.12)	(58) 12.50 ⟷	(47) 0.37:	+12.13		
P48	4 (0.10) ⟷	11 (0.26)	(58) 25.00 ⟷	(48) 0.81:	+24.19		
P49	56 (1.43) ⟷	74 (1.74)	(58) 34.36 ⟷	(49) 5.45:	+28.91		
P50	31 (0.80) ⟷	48 (1.13)	(58) 43.06 ⟷	(50) 3.53:	+39.53		
P51	192 (4.92) ⟷	264 (6.22)	(58) 30.09 ⟷	(51) 19.43:	+10.66		
P52	95 (2.44) ⟷	111 (2.62)	(58) 20.74 ⟷	(52) 8.17:	+12.57		
P53	7 (0.18) ⟷	17 (0.40)	(58) 19.44 ⟷	(53) 1.25:	+18.19		
P54	63 (1.62) ⟷	82 (1.93)	(58) 39.13 ⟷	(54) 6.03:	+33.10		
P55	12 (0.31) ⟷	9 (0.21)	(58) 41.38 ⟷	(55) 0.66:	+40.72		
P56	171 (4.39) ⟷	278 (6.56)	(58) 31.96 ⟷	(56) 20.46:	+11.50		
P57	417 (10.70) ⟷	403 (9.50)	(58) 32.48 ⟷	(57) 29.65:	+2.83		
P59	345 (8.85) ⟷	425 (10.02)	(58) 29.84 ⟷	(59) 31.27:	−1.43		
P60	11 (0.28) ⟷	13 (0.31)	(58) 32.35 ⟷	(60) 0.96:	+31.39		
P61	1,097 (28.13) ⟷	1,170 (27.59)	(58) 20.10 ⟷	(61) 86.09:	−65.99		
P62	798 (20.46) ⟷	644 (15.19)	(58) 32.61 ⟷	(62) 47.39:	−14.78		
P63	430 (11.03) ⟷	442 (10.42)	(58) 30.01 ⟷	(63) 32.52:	−2.51		
P64	55 (1.41) ⟷	71 (1.67)	(58) 18.84 ⟷	(64) 5.22:	+13.62		

TABLE 18 (Continued)

POSITION 59
Total ACF: 1,156
Total Out: 4,048
Total In: 3,539

	Horizontal					Vertical	
	Direct and external connections which each position has with all others in its class					Connections which are direct and internal	
	Per cent of *total* outgoing and incoming connections for each position		Per cent of totals between a position and totals of one other position				
	Outgoing	Incoming	Outgoing	Incoming	Difference		
P45	106 (2.62) ⟷	134 (3.79)	(59) 20.91 ⟷	(45) 11.59:	+9.32	(59) ⟷ (41)	+58.90
P46			(59) 0.00 ⟷	(46) 0.00:	0.00	(59) ⟷ (74)	−20.94
P47	1 (0.02) ⟷	2 (0.06)	(59) 6.25 ⟷	(47) 0.17:	+6.08	(59) ⟷ (82)	+11.80
P48	6 (0.15) ⟷	7 (0.20)	(59) 37.50 ⟷	(48) 0.61:	+36.89		
P49	32 (0.79) ⟷	49 (1.38)	(59) 19.63 ⟷	(49) 4.24:	+15.39		
P50	17 (0.42) ⟷	17 (0.48)	(59) 23.61 ⟷	(50) 1.47:	+22.14		
P51	174 (4.30) ⟷	199 (5.62)	(59) 27.27 ⟷	(51) 17.21:	+10.06		
P52	83 (2.05) ⟷	102 (2.88)	(59) 18.12 ⟷	(52) 8.82:	+9.30		
P53	7 (0.17) ⟷	9 (0.25)	(59) 19.44 ⟷	(53) 0.78:	+18.66		
P54	61 (1.51) ⟷	71 (2.01)	(59) 37.89 ⟷	(54) 6.14:	+31.75		
P55	8 (0.20) ⟷	9 (0.25)	(59) 27.59 ⟷	(55) 0.78:	+26.81		
P56	216 (5.34) ⟷	250 (7.06)	(59) 40.37 ⟷	(56) 21.63:	+18.74		
P57	365 (9.02) ⟷	306 (8.65)	(59) 28.43 ⟷	(57) 26.47:	+1.96		
P58	425 (10.50) ⟷	345 (9.75)	(59) 31.27 ⟷	(58) 29.84:	+1.43		
P60	3 (0.07) ⟷	4 (0.11)	(59) 8.82 ⟷	(60) 0.35:	+8.47		
P61	1,125 (27.78) ⟷	1,025 (28.96)	(59) 20.62 ⟷	(61) 88.67:	−68.05		
P62	797 (19.69) ⟷	526 (14.86)	(59) 32.57 ⟷	(62) 45.50:	−12.93		
P63	520 (12.85) ⟷	391 (11.05)	(59) 36.29 ⟷	(63) 33.82:	+2.47		
P64	102 (2.52) ⟷	93 (2.63)	(59) 34.93 ⟷	(64) 8.04:	+26.89		

TABLE 18 (Continued)

	Horizontal					Vertical	
	Direct and external connections which each position has with all others in its class					Connections which are direct and internal	
	Per cent of *total* outgoing and incoming connections for each position		Per cent of totals between a position and totals of one other position				
Position 60 Total ACF: 34 Total Out: 142 Total In: 121							
	Outgoing	Incoming	Outgoing	Incoming	Difference		
P45	4 (2.82) ⟷	4 (3.31)	(60) 0.79 ⟷	(45) 11.76:	−10.97	(60) ⟷ (42)	+25.42
P46			(60) 0.00 ⟷	(46) 0.00:	0.00	(60) ⟷ (83)	+17.46
P47			(60) 0.00 ⟷	(47) 0.00:	0.00		
P48			(60) 0.00 ⟷	(48) 0.00:	0.00		
P49	5 (3.52) ⟷	4 (3.31)	(60) 3.07 ⟷	(49) 11.76:	−8.69		
P50			(60) 0.00 ⟷	(50) 0.00:	0.00		
P51	12 (8.45) ⟷	13 (10.74)	(60) 1.88 ⟷	(51) 38.24:	−36.36		
P52	6 (4.23) ⟷	6 (4.96)	(60) 1.31 ⟷	(52) 17.65:	−16.34		
P53			(60) 0.00 ⟷	(53) 0.00:	0.00		
P54	2 (1.41) ⟷	2 (1.65)	(60) 1.24 ⟷	(54) 5.88:	−4.64		
P55			(60) 0.00 ⟷	(55) 0.00:	0.00		
P56	5 (3.52) ⟷	5 (4.13)	(60) 0.93 ⟷	(56) 14.71:	−13.78		
P57	16 (11.27) ⟷	12 (9.92)	(60) 1.25 ⟷	(57) 35.29:	−34.04		
P58	13 (9.15) ⟷	11 (9.09)	(60) 0.96 ⟷	(58) 32.35:	−31.39		
P59	4 (2.82) ⟷	3 (2.48)	(60) 0.35 ⟷	(59) 8.82:	−8.47		
P61	38 (26.75) ⟷	33 (27.27)	(60) 0.70 ⟷	(61) 97.06:	−96.36		
P62	17 (11.97) ⟷	11 (9.09)	(60) 0.69 ⟷	(62) 32.35:	−31.66		
P63	9 (6.34) ⟷	9 (7.44)	(60) 0.63 ⟷	(63) 26.47:	−25.84		
P64	11 (7.75) ⟷	8 (6.61)	(60) 3.77 ⟷	(64) 23.53:	−19.76		

TABLE 18 (Continued)

Horizontal												Vertical		
Direct and external connections which each position has with all others in its class												Connections which are direct and internal		
Per cent of *total* outgoing and incoming connections for each position						Per cent of totals between a position and totals of one other position								
Position 62 Total ACF: 2,447 Total Out: 5,038 Total In: 6,944														
	Outgoing			Incoming		Outgoing			Incoming		Difference			
P45	154	(3.06)	⟷	294	(4.23)	(62)	30.37 ⟷	(45)	12.01:		+18.36	(62) ⟷	(76)	−5.97
P46						(62)	0.00 ⟷	(46)	0.00:		0.00			
P47	7	(0.14)	⟷	6	(0.09)	(62)	43.75 ⟷	(47)	0.25:		+43.50			
P48	10	(0.20)	⟷	14	(0.20)	(62)	62.50 ⟷	(48)	0.57:		+61.93			
P49	44	(0.87)	⟷	73	(1.05)	(62)	26.99 ⟷	(49)	2.98:		+24.01			
P50	34	(0.67)	⟷	41	(0.59)	(62)	47.22 ⟷	(50)	1.68:		+45.54			
P51	216	(4.29)	⟷	410	(5.90)	(62)	33.86 ⟷	(51)	16.76:		+17.10			
P52	100	(1.98)	⟷	150	(2.16)	(62)	21.83 ⟷	(52)	6.13:		+15.70			
P53	5	(0.10)	⟷	5	(0.07)	(62)	13.89 ⟷	(53)	0.20:		+13.69			
P54	81	(1.61)	⟷	144	(2.07)	(62)	50.31 ⟷	(54)	5.88:		+44.43			
P55	17	(0.34)	⟷	35	(0.50)	(62)	58.62 ⟷	(55)	1.43:		+57.19			
P56	262	(5.20)	⟷	515	(7.42)	(62)	48.97 ⟷	(56)	21.05:		+27.92			
P57	479	(9.51)	⟷	549	(7.91)	(62)	37.31 ⟷	(57)	22.44:		+14.87			
P58	644	(12.78)	⟷	798	(11.49)	(62)	47.39 ⟷	(58)	32.61:		+14.78			
P59	526	(10.44)	⟷	797	(11.48)	(62)	45.50 ⟷	(59)	32.57:		+12.93			
P60	11	(0.22)	⟷	17	(0.24)	(62)	32.35 ⟷	(60)	0.69:		+31.66			
P61	1,542	(30.61)	⟷	1,990	(28.66)	(62)	28.26 ⟷	(61)	81.32:		−53.06			
P63	794	(15.76)	⟷	903	(13.00)	(62)	55.41 ⟷	(63)	36.90:		+18.51			
P64	112	(2.22)	⟷	203	(2.92)	(62)	38.36 ⟷	(64)	8.30:		+30.06			

TABLE 18 (Continued)

	Horizontal					Vertical	
	Direct and external connections which each position has with all others in its class					Connections which are direct and internal	
	Per cent of *total* outgoing and incoming connections for each position		Per cent of totals between a position and totals of one other position				
Position 63 Total ACF: 1,433 Total Out: 3,838 Total In: 4,497							
	Outgoing	Incoming	Outgoing	Incoming	Difference		
P45	85 (2.21) ⟷	144 (3.20)	(63) 16.77 ⟷	(45) 10.05:	+6.72	(63) ⟷ (77)	−18.35
P46			(63) 0.00 ⟷	(46) 0.00:	0.00	(63) ⟷ (86)	+1.77
P47	1 (0.03) ⟷	1 (0.02)	(63) 6.25 ⟷	(47) 0.07:	+6.18		
P48	6 (0.16) ⟷	9 (0.20)	(63) 37.50 ⟷	(48) 0.63:	+36.87		
P49	31 (0.81) ⟷	42 (0.93)	(63) 19.02 ⟷	(49) 2.93:	+16.09		
P50	21 (0.55) ⟷	47 (1.05)	(63) 29.17 ⟷	(50) 3.28:	+25.89		
P51	171 (4.46) ⟷	261 (5.80)	(63) 26.80 ⟷	(51) 18.21:	+8.59		
P52	70 (1.82) ⟷	102 (2.27)	(63) 15.28 ⟷	(52) 7.12:	+8.16		
P53	4 (0.10) ⟷	7 (0.16)	(63) 11.11 ⟷	(53) 0.49:	+10.62		
P54	55 (1.43) ⟷	70 (1.56)	(63) 34.16 ⟷	(54) 4.88:	+29.28		
P55	11 (0.29) ⟷	19 (0.42)	(63) 37.93 ⟷	(55) 1.33:	+36.60		
P56	164 (4.27) ⟷	257 (5.71)	(63) 30.65 ⟷	(56) 17.93:	+12.72		
P57	273 (7.11) ⟷	311 (6.92)	(63) 21.26 ⟷	(57) 21.70:	−0.44		
P58	442 (11.52) ⟷	430 (9.56)	(63) 32.52 ⟷	(58) 30.01:	+2.51		
P59	391 (10.19) ⟷	520 (11.56)	(63) 33.82 ⟷	(59) 36.29:	−2.47		
P60	9 (0.23) ⟷	9 (0.20)	(63) 26.47 ⟷	(60) 0.63:	+25.84		
P61	1,064 (27.72) ⟷	1,257 (27.95)	(63) 19.50 ⟷	(61) 87.72:	−68.22		
P62	903 (23.53) ⟷	794 (17.66)	(63) 36.90 ⟷	(62) 55.41:	−18.51		
P64	137 (3.57) ⟷	217 (4.83)	(63) 46.92 ⟷	(64) 15.14:	+31.78		

TABLE 18 (Continued)

	Horizontal								Vertical	
	Direct and external connections which each position has with all others in its class								Connections which are direct and internal	
	Per cent of *total* outgoing and incoming connections for each position			Per cent of totals between a position and totals of one other position						
Position 64 Total ACF: 292 Total Out: 1,087 Total In: 880										
	Outgoing		Incoming	Outgoing			Incoming	Difference		
P45	22 (2.02)	⟷	26 (2.95)	(64) 4.34	⟷	(45)	8.90:	−4.56	(64) ⟷ (87)	−1.15
P46				(64) 0.00	⟷	(46)	0.00:	0.00		
P47				(64) 0.00	⟷	(47)	0.00:	0.00		
P48	1 (0.09)	⟷	2 (0.23)	(64) 6.25	⟷	(48)	0.68:	+5.57		
P49	6 (0.55)	⟷	7 (0.80)	(64) 3.68	⟷	(49)	2.40:	+1.28		
P50	5 (0.46)	⟷	5 (0.57)	(64) 6.94	⟷	(50)	1.71:	+5.23		
P51	41 (3.77)	⟷	51 (5.80)	(64) 6.43	⟷	(51)	17.47:	−11.04		
P52	16 (1.47)	⟷	19 (2.16)	(64) 3.49	⟷	(52)	6.51:	−3.02		
P53				(64) 0.00	⟷	(53)	0.00:	0.00		
P54	8 (0.74)	⟷	11 (1.25)	(64) 4.97	⟷	(54)	3.77:	+1.20		
P55	6 (0.55)	⟷	4 (0.45)	(64) 20.69	⟷	(55)	1.37:	+19.32		
P56	37 (3.40)	⟷	33 (3.75)	(64) 6.92	⟷	(56)	11.30:	−4.38		
P57	65 (5.98)	⟷	52 (5.91)	(64) 5.06	⟷	(57)	17.81:	−12.75		
P58	71 (6.53)	⟷	55 (6.25)	(64) 5.22	⟷	(58)	18.84:	−13.62		
P59	93 (8.56)	⟷	102 (11.59)	(64) 8.04	⟷	(59)	34.93:	−26.89		
P60	8 (0.74)	⟷	11 (1.25)	(64) 23.53	⟷	(60)	3.77:	+19.76		
P61	288 (26.50)	⟷	253 (28.75)	(64) 5.28	⟷	(61)	86.64:	−81.36		
P62	203 (18.68)	⟷	112 (12.73)	(64) 8.30	⟷	(62)	38.36:	−30.06		
P63	217 (19.96)	⟷	137 (15.57)	(64) 15.14	⟷	(63)	46.92:	−31.78		

TABLE 18 (Continued)

Horizontal											Vertical
Direct and external connections which each position has with all others in its class											Connections which are direct and internal
Per cent of *total* outgoing and incoming connections for each position					Per cent of totals between a position and totals of one other position						
Position 78 Total ACF: 6,146 Total Out: 8,582 Total In: 8,507											
	Outgoing		Incoming		Outgoing		Incoming			Difference	
P65	47	(0.55) ⟷	55	(0.65)	(78)	92.16 ⟷	(65)	0.89:		+91.27	0
P66	46	(0.54) ⟷	62	(0.73)	(78)	80.70 ⟷	(66)	1.01:		+79.69	
P67	332	(3.87) ⟷	424	(4.98)	(78)	91.46 ⟷	(67)	6.90:		+84.56	
P68	184	(2.14) ⟷	231	(2.72)	(78)	90.64 ⟷	(68)	3.76:		+86.88	
P69	33	(0.38) ⟷	41	(0.48)	(78)	91.67 ⟷	(69)	0.67:		+91.00	
P70	3	(0.03) ⟷	5	(0.06)	(78)	100.00 ⟷	(70)	0.08:		+99.92	
P71	514	(5.99) ⟷	727	(8.55)	(78)	78.83 ⟷	(71)	11.83:		+67.00	
P72	794	(9.25) ⟷	846	(9.94)	(78)	84.47 ⟷	(72)	13.77:		+70.70	
P73	150	(1.75) ⟷	249	(2.93)	(78)	86.71 ⟷	(73)	4.05:		+82.66	
P74	1,444	(16.83) ⟷	1,491	(17.53)	(78)	87.67 ⟷	(74)	24.26:		+63.41	
P75	41	(0.48) ⟷	55	(0.65)	(78)	93.18 ⟷	(75)	0.89:		+92.29	
P76	2,047	(23.85) ⟷	1,442	(16.95)	(78)	73.90 ⟷	(76)	23.46:		+50.44	
P77	1,865	(21.73) ⟷	1,779	(20.91)	(78)	88.73 ⟷	(77)	28.95:		+59.78	
P79	1,082	(12.61) ⟷	1,100	(12.93)	(78)	84.33 ⟷	(79)	17.90:		+66.43	

TABLE 18 (Continued)

	Horizontal				Vertical	
	Direct and external connections which each position has with all others in its class				Connections which are direct and internal	
	Per cent of *total* outgoing and incoming connections for each position		Per cent of totals between a position and totals of one other position			
Position 65 Total ACF: 51 Total Out: 173 Total In: 127						
	Outgoing	Incoming	Outgoing ⟷ Incoming	Difference		
P66			(65) 0.00 ⟷ (66) 0.00:	0.00	(65) ⟷ (9)	+1.92
P67	7 (4.05) ⟷	7 (5.51)	(65) 1.93 ⟷ (67) 13.73:	−11.80	(65) ⟷ (16)	+10.42
P68	2 (1.16) ⟷	3 (2.36)	(65) 0.99 ⟷ (68) 5.88:	−4.89	(65) ⟷ (30)	−62.54
P69			(65) 0.00 ⟷ (69) 0.00:	0.00	(65) ⟷ (49)	−52.68
P70			(65) 0.00 ⟷ (70) 0.00:	0.00		
P71	8 (4.62) ⟷	7 (5.51)	(65) 1.23 ⟷ (71) 13.73:	−12.50		
P72	16 (9.25) ⟷	11 (8.66)	(65) 1.70 ⟷ (72) 21.57:	−19.87		
P73	4 (2.31) ⟷	2 (1.57)	(65) 2.31 ⟷ (73) 3.92:	−1.61		
P74	19 (10.98) ⟷	13 (10.24)	(65) 1.15 ⟷ (74) 25.49:	−24.34		
P75	2 (1.16) ⟷	2 (1.57)	(65) 4.55 ⟷ (75) 3.92:	+0.63		
P76	25 (14.45) ⟷	14 (11.02)	(65) 0.90 ⟷ (76) 27.45:	−26.55		
P77	17 (9.83) ⟷	10 (7.87)	(65) 0.81 ⟷ (77) 19.61:	−18.80		
P78	55 (31.79) ⟷	47 (37.01)	(65) 0.89 ⟷ (78) 92.16:	−91.27		
P79	18 (10.40) ⟷	11 (8.66)	(65) 1.40 ⟷ (79) 21.57:	−20.17		

TABLE 18 (Continued)

Horizontal						Vertical	
Direct and external connections which each position has with all others in its class						Connections which are direct and internal	
Per cent of *total* outgoing and incoming connections for each position			Per cent of totals between a position and totals of one other position				
POSITION 66 Total ACF: 57 Total Out: 245 Total In: 172							
	Outgoing	Incoming	Outgoing	Incoming	Difference		
P65			(66) 0.00 ⟷	(65) 0.00:	0.00	(66) ⟷ (10)	+63.89
P67	3 (1.22) ⟷	3 (1.74)	(66) 0.83 ⟷	(67) 5.26:	−4.43	(66) ⟷ (31)	+22.92
P68	5 (2.04) ⟷	3 (1.74)	(66) 2.46 ⟷	(68) 5.26:	−2.80	(66) ⟷ (50)	−10.61
P69	4 (1.63) ⟷	3 (1.74)	(66) 11.11 ⟷	(69) 5.26:	+5.85		
P70			(66) 0.00 ⟷	(70) 0.00:	0.00		
P71	17 (6.94) ⟷	14 (8.14)	(66) 2.61 ⟷	(71) 24.56:	−21.95		
P72	27 (11.02) ⟷	21 (12.21)	(66) 2.87 ⟷	(72) 36.84:	−33.97		
P73	6 (2.45) ⟷	4 (2.33)	(66) 3.47 ⟷	(73) 7.02:	−3.55		
P74	28 (11.43) ⟷	24 (13.95)	(66) 1.70 ⟷	(74) 42.11:	−40.41		
P75			(66) 0.00 ⟷	(75) 0.00:	0.00		
P76	56 (22.86) ⟷	23 (13.37)	(66) 2.02 ⟷	(76) 40.35:	−38.33		
P77	23 (9.39) ⟷	19 (11.05)	(66) 1.09 ⟷	(77) 33.33:	−32.24		
P78	62 (25.31) ⟷	46 (26.74)	(66) 1.01 ⟷	(78) 80.70:	−79.69		
P79	14 (5.71) ⟷	12 (6.98)	(66) 1.09 ⟷	(79) 21.05:	−19.96		

TABLE 18 (Continued)

	Horizontal						Vertical	
	Direct and external connections which each position has with all others in its class						Connections which are direct and internal	
	Per cent of *total* outgoing and incoming connections for each position			Per cent of totals between a position and totals of one other position				
Position 67 Total ACF: 363 Total Out: 1,461 Total In: 1,040	Outgoing		Incoming	Outgoing	Incoming	Difference		
P65	7 (0.48)	⟷	7 (0.67)	(67) 13.73 ⟷	(65) 1.93:	+11.80	(67) ⟷ (11)	+87.01
P66	3 (0.21)	⟷	3 (0.29)	(67) 5.26 ⟷	(66) 0.83:	+4.43	(67) ⟷ (17)	+85.33
P68	25 (1.71)	⟷	24 (2.31)	(67) 12.32 ⟷	(68) 6.61:	+5.71	(67) ⟷ (32)	+28.36
P69	6 (0.41)	⟷	7 (0.67)	(67) 16.67 ⟷	(69) 1.93:	+14.74	(67) ⟷ (51)	−8.43
P70	2 (0.14)	⟷	2 (0.19)	(67) 66.67 ⟷	(70) 0.55:	+66.12	(67) ⟷ (80)	+31.82
P71	80 (5.48)	⟷	72 (6.92)	(67) 12.27 ⟷	(71) 19.83:	−7.56		
P72	132 (9.03)	⟷	101 (9.71)	(67) 14.04 ⟷	(72) 27.82:	−13.78		
P73	25 (1.71)	⟷	19 (1.83)	(67) 14.45 ⟷	(73) 5.23:	+9.22		
P74	164 (11.23)	⟷	130 (12.50)	(67) 9.96 ⟷	(74) 35.81:	−25.85		
P75				(67) 0.00 ⟷	(75) 0.28:	−0.28		
P76	294 (20.12)	⟷	160 (15.38)	(67) 10.61 ⟷	(76) 44.08:	−33.47		
P77	222 (15.20)	⟷	127 (12.21)	(67) 10.56 ⟷	(77) 34.99:	−24.43		
P78	424 (29.02)	⟷	332 (31.92)	(67) 6.90 ⟷	(78) 91.46:	−84.56		
P79	77 (5.27)	⟷	55 (5.29)	(67) 6.00 ⟷	(79) 15.15:	−9.15		

TABLE 18 (Continued)

Horizontal											Vertical			
Direct and external connections which each position has with all others in its class											Connections which are direct and internal			
Per cent of *total* outgoing and incoming connections for each position				Per cent of totals between a position and totals of one other position										
Position 68 Total ACF: 203 Total Out: 786 Total In: 598														
	Outgoing		Incoming	Outgoing			Incoming		Difference					
P65	3 (0.38)	⟷	2 (0.33)	(68)	5.88	⟷	(65)	0.99:	+4.89		(68)	⟷	(22)	+77.02
P66	3 (0.38)	⟷	5 (0.84)	(68)	5.26	⟷	(66)	2.46:	+2.80		(68)	⟷	(35)	+24.92
P67	24 (3.05)	⟷	25 (4.18)	(68)	6.61	⟷	(67)	12.32:	−5.71		(68)	⟷	(54)	+10.05
P69	2 (0.25)	⟷	3 (0.50)	(68)	5.56	⟷	(69)	1.48:	+4.08					
P70				(68)	0.00	⟷	(70)	0.00:	0.00					
P71	46 (5.85)	⟷	45 (7.53)	(68)	7.06	⟷	(71)	22.17:	−15.11					
P72	58 (7.38)	⟷	44 (7.36)	(68)	6.17	⟷	(72)	21.67:	−15.50					
P73	10 (1.27)	⟷	8 (1.34)	(68)	5.78	⟷	(73)	3.94:	+1.84					
P74	80 (10.18)	⟷	69 (11.54)	(68)	4.86	⟷	(74)	33.99:	−29.13					
P75				(68)	0.00	⟷	(75)	0.00:	0.00					
P76	134 (17.05)	⟷	77 (12.88)	(68)	4.84	⟷	(76)	37.93:	−33.09					
P77	148 (18.83)	⟷	103 (17.22)	(68)	7.04	⟷	(77)	50.74:	−43.70					
P78	231 (29.39)	⟷	184 (30.77)	(68)	3.76	⟷	(78)	90.64:	−86.88					
P79	47 (5.98)	⟷	33 (5.52)	(68)	3.66	⟷	(79)	16.26:	−12.60					

TABLE 18 (Continued)

Position 69
Total ACF: 36
Total Out: 168
Total In: 136

	Horizontal							Vertical
	Direct and external connections which each position has with all others in its class							Connections which are direct and internal
	Per cent of *total* outgoing and incoming connections for each position			Per cent of totals between a position and totals of one other position				
	Outgoing		Incoming	Outgoing		Incoming	Difference	
P65				(69) 0.00	⟷	(65) 0.00:	0.00	(69) ⟷ (23) +35.85
P66	3 (1.79)	⟷	4 (2.94)	(69) 5.26	⟷	(66) 11.11:	−5.85	(69) ⟷ (55) +10.77
P67	7 (4.17)	⟷	6 (4.41)	(69) 1.93	⟷	(67) 16.67:	−14.74	
P68	3 (1.79)	⟷	2 (1.47)	(69) 1.48	⟷	(68) 5.56:	−4.08	
P70				(69) 0.00	⟷	(70) 0.00:	0.00	
P71	15 (8.93)	⟷	22 (16.18)	(69) 2.30	⟷	(71) 61.11:	−58.81	
P72	9 (5.36)	⟷	9 (6.62)	(69) 0.96	⟷	(72) 25.00:	−24.04	
P73	5 (2.98)	⟷	3 (2.21)	(69) 2.89	⟷	(73) 8.33:	−5.44	
P74	15 (8.93)	⟷	12 (8.82)	(69) 0.91	⟷	(74) 33.33:	−32.42	
P75				(69) 0.00	⟷	(75) 0.00:	0.00	
P76	39 (23.21)	⟷	24 (17.65)	(69) 1.41	⟷	(76) 66.67:	−65.26	
P77	22 (13.10)	⟷	13 (9.56)	(69) 1.05	⟷	(77) 36.11:	−35.06	
P78	41 (24.40)	⟷	33 (24.26)	(69) 0.67	⟷	(78) 91.67:	−91.00	
P79	9 (5.36)	⟷	8 (5.88)	(69) 0.70	⟷	(79) 22.22:	−21.52	

TABLE 18 (Continued)

Horizontal										Vertical		
Direct and external connections which each position has with all others in its class										Connections which are direct and internal		
Per cent of *total* outgoing and incoming connections for each position				Per cent of totals between a position and totals of one other position								
Position 70 Total ACF: 3 Total Out: 14 Total In: 10	Outgoing		Incoming	Outgoing			Incoming		Difference			
P65				(70)	0.00	⟷	(65)	0.00:	0.00	(70) ⟷ (24)		−25.00
P66				(70)	0.00	⟷	(66)	0.00:	0.00			
P67	2 (14.29)	⟷	2 (20.00)	(70)	0.55	⟷	(67)	66.67:	−66.12			
P68				(70)	0.00	⟷	(68)	0.00:	0.00			
P69				(70)	0.00	⟷	(69)	0.00:	0.00			
P71				(70)	0.00	⟷	(71)	0.00:	0.00			
P72	1 (7.14)	⟷	1 (10.00)	(70)	0.11	⟷	(72)	33.33:	−33.22			
P73				(70)	0.00	⟷	(73)	0.00:	0.00			
P74	1 (7.14)	⟷	1 (10.00)	(70)	0.06	⟷	(74)	33.33:	−33.27			
P75				(70)	0.00	⟷	(75)	0.00:	0.00			
P76	4 (28.57)	⟷	2 (20.00)	(70)	0.15	⟷	(76)	66.67:	−66.52			
P77				(70)	0.00	⟷	(77)	0.00:	0.00			
P78	5 (35.71)	⟷	3 (30.00)	(70)	0.08	⟷	(78)	100.00:	−99.92			
P79	1 (7.14)	⟷	1 (10.00)	(70)	8.08	⟷	(79)	33.33:	−33.25			

TABLE 18 (Continued)

Horizontal											Vertical			
Direct and external connections which each position has with all others in its class											Connections which are direct and internal			
Per cent of *total* outgoing and incoming connections for each position				Per cent of totals between a position and totals of one other position										
Position 71 Total ACF: 652 Total Out: 2,615 Total In: 1,897														
	Outgoing		Incoming	Outgoing			Incoming			Difference				
P65	7 (0.27)	⟷	8 (0.42)	(71)	13.73	⟷	(65)	1.23:		+12.50	(71)	⟷	(25)	+95.05
P66	14 (0.54)	⟷	17 (0.90)	(71)	24.56	⟷	(66)	2.61:		+21.95	(71)	⟷	(36)	+65.15
P67	72 (2.75)	⟷	80 (4.22)	(71)	19.83	⟷	(67)	12.27:		+7.56	(71)	⟷	(56)	+17.10
P68	45 (1.72)	⟷	46 (2.42)	(71)	22.17	⟷	(68)	7.06:		+15.11	(71)	⟷	(81)	+48.06
P69	22 (0.84)	⟷	15 (0.79)	(71)	61.11	⟷	(69)	2.30:		+58.81				
P70				(71)	0.00	⟷	(70)	0.00:		0.00				
P72	195 (7.46)	⟷	157 (8.28)	(71)	20.74	⟷	(72)	24.08:		−3.34				
P73	66 (2.52)	⟷	69 (3.64)	(71)	38.15	⟷	(73)	10.58:		+27.57				
P74	308 (11.78)	⟷	262 (13.81)	(71)	18.70	⟷	(74)	40.18:		−21.48				
P75	7 (0.27)	⟷	5 (0.26)	(71)	15.91	⟷	(75)	0.77:		+15.14				
P76	612 (23.40)	⟷	322 (16.97)	(71)	22.09	⟷	(76)	49.39:		−27.30				
P77	342 (13.08)	⟷	257 (13.55)	(71)	16.27	⟷	(77)	39.42:		−23.15				
P78	727 (27.80)	⟷	514 (27.09)	(71)	11.83	⟷	(78)	78.83:		−67.00				
P79	198 (7.57)	⟷	145 (7.64)	(71)	15.43	⟷	(79)	22.24:		−6.81				

TABLE 18 (Continued)

	Horizontal					Vertical	
	Direct and external connections which each position has with all others in its class					Connections which are direct and internal	
	Per cent of *total* outgoing and incoming connections for each position		Per cent of totals between a position and totals of one other position				
Position 72 Total ACF: 940 Total Cut: 2,854 Total In: 2,722							
	Outgoing	Incoming	Outgoing	Incoming	Difference		
P65	11 (0.39) ⟷	16 (0.59)	(72) 21.57 ⟷	(65) 1.70:	+19.87	(72) ⟷ (39)	+21.05
P66	21 (0.74) ⟷	27 (0.99)	(72) 36.84 ⟷	(66) 2.87:	+33.97	(72) ⟷ (58)	−17.80
P67	101 (3.54) ⟷	132 (4.85)	(72) 27.82 ⟷	(67) 14.04:	+13.78		
P68	44 (1.54) ⟷	58 (2.13)	(72) 21.67 ⟷	(68) 6.17:	+15.50		
P69	9 (0.32) ⟷	9 (0.33)	(72) 25.00 ⟷	(69) 0.96:	+24.04		
P70	1 (0.04) ⟷	1 (0.04)	(72) 33.33 ⟷	(70) 0.11:	+33.22		
P71	157 (5.50) ⟷	195 (7.16)	(72) 24.08 ⟷	(71) 20.74:	+3.34		
P73	63 (2.21) ⟷	93 (3.42)	(72) 36.42 ⟷	(73) 9.89:	+26.53		
P74	315 (11.04) ⟷	349 (12.82)	(72) 19.13 ⟷	(74) 37.13:	−18.00		
P75	3 (0.11) ⟷	3 (0.11)	(72) 6.82 ⟷	(75) 0.32:	+6.50		
P76	693 (24.28) ⟷	491 (18.04)	(72) 25.02 ⟷	(76) 52.23:	−27.21		
P77	408 (14.30) ⟷	378 (13.89)	(72) 19.41 ⟷	(77) 40.21:	−20.80		
P78	846 (29.64) ⟷	794 (29.17)	(72) 13.77 ⟷	(78) 84.47:	−70.70		
P79	182 (6.38) ⟷	176 (6.47)	(72) 14.19 ⟷	(79) 18.72:	−4.53		

TABLE 18 (Continued)

	Horizontal								Vertical	
	Direct and external connections which each position has with all others in its class								Connections which are direct and internal	
	Per cent of *total* outgoing and incoming connections for each position			Per cent of totals between a position and totals of one other position						
Position 73 Total ACF: 173 Total Out: 996 Total In: 679										
	Outgoing		Incoming	Outgoing			Incoming	Difference		
P65	2 (0.20)	⟷	4 (0.59)	(73)	3.92	⟷	(65) 2.31:	+1.61	(73) ⟷ (40)	−5.70
P66	4 (0.40)	⟷	6 (0.88)	(73)	7.02	⟷	(66) 3.47:	+3.55		
P67	19 (1.91)	⟷	25 (3.68)	(73)	5.23	⟷	(67) 14.45:	−9.22		
P68	8 (0.80)	⟷	10 (1.47)	(73)	3.94	⟷	(68) 5.78:	−1.84		
P69	3 (0.30)	⟷	5 (0.74)	(73)	8.33	⟷	(69) 2.89:	+5.44		
P70				(73)	0.00	⟷	(70) 0.00:	0.00		
P71	69 (6.93)	⟷	66 (9.72)	(73)	10.58	⟷	(71) 38.15:	−27.57		
P72	93 (9.34)	⟷	63 (9.28)	(73)	9.89	⟷	(72) 36.42:	−26.53		
P74	93 (9.34)	⟷	87 (12.81)	(73)	5.65	⟷	(74) 50.29:	−44.64		
P75	10 (1.00)	⟷	11 (1.62)	(73)	22.73	⟷	(75) 6.36:	+16.37		
P76	250 (25.10)	⟷	111 (16.35)	(73)	9.03	⟷	(76) 64.16:	−55.13		
P77	105 (10.54)	⟷	83 (12.22)	(73)	5.00	⟷	(77) 47.98:	−42.98		
P78	249 (25.00)	⟷	150 (22.09)	(73)	4.05	⟷	(78) 86.71:	−82.66		
P79	91 (9.14)	⟷	58 (8.54)	(73)	7.09	⟷	(79) 33.53:	−26.44		

TABLE 18 (Continued)

Horizontal								Vertical	
Direct and external connections which each position has with all others in its class								Connections which are direct and internal	
Per cent of *total* outgoing and incoming connections for each position				Per cent of totals between a position and totals of one other position					
Position 74 Total ACF: 1,647 Total Out: 4,604 Total In: 4,157									
	Outgoing		Incoming	Outgoing		Incoming	Difference		
P65	13 (8.28)	⟷	19 (0.46)	(74) 25.49	⟷	(65) 1.15:	+24.34	(74) ⟷ (41)	+71.07
P66	24 (0.52)	⟷	28 (0.67)	(74) 42.11	⟷	(66) 1.70:	+40.41	(74) ⟷ (59)	+20.94
P67	130 (2.82)	⟷	164 (3.95)	(74) 35.81	⟷	(67) 9.96:	+25.85	(74) ⟷ (82)	+31.95
P68	69 (1.50)	⟷	80 (1.92)	(74) 33.99	⟷	(68) 4.86:	+29.13		
P69	12 (0.26)	⟷	15 (0.36)	(74) 33.33	⟷	(69) 0.91:	+32.42		
P70	1 (0.02)	⟷	1 (0.02)	(74) 33.33	⟷	(70) 0.06:	+33.27		
P71	262 (5.69)	⟷	308 (7.41)	(74) 40.18	⟷	(71) 18.70:	+21.48		
P72	349 (7.58)	⟷	315 (7.58)	(74) 37.13	⟷	(72) 19.13:	+18.00		
P73	87 (1.89)	⟷	93 (2.24)	(74) 50.29	⟷	(73) 5.65:	+44.64		
P75	16 (0.35)	⟷	22 (0.53)	(74) 36.36	⟷	(75) 1.34:	+35.02		
P76	942 (20.46)	⟷	626 (15.06)	(74) 34.01	⟷	(76) 38.01:	−4.00		
P77	803 (17.44)	⟷	681 (16.38)	(74) 38.20	⟷	(77) 41.35:	−3.15		
P78	1,491 (32.38)	⟷	1,444 (34.74)	(74) 24.26	⟷	(78) 87.67:	−63.41		
P79	405 (8.80)	⟷	361 (8.68)	(74) 31.57	⟷	(79) 21.92:	+9.65		

TABLE 18 (Continued)

	Horizontal									Vertical	
	Direct and external connections which each position has with all others in its class									Connections which are direct and internal	
	Per cent of *total* outgoing and incoming connections for each position			Per cent of totals between a position and totals of one other position							
Position 75 Total ACF: 44 Total Out: 208 Total In: 141											
	Outgoing		Incoming	Outgoing			Incoming		Difference		
P65	2 (8.96)	⟷	2 (1.42)	(75)	3.92	⟷	(65)	4.55:	−0.63	(75) ⟷ (43)	+24.14
P66				(75)	0.00	⟷	(66)	0.00:	0.00	(75) ⟷ (84)	+18.68
P67				(75)	0.28	⟷	(67)	0.00:	+0.28		
P68				(75)	0.00	⟷	(68)	0.00:	0.00		
P69				(75)	0.00	⟷	(69)	0.00:	0.00		
P70				(75)	0.00	⟷	(70)	0.00:	0.00		
P71	5 (2.40)	⟷	7 (4.96)	(75)	0.77	⟷	(71)	15.91:	−15.14		
P72	3 (1.44)	⟷	3 (2.13)	(75)	0.32	⟷	(72)	6.82:	−6.50		
P73	11 (5.29)	⟷	10 (7.09)	(75)	6.36	⟷	(73)	22.73:	−16.37		
P74	22 (10.58)	⟷	16 (11.35)	(75)	1.34	⟷	(74)	36.36:	−35.02		
P76	30 (14.42)	⟷	16 (11.35)	(75)	1.08	⟷	(76)	36.36:	−35.28		
P77	31 (14.90)	⟷	21 (14.89)	(75)	1.47	⟷	(77)	47.73:	−46.26		
P78	55 (26.44)	⟷	41 (29.08)	(75)	0.89	⟷	(78)	93.18:	−92.29		
P79	48 (23.08)	⟷	25 (17.73)	(75)	3.74	⟷	(79)	56.82:	−53.08		

TABLE 18 (Continued)

Horizontal													Vertical				
Direct and external connections which each position has with all others in its class													Connections which are direct and internal				
Per cent of *total* outgoing and incoming connections for each position						Per cent of totals between a position and totals of one other position											
Position 76 Total ACF: 2,770 Total Out: 4,642 Total In: 6,772																	
	Outgoing			Incoming		Outgoing			Incoming		Difference						
P65	14	(0.30)	⟷	25	(0.37)	(76)	27.45	⟷	(65)	0.90:	+26.55		(76)	⟷	(62)	+5.97	
P66	23	(0.50)	⟷	56	(0.83)	(76)	40.35	⟷	(66)	2.02:	+38.33						
P67	160	(3.45)	⟷	294	(4.34)	(76)	44.08	⟷	(67)	10.61:	+33.47						
P68	77	(1.66)	⟷	134	(1.98)	(76)	37.93	⟷	(68)	4.84:	+33.09						
P69	24	(0.52)	⟷	39	(0.58)	(76)	66.67	⟷	(69)	1.41:	+65.26						
P70	2	(0.04)	⟷	4	(0.06)	(76)	66.67	⟷	(70)	0.15:	+66.52						
P71	322	(6.94)	⟷	612	(9.04)	(76)	49.39	⟷	(71)	22.09:	+27.30						
P72	491	(10.58)	⟷	693	(10.23)	(76)	52.23	⟷	(72)	25.02:	+27.21						
P73	111	(2.39)	⟷	250	(3.69)	(76)	64.16	⟷	(73)	9.03:	+55.13						
P74	626	(13.49)	⟷	942	(13.91)	(76)	38.01	⟷	(74)	34.01:	+4.00						
P75	16	(0.34)	⟷	30	(0.44)	(76)	36.36	⟷	(75)	1.08:	+35.28						
P77	905	(19.50)	⟷	1,105	(16.32)	(76)	43.05	⟷	(77)	39.89:	+3.16						
P78	1,442	(31.06)	⟷	2,047	(30.23)	(76)	23.46	⟷	(78)	73.90:	−50.44						
P79	429	(9.24)	⟷	541	(7.99)	(76)	33.44	⟷	(79)	19.53:	+13.91						

TABLE 18 (Continued)

	Horizontal							Vertical	
	Direct and external connections which each position has with all others in its class							Connections which are direct and internal	
	Per cent of *total* outgoing and incoming connections for each position			Per cent of totals between a position and totals of one other position					
Position 77 Total ACF: 2,102 Total Out: 5,122 Total In: 5,409	Outgoing		Incoming	Outgoing		Incoming	Difference		
P65	10 (0.20)	⟷	17 (0.31)	(77) 19.61	⟷	(65) 0.81:	+18.80	(77) ⟷ (63)	+18.35
P66	19 (0.37)	⟷	23 (0.43)	(77) 33.33	⟷	(66) 1.09:	+32.24	(77) ⟷ (86)	+20.06
P67	127 (2.48)	⟷	222 (4.10)	(77) 34.99	⟷	(67) 10.56:	+24.43		
P68	103 (2.01)	⟷	148 (2.74)	(77) 50.74	⟷	(68) 7.04:	+43.70		
P69	13 (0.25)	⟷	22 (0.41)	(77) 36.11	⟷	(69) 1.05:	+35.06		
P70				(77) 0.00	⟷	(70) 0.00:	0.00		
P71	257 (5.02)	⟷	342 (6.32)	(77) 39.42	⟷	(71) 16.27:	+23.15		
P72	378 (7.38)	⟷	408 (7.54)	(77) 40.21	⟷	(72) 19.41:	+20.80		
P73	83 (1.62)	⟷	105 (1.94)	(77) 47.98	⟷	(73) 5.00:	+42.98		
P74	681 (13.30)	⟷	803 (14.85)	(77) 41.35	⟷	(74) 38.20:	+3.15		
P75	21 (0.41)	⟷	31 (0.57)	(77) 47.73	⟷	(75) 1.47:	+46.26		
P76	1,105 (21.57)	⟷	905 (16.73)	(77) 39.89	⟷	(76) 43.05:	−3.16		
P78	1,779 (34.73)	⟷	1,865 (34.48)	(77) 28.95	⟷	(78) 88.73:	−59.78		
P79	546 (10.66)	⟷	518 (9.58)	(77) 42.56	⟷	(79) 24.64:	+17.92		

TABLE 18 (Continued)

Horizontal								Vertical
Direct and external connections which each position has with all others in its class								Connections which are direct and internal
Per cent of *total* outgoing and incoming connections for each position			Per cent of totals between a position and totals of one other position					
POSITION 79 Total ACF: 1,283 Total Out: 3,044 Total In: 3,147								
	Outgoing		Incoming	Outgoing		Incoming	Difference	
P65	11 (0.36)	⟷	18 (0.57)	(79) 21.57	⟷	(65) 1.40:	+20.17	(79) ⟷ (88) +0.27
P66	12 (0.39)	⟷	14 (0.44)	(79) 21.05	⟷	(66) 1.09:	+19.96	
P67	55 (1.81)	⟷	77 (2.45)	(79) 15.15	⟷	(67) 6.00:	+9.15	
P68	33 (1.08)	⟷	47 (1.49)	(79) 16.26	⟷	(68) 3.66:	+12.60	
P69	8 (0.26)	⟷	9 (0.29)	(79) 22.22	⟷	(69) 0.70:	+21.52	
P70	1 (0.03)	⟷	1 (0.03)	(79) 33.33	⟷	(70) 0.08:	+33.25	
P71	145 (4.76)	⟷	198 (6.29)	(79) 22.24	⟷	(71) 15.43:	+6.81	
P72	176 (5.78)	⟷	182 (5.78)	(79) 18.72	⟷	(72) 14.19:	+4.53	
P73	58 (1.91)	⟷	91 (2.89)	(79) 33.53	⟷	(73) 7.09:	+26.44	
P74	361 (11.86)	⟷	405 (12.87)	(79) 21.92	⟷	(74) 31.57:	−9.65	
P75	25 (0.82)	⟷	48 (1.53)	(79) 56.82	⟷	(75) 3.74:	+53.08	
P76	541 (17.77)	⟷	429 (13.63)	(79) 19.53	⟷	(76) 33.44:	−13.91	
P77	518 (17.02)	⟷	546 (17.35)	(79) 24.64	⟷	(77) 42.56:	−17.92	
P78	1,100 (36.14)	⟷	1,082 (34.38)	(79) 17.90	⟷	(78) 84.33:	−66.43	

TABLE 18 (Continued)

Horizontal									Vertical
Direct and external connections which each position has with all others in its class									Connections which are direct and internal
Per cent of *total* outgoing and incoming connections for each position				Per cent of totals between a position and totals of one other position					
POSITION 89 Total ACF: 5,146 Total Out: 3,574 Total In: 3,511									
	Outgoing		Incoming	Outgoing		Incoming		Difference	
P80	150 (4.20)	⟷	168 (4.78)	(89) 96.15	⟷	(80)	3.26:	+92.89	0
P81	131 (3.67)	⟷	167 (4.76)	(89) 94.24	⟷	(81)	3.25:	+90.99	
P82	571 (15.98)	⟷	576 (16.41)	(89) 95.01	⟷	(82)	11.19:	+83.82	
P83	19 (0.53)	⟷	14 (0.40)	(89) 79.17	⟷	(83)	0.27:	+79.80	
P84	22 (0.62)	⟷	23 (0.66)	(89) 81.48	⟷	(84)	0.45:	+81.03	
P85	12 (0.34)	⟷	16 (0.46)	(89) 92.31	⟷	(85)	0.31:	+92.00	
P86	1,321 (36.96)	⟷	1,176 (33.49)	(89) 94.70	⟷	(86)	22.85:	+71.85	
P87	257 (7.19)	⟷	310 (8.83)	(89) 85.67	⟷	(87)	6.02:	+79.65	
P88	1,091 (30.53)	⟷	1,061 (30.22)	(89) 80.99	⟷	(88)	20.62:	+60.37	

TABLE 18 (Continued)

Horizontal							Vertical	
Direct and external connections which each position has with all others in its class							Connections which are direct and internal	
Per cent of *total* outgoing and incoming connections for each position			Per cent of totals between a position and totals of one other position					
Position 80 Total ACF: 156 Total Out: 428 Total In: 332								
	Outgoing	Incoming	Outgoing		Incoming	Difference		
P81	17 (3.97) ⟷	15 (4.52)	(80) 12.23 ⟷		(81) 9.62:	+2.61	(80) ⟷ (11)	+76.32
P82	44 (10.28) ⟷	36 (10.84)	(80) 7.32 ⟷		(82) 23.08:	−15.76	(80) ⟷ (17)	+73.45
P83	9 (2.10) ⟷	5 (1.51)	(80) 37.50 ⟷		(83) 3.21:	+34.29	(80) ⟷ (32)	−3.80
P84	1 (0.23) ⟷	1 (0.30)	(80) 3.70 ⟷		(84) 0.64:	+3.06	(80) ⟷ (51)	−39.20
P85	1 (0.23) ⟷	2 (0.60)	(80) 7.69 ⟷		(85) 1.28:	+6.41	(80) ⟷ (67)	−31.82
P86	90 (21.03) ⟷	55 (16.57)	(80) 6.45 ⟷		(86) 35.26:	−28.81		
P87	15 (3.50) ⟷	16 (4.82)	(80) 5.00 ⟷		(87) 10.26:	−5.26		
P88	83 (19.39) ⟷	52 (15.66)	(80) 6.16 ⟷		(88) 33.33:	−27.17		
P89	168 (39.25) ⟷	150 (45.18)	(80) 3.26 ⟷		(89) 96.15:	−92.89		

TABLE 18 (Continued)

Horizontal								Vertical	
Direct and external connections which each position has with all others in its class								Connections which are direct and internal	
Per cent of *total* outgoing and incoming connections for each position				Per cent of totals between a position and totals of one other position					
POSITION 81 Total ACF: 139 Total Out: 491 Total In: 353									
	Outgoing		Incoming	Outgoing		Incoming	Difference		
P80	15 (3.05)	⟷	17 (4.82)	(81) 9.62	⟷	(80) 12.23:	−2.61	(81) ⟷ (25)	+86.51
P82	70 (14.26)	⟷	50 (14.16)	(81) 11.65	⟷	(82) 35.97:	−24.32	(81) ⟷ (36)	+24.87
P83	3 (0.61)	⟷	2 (0.57)	(81) 12.50	⟷	(83) 1.44:	+11.06	(81) ⟷ (56)	−33.74
P84	2 (0.41)	⟷	2 (0.57)	(81) 7.41	⟷	(84) 1.44:	+5.97	(81) ⟷ (71)	−48.06
P85	1 (0.20)	⟷	2 (0.57)	(81) 7.69	⟷	(85) 1.44:	+6.25		
P86	123 (25.05)	⟷	67 (18.98)	(81) 8.82	⟷	(86) 48.20:	−39.38		
P87	30 (6.11)	⟷	21 (5.95)	(81) 10.00	⟷	(87) 15.11:	−5.11		
P88	80 (16.29)	⟷	61 (17.28)	(81) 5.94	⟷	(88) 43.88:	−37.94		
P89	167 (34.01)	⟷	131 (37.11)	(81) 3.25	⟷	(89) 94.24:	−90.99		

TABLE 18 (Continued)

	Horizontal						Vertical	
	Direct and external connections which each position has with all others in its class						Connections which are direct and internal	
	Per cent of *total* outgoing and incoming connections for each position		Per cent of totals between a position and totals of one other position					
POSITION 82 Total ACF: 601 Total Out: 1,256 Total In: 1,169								
	Outgoing	Incoming	Outgoing		Incoming	Difference		
P80	36 (2.87) ⟷	44 (3.76)	(82) 23.08 ⟷		(80) 7.32:	+15.76	(82) ⟷ (41)	+50.62
P81	50 (3.98) ⟷	70 (5.99)	(82) 35.97 ⟷		(81) 11.65:	+24.32	(82) ⟷ (59)	−11.80
P83	2 (0.16) ⟷	2 (0.17)	(82) 8.33 ⟷		(83) 0.33:	+8.00	(82) ⟷ (74)	−31.95
P84	4 (0.32) ⟷	9 (0.77)	(83) 14.81 ⟷		(84) 1.50:	+13.31		
P85	2 (0.16) ⟷	7 (0.60)	(82) 15.38 ⟷		(85) 1.16:	+14.22		
P86	332 (26.43) ⟷	244 (20.87)	(82) 23.80 ⟷		(86) 40.60:	−16.80		
P87	44 (3.50) ⟷	42 (3.59)	(82) 14.67 ⟷		(87) 6.99:	+7.68		
P88	210 (16.72) ⟷	180 (15.40)	(82) 15.59 ⟷		(88) 29.95:	−14.36		
P89	576 (45.86) ⟷	571 (48.85)	(82) 11.19 ⟷		(89) 95.01:	−83.82		

TABLE 18 (Continued)

Horizontal									Vertical			
Direct and external connections which each position has with all others in its class									Connections which are direct and internal			
Per cent of *total* outgoing and incoming connections for each position			Per cent of totals between a position and totals of one other position									
Position 83 Total ACF: 24 Total Out: 43 Total In: 56												
	Outgoing	Incoming	Outgoing			Incoming		Difference				
P80	5 (11.63) ⟷	9 (16.07)	(83)	3.21 ⟷	(80)	37.50:		−34.29	(83) ⟷	(42)	+8.33	
P81	2 (4.65) ⟷	3 (5.36)	(83)	1.44 ⟷	(81)	12.50:		−11.06	(83) ⟷	(60)	−17.46	
P82	2 (4.65) ⟷	2 (3.57)	(83)	0.33 ⟷	(82)	8.33:		−8.00				
P84			(83)	0.00 ⟷	(84)	0.00:		0.00				
P85	1 (2.33) ⟷	2 (3.57)	(83)	7.69 ⟷	(85)	8.33:		−0.64				
P86	7 (16.28) ⟷	7 (12.50)	(83)	0.50 ⟷	(86)	29.17:		−28.67				
P87	3 (6.98) ⟷	4 (7.14)	(83)	1.00 ⟷	(87)	16.67:		−15.67				
P88	9 (20.93) ⟷	10 (17.86)	(83)	0.67 ⟷	(88)	41.67:		−41.00				
P89	14 (32.56) ⟷	19 (33.93)	(83)	0.27 ⟷	(89)	79.17:		−78.90				

TABLE 18 (Continued)

	Horizontal					Vertical	
	Direct and external connections which each position has with all others in its class					Connections which are direct and internal	
	Per cent of *total* outgoing and incoming connections for each position		Per cent of totals between a position and totals of one other position				
Position 84 Total ACF: 27 Total Out: 76 Total In: 50							
	Outgoing	Incoming	Outgoing	Incoming	Difference		
P80	1 (1.32) ⟷	1 (2.00)	(84) 0.64 ⟷	(80) 3.70:	−3.06	(84) ⟷ (43)	+5.71
P81	2 (2.63) ⟷	2 (4.00)	(84) 1.44 ⟷	(81) 7.41:	−5.97	(84) ⟷ (75)	−18.68
P82	9 (11.84) ⟷	4 (8.00)	(84) 1.50 ⟷	(82) 14.81:	−13.31		
P83			(84) 0.00 ⟷	(83) 0.00:	0.00		
P85			(84) 0.00 ⟷	(85) 0.00:	0.00		
P86	13 (17.11) ⟷	6 (12.00)	(84) 0.93 ⟷	(86) 22.22:	−21.29		
P87	4 (5.26) ⟷	4 (8.00)	(84) 1.33 ⟷	(87) 14.81:	−13.48		
P88	24 (31.58) ⟷	11 (22.00)	(84) 1.78 ⟷	(88) 40.74:	−38.96		
P89	23 (30.26) ⟷	22 (44.00)	(84) 0.45 ⟷	(89) 81.48:	−81.03		

TABLE 18 (Continued)

	Horizontal									Vertical
	Direct and external connections which each position has with all others in its class									Connections which are direct and internal
	Per cent of *total* outgoing and incoming connections for each position			Per cent of totals between a position and totals of one other position						
POSITION 85 Total ACF: 13 Total Out: 49 Total In: 28										
	Outgoing		Incoming	Outgoing			Incoming		Difference	
P80	2 (4.08)	⟷	1 (3.57)	(85)	1.28	⟷	(80)	7.69:	−6.41	(85) ⟷ (44) +10.34
P81	2 (4.08)	⟷	1 (3.57)	(85)	1.44	⟷	(81)	7.69:	−6.25	
P82	7 (14.29)	⟷	2 (7.14)	(85)	1.16	⟷	(82)	15.38:	−14.22	
P83	2 (4.08)	⟷	1 (3.57)	(85)	8.33	⟷	(83)	7.69:	+0.64	
P84				(85)	0.00	⟷	(84)	0.00:	0.00	
P86	11 (22.45)	⟷	6 (21.43)	(85)	0.79	⟷	(86)	46.15:	−45.36	
P87				(85)	0.00	⟷	(87)	0.00:	0.00	
P88	9 (18.37)	⟷	5 (17.86)	(85)	0.67	⟷	(88)	38.46:	−37.79	
P89	16 (32.65)	⟷	12 (42.86)	(85)	0.31	⟷	(89)	92.31:	−92.00	

TABLE 18 (Continued)

Horizontal								Vertical	
Direct and external connections which each position has with all others in its class								Connections which are direct and internal	
Per cent of *total* outgoing and incoming connections for each position				Per cent of totals between a position and totals of one other position					
Position 86 Total ACF: 1,395 Total Out: 2,135 Total In: 2,577	Outgoing		Incoming	Outgoing		Incoming	Difference		
P80	55 (2.58)	⟷	90 (3.49)	(86) 35.26	⟷	(80) 6.45:	+28.81	(86) ⟷ (63)	−1.77
P81	67 (3.14)	⟷	123 (4.77)	(86) 48.20	⟷	(81) 8.82:	+39.38	(86) ⟷ (77)	−20.06
P82	244 (11.43)	⟷	332 (12.88)	(86) 40.60	⟷	(82) 23.80:	+16.80		
P83	7 (0.33)	⟷	7 (0.27)	(86) 29.17	⟷	(83) 0.50:	+28.67		
P84	6 (0.28)	⟷	13 (0.50)	(86) 22.22	⟷	(84) 0.93:	+21.29		
P85	6 (0.28)	⟷	11 (0.43)	(86) 46.15	⟷	(85) 0.79:	+45.36		
P87	126 (5.90)	⟷	185 (7.18)	(86) 42.00	⟷	(87) 13.26:	+28.74		
P88	448 (20.98)	⟷	495 (19.21)	(86) 33.26	⟷	(88) 35.48:	−2.22		
P89	1,176 (55.08)	⟷	1,321 (51.26)	(86) 22.85	⟷	(89) 94.70:	−71.85		

TABLE 18 (Continued)

	Horizontal								Vertical	
	Direct and external connections which each position has with all others in its class								Connections which are direct and internal	
	Per cent of *total* outgoing and incoming connections for each position			Per cent of totals between a position and totals of one other position						
Position 87 Total ACF: 300 Total Out: 739 Total In: 591										
	Outgoing		Incoming	Outgoing		Incoming		Difference		
P80	16 (2.17)	⟷	15 (2.54)	(87) 10.26	⟷	(80)	5.00:	+5.26	(87) ⟷ (64)	+1.15
P81	21 (2.84)	⟷	30 (5.08)	(87) 15.11	⟷	(81)	10.00:	+5.11		
P82	42 (5.68)	⟷	44 (7.45)	(87) 6.99	⟷	(82)	14.67:	−7.68		
P83	4 (0.54)	⟷	3 (0.51)	(87) 16.67	⟷	(83)	1.00:	+15.67		
P84	4 (0.54)	⟷	4 (0.68)	(87) 14.81	⟷	(84)	1.33:	+13.48		
P85				(87) 0.00	⟷	(85)	0.00:	0.00		
P86	185 (25.03)	⟷	126 (21.32)	(87) 13.26	⟷	(86)	42.00:	−28.74		
P88	157 (21.24)	⟷	112 (18.95)	(87) 11.66	⟷	(88)	37.33:	−25.67		
P89	310 (41.95)	⟷	257 (43.49)	(87) 6.02	⟷	(89)	85.67:	−79.65		

TABLE 18 (Continued)

Horizontal					Vertical	
Direct and external connections which each position has with all others in its class					Connections which are direct and internal	
Per cent of *total* outgoing and incoming connections for each position		Per cent of totals between a position and totals of one other position				
Position 88 Total ACF: 1,276 Total Out: 1,987 Total In: 2,111						
	Outgoing	Incoming	Outgoing	Incoming	Difference		
P80	52 (2.62) ⟷	83 (3.93)	(88) 33.33 ⟷	(80) 6.16:	+27.17	(88) ⟷ (79)	−0.27
P81	61 (3.07) ⟷	80 (3.79)	(88) 43.88 ⟷	(81) 5.94:	+37.94		
P82	180 (9.06) ⟷	210 (9.95)	(88) 29.95 ⟷	(82) 15.59:	+14.36		
P83	10 (0.50) ⟷	9 (0.43)	(88) 41.67 ⟷	(83) 0.67:	+41.00		
P84	11 (0.55) ⟷	24 (1.14)	(88) 40.74 ⟷	(84) 1.78:	+38.96		
P85	5 (0.25) ⟷	9 (0.43)	(88) 38.46 ⟷	(85) 0.67:	+37.79		
P86	495 (24.91) ⟷	448 (21.22)	(88) 35.48 ⟷	(86) 33.26:	+2.22		
P87	112 (5.64) ⟷	157 (7.44)	(88) 37.33 ⟷	(87) 11.66:	+25.67		
P89	1,061 (53.40) ⟷	1,091 (51.68)	(88) 20.62 ⟷	(89) 80.99:	−60.37		

see what his relative position is within the whole; and (3) the meaning of a particular event or series of events in his life in relation to his whole social behavior may be understood. Furthermore, it provides a means of systematically eliminating all other relations except those which are being analyzed. When an individual's behavior as a member of Position 1 is being compared with his behavior as a member of Position 3, certain differences immediately become apparent; in Position 1 he expresses a set of sentiments about members in his own class which are quite different from those he will state as a member of Position 3. Yet the sentiments in 1 and 3 will be those of the upper-upper class and not of another class. Further, if the sentiments are expressed in a family relation rather than in an associational or other relation, the values proper to the family will be involved, but they will be in a particular class context.

The positional system, as a method of analysis, cannot give the investigator the *strength* or *intensity* of the relation involved; it fails to do this for the different types of structural relations within the general type of relation and for a particular relation within the type for two or more individuals. For instance, the association, clique, and family relations of Position 3 with other positions are assumed to be of equal strength. Only very general and approximate weightings can be given to each type of structural relations. It is probable that relations which are observably more frequent and direct (face-to-face) are likely to be more intense and strong, while those which are less frequent and provide fewer face-to-face contacts will be less intense. However, this is only approximately true and will not do as a general principle. Such a rough measurement would regard family relations as the strongest, clique relations next, and associational relations as last. The relations of particular individuals might very easily reverse this order. It is conceivable that certain men would have stronger relations with the members of their clubs than with the members of their family.

Although such an analysis of the behavior and verbalizations of individuals in these various relations is useful and gives us a means for evaluating the amount of control exercised by the various relations, it must be admitted that this measurement is only approximate and that there is no way of *accurately* measuring the strength or intensity of the relation except by the use of arbitrary mechanical devices. Thousands of relations must be examined among hundreds of positions and subpositions in order to establish the typical intensity in different relations and positions.

In spite of these limitations to the usefulness of the positional method, it supplies a relevant social framework for the analysis of particular relations and events and allows the investigator to include or exclude all, some, or none of the other types of relations which compose the social system of Yankee City. It also allows a psychologist to examine the behavior of a particular individual by comparing it with that of others in a similar and comparable situation and facing similar problems. The psychiatrist, for instance, can compare the behavior of a particular upper-upper individual not only with that of other upper-uppers (which gives him a first delimitation of the field) but also with other upper-uppers who participate in the same part of the relational system. Such comparisons will provide a far more accurate method of estimating the degree of individual deviance and a much better understanding of the problems which the patient is attempting to solve than present-day psychiatry possesses.

APPENDICES

The Appendices attached to this volume represent only a small part of the detailed material, charts, and tables on which the analysis in the foregoing chapters was based. The *Data Book for the Yankee City Series* (Volume VI) will supply the rest. The Appendices are placed here primarily as samples of the type of evidence available.

APPENDIX 1.

ANALYSIS OF POSITION 26

THE following analysis of one specific position is offered as an example of the method which has been applied to the eighty-nine positions. (See pages 53–66.)

Position 26 belongs to the upper-middle class and to Class Type 3, which also consists of Positions 3 in the upper-upper class and 13 in the lower-upper. Its 632 members represent 0.89% of the Positional System, ranking twenty-seven of eighty-one possible places, 44.32% of its vertical extension, and 6.59% of the upper-middle class, ranking five of nineteen.

The association, clique, and family are the structures represented.

a. The Structural Organization

There are 89.25% (564) members in associations, 10.28% (65) in cliques, and 0.47% (3) in the family. In its vertical extension this position comprises 47.80% (564) of the associational, 27.08% (65) of the clique, and 50% (3) of the family members.

It holds 20.04% (564) of the associational members of the upper-middle class (rank two of eleven), 2.37% (65) of the clique (rank nine of sixteen), and 0.17% (3) of the family (rank seven of nine).

b. The Characteristics of the Total Membership

Adults comprise 97.31% (615) and subadults 2.69% (17), ranking six of eighty-four and seventy-nine of eighty-three. Males have 38.92% (246), and females 61.08% (386), ranking seventy-nine of eighty-seven and ten of eighty-eight.

Catholics compose 5.54% (35), ranking fifty-eight of sixty-eight; Protestants 60.76% (384), ranking twenty-seven of eighty-six; Jewish religionists 0.63% (4), ranking thirty-five of forty-five; and those having no religion 33.07% (209), ranking forty-three of eighty-one.

There are 90.35% (571) natives and 9.65% (61) ethnics,

ranking eleven of seventy-two and sixty-two of seventy-one. There are 8.22% (52) Irish (rank fifty-nine of seventy), 0.32% (2) French (rank forty-nine of fifty), 0.95% (6) Jewish (rank thirty-four of forty-five), and 0.16% (1) Greek (rank forty of forty-one).

At this point in our analysis we know what characteristics are present but we do not know how they are interrelated. It is important to know how many of the males are adults or subadults, how many of the Catholics are Irish or French Canadians, as well as the other combinations which are possible among the several characteristics present. The reasons for this part of our analysis are fairly obvious and do not need further explanation. Let us once again examine Position 26.

c. The Amount of Interrelation among the Characteristics

Adult males comprise 38.29% (242) and females 59.02% (373); subadult males 0.63% (4), and females 2.06% (13).

Male Catholics represent 0.79% (5); Protestants 19.62% (124); Jews 0.63% (4); and males with no religion 17.88% (113). Female Catholics comprise 4.75% (30); Protestants 41.14% (260); and females with no religion 15.19% (96).

Adult Catholics represent 5.54% (35); Protestants 59.18% (374); Jews 0.63% (4); and adults with no religious affiliation 31.96% (202). Subadult Catholics are not represented; Protestant subadults have 1.58% (10) and subadults with no religion, 1.11% (7).

This position has 36.07% (228) male and 54.28% (343) female natives; 2.85% (18) male and 6.80% (43) female ethnics. It has 87.66% (554) adult and 2.69% (17) subadult natives; 9.65% (61) adult and no subadult ethnics.

There are 2.22% (14) male and 6% (38) female Irish members; no male and 0.32% (2) female French; 0.63% (4) male and 0.32% (2) female Jews; no male and 0.16% (1) female Greeks. All of the ethnic members are adults. There are 8.22% (52) Irish adults, 0.32% (2) French, 0.95% (6) Jewish, and 0.16% (1) Greek.

This position has 5.06% (32) Catholic, 0.63% (4) Protestant, and 2.53% (16) Irish with no religion. All of the French are Protestant. There are 0.63% (4) Jews of the Jewish religion and 0.32% (2) of no religion. There are 0.16% (1) Protestant Greeks.

We now have fairly exact information concerning the characteristics of the position, but we still know nothing of the comparative place of the characteristics of Position 26 in the upper-middle class and within its class type. These analyses provide the same kind of knowledge for the characteristics as they did for the seven structures.

d. The Comparative Characteristics

In the upper-middle class Position 26 holds 7.58% (615) of the adults and 1.15% (17) of the subadults, ranking four of nineteen and eleven of seventeen; 4.88% (246) of the males and 8.50% (386) of the females, ranking seven of eighteen and four of nineteen; 3.09% (35) of the Catholic members (rank nine of sixteen), 7.24% (384) of the Protestant (rank four of nineteen), 5.19% (4) of the Jewish (rank six of eight), and 6.86% (209) of those not professing a religion (rank five of nineteen). It has 7.33% (571) of the natives and 3.39% (61) of the ethnics, ranking four of nineteen and nine of sixteen.

Of the Irish members of the upper-middle class 3.32% (52) are in Position 26, ranking nine of seventeen; of the French 3.03% (2), ranking five of six; of the Jewish 6.32% (6), ranking five of nine; and of the Greek 1.89% (1), ranking seven of seven.

In the vertical extension 79.55% (35) of the Catholics are in Position 26 (rank one of two), 40.63% (384) of the Protestants (rank one of three), all (4) of the Jews (rank one of one), and 48.27% (209) of those with no religious affiliation (rank one of three); 42.24% (571) of the natives and 82.43% (61) of the ethnics, ranking one of three and one of two.

Of the Irish members in its vertical extension, 80% (52) are in this position, ranking one of two; of the French 100% (2), ranking one of one; of the Jewish 100% (6), ranking one of one; and of the Greek 100% (1), ranking one of one.

Although we are now aware of the comparative place of the position by structure and by characteristics, we have yet to determine the interrelation of these two types of social behavior. We know, for example, that there are so many Protestants in the position and so many members of associations, but we do not know how many members of association are Protestants or are affiliated with some other religious faith. To understand fully what is taking place in any particular event under analysis, we should know the composition by characteristic of each structure. Once this is known any given status has a sufficient number of interrelated social facts to give the interested person a clear understanding of the kind of general behavior he may normally expect there.

e. The Characteristics of Each Structure

In the association 97.16% (548) of the members are adult and 2.84% (16) subadult; 37.94% (214) male and 62.06% (350) female; 6.03% (34) Catholic, 62.59% (353) Protestant, 0.53% (3) Jewish, and 30.85% (174) with no religion; 90.78% (512) native and 9.22% (52) ethnic.

Clique members are 98.46% (64) adult and 1.54% (1) subadult; 46.15% (30) male and 53.85% (35) female; 1.54% (1) Catholic, 47.69% (31) Protestant, 1.54% (1) Jewish, and 49.23% (32) with no religion; 86.15% (56) native and 13.85% (9) ethnic.

All (3) of the family members are adult; 66.67% (2) male and 33.33% (1) female; all without religious affiliation; and all native.

There are 84.62% (44) of the Irish members in associations and 15.38% (8) in cliques; 100% (2) of the French in associations; 83.33% (5) of the Jews in associations and 16.67% (1) in cliques; and all (1) of the Greeks in associations.

The above analysis still lacks one fundamental set of facts to complete our study of the place of any position in the social system. We do not know how a position is interconnected with the other positions in the total system. We know by the above analysis how much of each structure and characteristic each position in a particular class possesses. We also know how much its membership is interconnected with the other positions in its vertical extension or class type. We do not know how much interconnection the members of a position have with the other positions of the class in which it is found. Because of the complexity of this part of the analysis, we have placed this discussion in Chapter Five in this volume.

A full analysis of each position's composition is far too long for this volume and has been placed in a separate data book.

APPENDIX 2

ANALYSIS BY DECILE OF THE AMOUNT OF STRUCTURAL MEMBERS IN THE SYSTEM

TABLE 19: *Associational Members*

Decile	1	2	3	4	5	6	7	8	9	10	Percentage Range	Positions per Class						
												UU	LU	UM	LM	UL	LL	Total
1	74	59	71	77	51	28	26	56	45	32	10.20–3.54			3	4	3		10
2	82	86	52	67	63	3	13	57	58	41	3.50–1.92	1	1	1	4	1	2	10
3	36	34	30	49	80	14	81	72	5	39 76	1.81–0.92	1	1	4	1	2	2	11
4	62	54	38	88	35	2 17	65	11	9 68	12 16	0.74–0.31	3	3	2	2	2	1	13
5	25	61	79	89	22	20	78	1	33	19	0.30–0.01	1	4	1	1	2	1	10
												6	9	11	12	10	6	54

TABLE 20: *Clique Members*

Decile	1	2	3	4	5	6	7	8	9	10	Percentage Range	Positions per Class						
												UU	LU	UM	LM	UL	LL	Total
1	76	62	77	78	79	58	63	88	61	57	9.36–4.15				5	4	1	10
2	38	89	72	37	39	74	12	59	2	1	3.69–1.26	2	1	3	1	2	1	10
3	87	64	33	18	40	42	19	73	68	82	1.22–0.68		2	3	1	2	2	10
4	13	41	27	34	4 50	54	3 26	52 66	75 35	20	0.50–0.18	2	2	5	3	2		14
5	31 69	60	43 55	53 84	21 83	8	23	47	22 48 29	10 85 14 44	0.16–0.05	2	4	4	5	1	3	19
6	7 86 28	5	24 15	70	6 45 46						0.04–0.005	3	2	1	2	1	1	10
												9	11	16	17	12	8	73

TABLE 21: *Family Members*

Decile	1	2	3	4	5	6	7	8	9	10	Percentage Range	Positions per Class: UU	LU	UM	LM	UL	LL	Total
1	78	61	89	37	76	62	1	18	79	88	28.66–0.79	1	1	1	2	3	2	10
2	38	57	87	77	64	19	40 63 73	72	33 58	53 86	0.60–0.05		1	3	5	3	2	14
3	2 27 21	42 39 26 20 8	75 74 59 52 48 41 34 13 12 4 3	44 43 85 84 83 82 60							0.03–0.006	4	4	8	4	2	4	26
												5	6	12	11	8	8	50

TABLE 22: *Economic Members*

Decile	1	2	3	4	5	6	7	8	9	10	Percentage Range	Positions per Class: UU	LU	UM	LM	UL	LL	Total
1	74	82	56	71	61	59	78	81	37	62	12.61–2.46			1	4	3	2	10
2	57	76	38	36	41 58	89	72	63	67	51	2.39–1.08			3	4	3	1	11
3	39	77	86	35	84 75	73 54	25 49 64	40 87	1 29 80	18 30 68	0.78–0.19	1	2	5	3	4	4	19
4	9 32 34 53 79 89	16 17 20 43 52 60 85	11 21 22 31 33 47 65 66 83	7 10 19 42 44 50							0.15–0.04	4	6	7	5	3	3	28
												5	8	16	16	13	10	68

TABLE 23: *School Members*

Decile	1	2	3	4	5	6	7	8	9	10	Percentage Range	Positions per Class						
												UU	LU	UM	LM	UL	LL	Total
1	67	51	80	74	82	32	59	41	17	11	28.37–0.18	1	1	2	2	2	2	10

TABLE 24: *Church Members*

Decile	1	2	3	4	5	6	7	8	9	10	Percentage Range	Positions per Class						
												UU	LU	UM	LM	UL	LL	Total
1	71	51	56	67	32	81	80	74	36	59	20.91–2.67			2	3	3	2	10
2	82	17	11	25	41						2.59–0.20	1	2	1			1	5
												1	2	3	3	3	3	15

TABLE 25: *Political Members*

Decile	1	2	3	4	5	6	7	8	9	10	Percentage Range	Positions per Class						
												UU	LU	UM	LM	UL	LL	Total
1	51	67	80	32	17	11					34.34–1.26	1	1	1	1	1	1	6

APPENDIX 3

ANALYSIS BY DECILE OF ETHNIC MEMBERSHIP

TABLE 26: *Native Members*

Decile	1	2	3	4	5	6	7	8	9	10	Percentage Range	Positions per Class						
												UU	LU	UM	LM	UL	LL	Total
1	1–11 15 16 24 42 43 46 70	13	12	17	18	23	34	22	14	19	100–90.48	11	11	3	1	1		27
2	26	21	28	32	52	20	60	33	38	29	90.35–84.21		2	6	2			10
3	30	27	37	31	35	44	25	49	65	45	83.91–72.98		1	6	2	1		10
4	53	47	51	57	83	41	61	39	40	36	72.50–57.25			4	5		1	10
5	48	54	50	64	80	58	87	62	67	59	56.25–42.41				7	1	2	10
6	66	63	56	89	75	84	86	78	73	55	42.37–31.03				3	4	3	10
7	72	76	77	81	82	88	68	79	69	74	30.56–21.91					7	3	10
8	71	85									15.87–12.50					1	1	2
												11	14	19	20	15	10	89

TABLE 27: *Combined Ethnic Members*

Decile	1	2	3	4	5	6	7	8	9	10	Percentage Range	Positions per Class						
												UU	LU	UM	LM	UL	LL	Total
1	85	71	74	69	79	68	88	82	81	77	87.50–72.76					6	4	10
2	76	72	55	73	78	86	84	75	89	56	70.52–60.69				2	5	3	10
3	63	66	59	67	62	87	58	80	64	50	57.86–46.58				6	2	2	10
4	54	48	36	40	39	61	41	83	57	51	44.71–28.65			4	5		1	10
5	47	53	45	65	49	25	44	35	31	37	27.78–18.26		1	4	4	1		10
6	27	30	29	38	33	60	20	52	32	28	16.67–11.62		1	7	2			10
7	21	26	19	14	22	34	23	18	17	12	10.00–3.57		8	2				10
8	13										3.29		1					1
													11	17	19	14	10	71

The 18 positions having no ethnic members are: 1–11, 15, 16, 24, 42, 43, 46, 70.

TABLE 28: *Irish Members*

Decile	1	2	3	4	5	6	7	8	9	10	Percentage Range	Positions per Class						
												UU	LU	UM	LM	UL	LL	Total
1	71	68	72	56	66	76	73	77	36	74	71.29–41.41			1	1	8		10
2	79	50	78	63	69	58	67	54	62	40	41.11–36.28			1	5	4		10
3	59	39	48	41	64	75	81	55	25	61	32.64–23.11		1	2	5	1	1	10
4	57	35	51	31	86	53	65	87	27	45	22.93–16.56			3	4	1	2	10
5	29	37	80	88	38	82	49	33	20	30	15.79–11.75		1	5	1		3	10
6	89	47	84	21	28	32	19	14	26	60	11.55– 8.11		3	3	2		2	10
7	83	44	22	52	34	23	18	17	12	13	7.70– 3.29		6	2	1		1	10
													11	17	19	14	9	70

The 19 positions having no Irish members are: 1–11, 15, 16, 24, 42, 43, 46, 70, 85.

TABLE 29: *French Members*

Decile	1	2	3	4	5	6	7	8	9	10	Percentage Range	Positions per Class						
												UU	LU	UM	LM	UL	LL	Total
1	55	82	84	74	86	77	89	80	48 85	88	44.83–12.03				2	2	7	11
2	78	47 69 75	64	81	87	79	67	59	63	83	11.51– 7.69				4	5	3	12
3	65	53	76	71	73	72	62	45	61	51	7.55– 4.12				5	5		10
4	68	56	54	52	66	58	31	57	49	41	3.85– 1.67			2	6	2		10
5	50	37	30	32	28	39	40	38	26 34	36	1.37– 0.19			10	1			11
														12	18	14	10	54

The 35 positions having no French members are: 1–25, 27, 29, 33, 35, 42–44, 46, 60, 70.

TABLE 30: *Jewish Members*

Decile	1	2	3	4	5	6	7	8	9	10	Percentage Range	Positions per Class						
												UU	LU	UM	LM	UL	LL	Total
1	59	62	58	74	75	76	73	49	85	61	13.40–5.47				5	4	1	10
2	72	63	78	57	64	39	41	45	51	79	4.73–2.80			2	5	3		10
3	69	50	60	82	53	67	54	30	77	52	2.78–1.30			1	5	3	1	10
4	33	37	40	26	86	89	88	28	32	68	1.29–0.48			6		1	3	10
5	38	71 80	56	36	87						0.47–0.33			2	1	1	2	6
														11	16	12	7	46

The 43 positions having no Jewish members are: 1–25, 27, 29, 31, 34, 35, 42–44, 46–48, 55, 65, 66, 70, 81, 83, 84.

TABLE 31: *Italian Members*

Decile	1	2	3	4	5	6	7	8	9	10	Percentage Range	Positions per Class						
												UU	LU	UM	LM	UL	LL	Total
1	83	85	84	79	86	88	87	81	89	82	7.69–2.90					1	9	10
2	71	60	76	78	63	77	58	75	56	80	2.82–1.73				4	5	1	10
3	74	62	67	61	45	59	64	54	68	72	1.57–0.93				6	4		10
4	51	57	49	34	37	28	39	32			0.86–0.09			5	3			8
														5	13	10	10	38

The 51 positions having no Italian members are: 1–27, 29–31, 33, 35, 36, 38, 40–44, 46–48, 50, 52, 53, 55, 65, 66, 69, 70, 73.

TABLE 32: *Greek Members*

Decile	1	2	3	4	5	6	7	8	9	10	Percentage Range	Positions per Class						
												UU	LU	UM	LM	UL	LL	Total
1	85	44	82	88	83	79	75	84	86	89	25.–6.47			1		2	7	10
2	74	78	80	87	73	77	67	66	41	64	4.32–1.33			1	1	6	2	10
3	76	39	59	32	81	49	37	62	72	61	1.20–0.48			3	4	2	1	10
4	38	30	51	34	71	52	45 63	36	28	26	0.47–0.16			6	4	1		11
5	57 58										0.07				2			2
														11	11	11	10	43

The 46 positions having no Greek members are: 1–25, 27, 29, 31, 33, 35, 40, 42, 43, 46–48, 50, 53–56, 60, 65, 68, 69, 70.

TABLE 33: *Armenian Members*

Decile	1	2	3	4	5	6	7	8	9	10	Percentage Range	Positions per Class						
												UU	LU	UM	LM	UL	LL	Total
1	69	85	84	47	75	77	66	73	86	67	25.–3.14				1	6	3	10
2	80	63	76	78	79	88	65	89	64	72	3.11–1.54				2	5	3	10
3	68	62	50	54	82	81	51	74	61	56	1.44–0.91				6	2	2	10
4	30	59	71	45	49	52	57	58	87	39	0.87–0.16			2	6	1	1	10
5	32	37									0.14–0.13			2				2
														4	15	14	9	42

The 47 positions having no Armenians are: 1–29, 31, 33–36, 38, 40–44, 46, 48, 53, 55, 60, 70, 83.

TABLE 34: *Polish Members*

Decile	1	2	3	4	5	6	7	8	9	10	Percentage Range	Positions per Class						
												UU	LU	UM	LM	UL	LL	Total
1	81	88	89	86	87	82	84	80	85	79	27.90–5.28					1	9	10
2	71	78	77	74	63	64 76	67	73	58 62	56	1.41–0.28				5	7		12
3	52	72	45	59	51	57	61				0.22–0.05				6	1		7
															11	9	9	29

The 60 positions having no Polish members are: 1–44, 46–50, 53–55, 60, 65, 66, 68–70, 75, 83.

TABLE 35: *Russian Members*

Decile	1	2	3	4	5	6	7	8	9	10	Percentage Range	Positions per Class						
												UU	LU	UM	LM	UL	LL	Total
1	85	88	87	86	89	82	79	80	75	81	6.25–1.49					2	8	10
2	78	77	49 67	74	76	62	61	71	56	63	0.94–0.07				5	6		11
3	59	51									0.06–0.04				2			2
															7	8	8	23

The 66 positions having no Russian members are: 1–48, 50, 52–55, 57, 58, 60, 64–66, 68–70, 72, 73, 83, 84.

TABLE 36: *Negro Members*

Decile	1	2	3	4	5	6	7	8	9	10	Percentage Range	Positions per Class						
												UU	LU	UM	LM	UL	LL	Total
1	85	81	84	80	89	87	88	82	86	64	12.50–0.33				1		9	10
2	76 61										0.04				1	1		2
															2	1	9	12

The 77 positions having no Negro members are: 1–60, 62, 63, 65–75, 77–79, 83.

APPENDIX 4

ANALYSIS BY CLASS OF ETHNIC PARTICIPATION IN BEHAVIORAL SITUATIONS

TABLE 37

Native Participation in Behavioral Situations in the Upper-upper Class

Structure	Natives
Association	21.4 6
Clique	32.1 9
Family	17.9 5
Economic	17.9 5
School	3.6 1
Church	3.6 1
Political	3.6 1
Totals	28

TABLE 38

Ethnic Participation in Behavioral Situations in the Lower-upper Class

Structure	Native	Irish	Total Places
Association	23.7 56.3 9	29.2 43.7 7	16
Clique	28.9 55. 11	37.5 45. 9	20
Family	15.8 66.7 6	12.5 33.3 3	9
Economic	21.1 88.9 8	4.2 11.1 1	9
School	2.6 50. 1	4.2 50. 1	2
Church	5.3 50. 2	8.3 50. 2	4
Political	2.6 50. 1	4.2 50. 1	2
Totals	38	24	62

TABLE 39: *Ethnic Participation in Behavioral Situations in the Upper-middle Class*

Structure	Native	Irish	French	Jewish	Italian	Greek	Armenian	Total Places
Association	19.0 23.4 11	24.4 21.3 10	33.3 14.9 7	36.8 14.9 7	33.3 4.3 2	42.1 17. 8	33.3 4.3 2	27.6 47
Clique	27.6 32. 16	31.7 26. 13	33.3 14. 7	26.3 10. 5	33.3 4. 2	26.3 10. 5	33.3 4. 2	29.4 50
Family	19.0 52.4 11	12.2 23.8 5	4.8 4.8 1	5.3 4.8 1	16.7 4.8 1	5.3 4.8 1	16.7 4.8 1	12.4 21
Economic	27.6 55.2 16	19.5 27.6 8	9.5 6.9 2	10.5 6.9 2		5.3 3.4 1		17.1 29
School	1.7 16.7 1	4.9 33.3 2	4.8 16.7 1	5.3 16.7 1		5.3 16.7 1		3.5 6
Church	3.4 20.0 2	4.9 20.0 2	9.5 20.0 2	10.5 20.0 2		10.5 20.0 2		5.9 10
Political	1.7 14.3 1	2.4 14.3 1	4.8 14.3 1	5.3 14.3 1	16.7 14.3 1	5.3 14.3 1	16.7 14.3 1	4.1 7
Totals	34.1 58	24.1 41	12.4 21	11.2 19	3.5 6	11.2 19	3.5 6	170

TABLE 40: *Ethnic Participation in Behavioral Situations in the Lower-middle Class*

Structure	Native	Irish	French	Jewish	Italian	Greek	Armenian	Polish	Russian	Negro	Total
Association	20.3 / 14.3 / 12	22.6 / 14.3 / 12	27.9 / 14.3 / 12	32.4 / 13.1 / 11	33.3 / 11.9 / 10	30.0 / 7.1 / 6	29.4 / 11.9 / 10	36.4 / 9.5 / 8	37.5 / 3.6 / 3		27.5 / 84
Clique	28.8 / 18.9 / 17	28.3 / 16.7 / 15	32.6 / 15.6 / 14	32.4 / 12.2 / 11	26.7 / 8.9 / 8	23.0 / 5.6 / 5	26.5 / 10. / 9	31.8 / 7.8 / 7	25.0 / 2.2 / 2	66.7 / 2.2 / 2	29.4 / 90
Family	16.9 / 28.6 / 10	11.3 / 17.1 / 6	9.3 / 11.4 / 4	8.8 / 8.6 / 3	6.7 / 5.7 / 2	10.0 / 5.7 / 2	11.8 / 11.4 / 4	9.1 / 5.7 / 2	12.5 / 2.9 / 1	33.3 / 2.9 / 1	11.4 / 35
Economic	25.4 / 25.4 / 15	26.4 / 23.7 / 14	16.3 / 11.9 / 7	14.7 / 8.5 / 5	20.0 / 10.2 / 6	15.0 / 5.1 / 3	20.6 / 11.9 / 7	4.5 / 1.7 / 1	12.5 / 1.7 / 1		19.3 / 59
School	3.4 / 16.7 / 2	3.8 / 16.7 / 2	4.7 / 16.7 / 2	2.9 / 8.3 / 1	3.3 / 8.3 / 1	5.0 / 8.3 / 1	2.9 / 8.3 / 1	4.5 / 8.3 / 1	12.5 / 8.3 / 1		3.9 / 12
Church	3.4 / 11.1 / 2	5.7 / 16.7 / 3	7.0 / 16.7 / 3	5.9 / 11.1 / 2	6.7 / 11.1 / 2	10.0 / 11.1 / 2	5.9 / 11.1 / 2	9.1 / 11.1 / 2			5.9 / 18
Political	1.7 / 12.5 / 1	1.9 / 12.5 / 1	2.3 / 12.5 / 1	2.9 / 12.5 / 1	3.3 / 12.5 / 1	5.0 / 12.5 / 1	2.9 / 12.5 / 1	4.5 / 12.5 / 1			2.6 / 8
Totals	19.3 / 59	17.3 / 53	14.1 / 43	11.1 / 34	9.8 / 30	6.5 / 20	11.1 / 34	7.2 / 22	2.6 / 8	1.0 / 3	306

TABLE 41: *Ethnic Participation in Behavioral Situations in the Upper-lower Class*

Structure	Native	Irish	French	Jewish	Italian	Greek	Armenian	Polish	Russian	Negro	Total
Association	21.7 14.9 10	21.3 14.9 10	20.5 11.9 8	20.0 9. 6	28.6 11.9 8	20.7 9. 6	29.0 13.4 9	29.2 10.4 7	15.0 4.5 3		22.7 67
Clique	26.1 14.3 12	23.4 13.1 11	28.2 13.1 11	30.0 10.7 9	25.0 8.3 7	31.0 10.7 9	35.5 13.1 11	29.2 8.3 7	30.0 7.1 6	100.0 1.2 1	28.5 84
Family	15.2 20. 7	14.9 20. 7	7.7 8.6 3	13.3 11.4 4	10.7 8.6 3	10.3 8.6 3	9.7 8.6 3	8.3 5.7 2	15.0 8.6 3		11.9 35
Economic	26.1 18.8 12	27.7 20.3 13	28.2 17.2 11	23.3 10.9 7	17.9 7.8 5	20.7 9.4 6	12.9 6.3 4	12.5 4.7 3	15.0 4.7 3		21.7 64
School	4.3 13.3 2	4.3 13.3 2	5.1 13.3 2	3.3 6.7 1	7.1 13.3 2	6.9 13.3 2	3.2 6.7 1	8.3 13.3 2	5.0 6.7 1		5.1 15
Church	4.3 9.5 2	6.4 14.3 3	7.7 14.3 3	6.7 9.5 2	7.1 9.5 2	6.9 9.5 2	6.5 9.5 2	8.3 9.5 2	15.0 14.3 3		7.1 21
Political	2.2 11.1 1	2.1 11.1 1	2.6 11.1 1	3.3 11.1 1	3.6 11.1 1	3.4 11.1 1	3.2 11.1 1	4.2 11.1 1	5.0 11.1 1		3.1 9
Totals	46 15.6	47 15.9	39 13.2	30 10.2	28 9.5	29 9.8	31 10.5	24 8.1	20 6.8	1 0.3	295

TABLE 42: *Ethnic Participation in Behavioral Situations in the Lower-lower Class*

Structure	Native	Irish	French	Jewish	Italian	Greek	Armenian	Polish	Russian	Negro	Total
Association	17.1 12. 6	18.8 12. 6	16.7 10. 5	16.7 4. 2	22.7 10. 5	22.7 10. 5	21.1 8. 4	24.0 12. 6	29.4 10. 5	30.0 12. 6	21.4 50
Clique	20.0 10.4 7	21.9 10.4 7	26.7 11.9 8	33.3 6. 4	31.8 10.4 7	36.4 11.9 8	36.8 10.4 7	28.0 10.4 7	35.3 9. 6	30.0 9. 6	28.6 67
Family	17.1 22.2 6	15.6 18.5 5	10.0 11.1 3	16.7 7.4 2	9.1 7.4 2	13.6 11.1 3	10.5 7.4 2	8.0 7.4 2	5.9 3.7 1	5.0 3.7 1	11.5 27
Economic	28.6 22.7 10	25.0 18.2 8	26.7 18.2 8	8.3 2.3 1	13.6 6.8 3	13.6 6.8 3	15.8 6.8 3	16.0 9.1 4	5.9 2.3 1	15.0 6.8 3	18.8 44
School	5.7 13.3 2	6.3 13.3 2	6.7 13.3 2	8.3 6.7 1	9.1 13.3 2	4.5 6.7 1	5.3 6.7 1	8.0 13.3 2	5.9 6.7 1	5.0 6.7 1	6.4 15
Church	8.6 13.6 3	9.4 13.6 3	10.0 13.6 3	8.3 4.5 1	9.1 9.1 2	4.5 4.5 1	5.3 4.5 1	12.0 13.6 3	17.6 13.6 3	10.0 9.1 2	9.8 22
Political	2.9 11.1 1	3.1 11.1 1	3.3 11.1 1	8.3 11.1 1	4.5 11.1 1	4.5 11.1 1	5.3 11.1 1	4.0 11.1 1		5.0 11.1 1	3.8 9
Totals	35 15.0	32 13.7	30 12.8	12 5.1	22 9.4	22 9.4	19 8.1	25 10.7	17 7.3	20 8.5	234

APPENDIX 5

ANALYSIS BY DECILE OF SEX AND AGE

TABLE 43: *Male Members*

Decile	1	2	3	4	5	6	7	8	9	10	Percentage Range	Positions per Class						
												UU	LU	UM	LM	UL	LL	Total
1	60	83	10	43	15	22	21	50	66	85	86.49–68.75	1	3	1	2	1	2	10
2	33	42	31	16	45	70	52	20	40	30	68.53–64.78		2	5	2	1		10
3	19	69	38	64	53	88	39	34	25	79	64.02–59.21		2	3	2	2	1	10
4	87	4	73	27	80	36	18	28	57	84	57.33–54.05	1	1	3	1	1	3	10
5	67	72	89	41	23	82	86	63	62	59	53.97–51.66		1	1	3	2	3	10
6	14	35	61	56	58	81	76	74	13	49	51.23–50.29		2	1	4	2	1	10
7	48	77	17	78	51	37	54	29	2	71	50. –46.40	1	1	2	3	3		10
8	32	1	12	55	9	7	11	68	26	3	46.04–36.34	5	1	2	1	1		10
9	5	8	44	75	47	65	24				34.29–20.	2	1	1	1	2		7
												10	14	19	19	15	10	87

TABLE 44: *Female Members*

Decile	1	2	3	4	5	6	7	8	9	10	Percentage Range	Positions per Class						
												UU	LU	UM	LM	UL	LL	Total
1	46 6	24	65	47	75	44	8	5	3	26	100. –61.08	4	1	2	2	2		11
2	68	11	7	9	55	12	1	32	71	2	61.06–52.91	5	1	1	1	2		10
3	29	54	37	51	78	17	77	48	49	13	52.63–49.62		2	2	4	2		10
4	74	76	81	58	56	61	35	14	59	62	49.39–48.31		1	1	5	2	1	10
5	63	86	82	23	41	89	72	67	84	57	48.02–45.85		1	1	2	2	4	10
6	28	18	36	80	27	73	4	87	79	25	45.81–39.68	1	2	3		2	2	10
7	34	39	88	53	64	38	69	19	30	40	39.23–34.31		1	5	2	1	1	10
8	20	52	70	45	16	31	42	33	85	66	33.96–30.51		2	3	2	2	1	10
9	50	21	22	15	43	10	83	60			28.77–13.51	1	3	1	2		1	8
												11	14	19	20	15	10	89

TABLE 45: *Adult Members*

Decile	1	2	3	4	5	6	7	8	9	10	Percentage Range	Positions per Class						
												UU	LU	UM	LM	UL	LL	Total
1	6 15 16 46	5	14	12	9	26	28	2	34	13	100. –94.94	4	5	3	1			13
2	52	3	45	30	33	1	4	27	60	11	94.79–88.60	4		3	3			10
3	17	32	18	19	42	49	83	37	38	36	88.39–80.73		3	5	1		1	10
4	51	68	22	44	21	57	61	56 67	50	71	79.34–73.86		2	1	5	3		11
5	54	35	39	53	20 65	58	72	40	29	25	73.53–68.25		2	4	3	2		11
6	66	78	31	70	74	59	80	41	43	85	67.80–62.50			3	1	4	2	10
7	84	89	81	77	62	7	8	63	76	47	62.16–55.55	2			3	2	3	10
8	86	82	48	64	87	10	79	73	88	75	54.92–40.74	1			2	3	4	10
9	24	69	55	23							40. –29.41		2		1	1		4
												11	14	19	20	15	10	89

TABLE 46: *Subadult Members*

Decile	1	2	3	4	5	6	7	8	9	10	Percentage Range	Positions per Class						
												UU	LU	UM	LM	UL	LL	Total
1	23	55	69	24	75	88	73	79	10	87	70.59–53.09	1	2		1	4	2	10
2	64	48	82	86	47	76	63	8	7	62	52.67–39.67	2			5	1	2	10
3	77	81	89	84	85	43	41	80	59	74	39.54–35.07			2	1	2	5	10
4	70	31	78	66	25	29	40	72	58	20 65	33.33–28.30		2	3	1	5		11
5	53	39	35	54	71	50	56 67	61	57	21	27.50–23.33		1	2	6	2		11
6	44	22	68	51	36	38	37	83	49	42	23.07–13.64		1	5	2	1	1	10
7	19	18	32	17	11	60	27	4	1	33	13.23– 7.33	3	3	3	1			10
8	30	45	3	52	13	34	2	28	26	9	6.52– 1.96	3	1	4	2			10
9	12	14	5								1.92– 1.43	1	2					3
												10	12	19	19	15	10	85

The 4 positions having no subadult members are: 6, 15, 16, 46.

APPENDIX 6

ANALYSIS BY DECILE OF RELIGIOUS FAITH

TABLE 47: *Protestant Members*

Decile	1	2	3	4	5	6	7	8	9	10	Percentage Range	Positions per Class						
												UU	LU	UM	LM	UL	LL	Total
1	6	16	11	17	8	24	14	42	10 12	5	100. –76.43	5	5	1				11
2	2	9	4	32	13	3	44	34	43	1	74.79–65.71	5	1	4				10
3	19	28	18	22	65	55	26	30	20	7	65.61–60.	1	4	3	1	1		10
4	25	31	60	51	23	33	38	35	49	15	58.73–50.		3	4	3			10
5	37	27	52	48	54	41	36	29	69	40	47.96–40.20			6	3	1		10
6	21	57	47	53	39	80	67	45	61	83	40. –30.76		1	1	5	1	2	10
7	58	64	87	62	59	56	63	73	50	75	30.37–20.37				7	2	1	10
8	81	72	84	77	76	78	66	68	79	86	16.76–13.45					7	3	10
9	85	88	89	74	71	82					12.50– 9.39					2	4	6
												11	14	19	19	14	10	87

The 2 positions having no Protestant members are 46 and 70.

TABLE 48: *Catholic Members*

Decile	1	2	3	4	5	6	7	8	9	10	Percentage Range	Positions per Class						
												UU	LU	UM	LM	UL	LL	Total
1	71	81	56	36	68	76	72	66	69	74	73.54–35.83			1	1	7	1	10
2	73	77	79	54	63	78	58	50	59	40	34.62–26.47			1	5	4		10
3	62	48	67	39	25	75	41	88	84	64	25.94–18.33		1	2	3	2	2	10
4	82	57	61	35	53	87	86	89	45	51	18.08–12.70			1	5		4	10
5	83	20	47 49	31	80	37	21	65	30 38	19 22	11.54–7.41		4	4	2	1	2	13
6	28	55	14	32	33	85	23	26	60	29	7.18– 5.26		2	5	2		1	10
7	42	27	52	34	18	17	13	12			4.55– 1.65		4	3	1			8
													11	17	19	14	10	71

The 18 positions having no Catholic members are: 1–11, 15, 16, 24, 43, 44, 46, 70.

TABLE 49: *Jewish Members*

Decile	1	2	3	4	5	6	7	8	9	10	Percentage Range	Positions per Class						
												UU	LU	UM	LM	UL	LL	Total
1	59	62	58	74	49	85	76	73	61	57	13.27–3.56				6	3	1	10
2	63	72	41	78	39	69	50	60	51	82	3.55–2.58			2	4	3	1	10
3	45	53	64	75	79	54	30 67	33	52	77	2.56–0.94			2	5	4		11
4	86	89	37	88	26	28	40	68	38	80	0.85–0.44			5		1	4	10
5	32	71	56	87	36						0.41–0.19			2	1	1	1	5
														11	16	12	7	46

The 43 positions having no Jewish members are: 1–25, 27, 29, 31, 34, 35, 42–44, 46–48, 55, 65, 66, 70, 81, 83, 84.

TABLE 50: *Greek Orthodox Members*

Decile	1	2	3	4	5	6	7	8	9	10	Percentage Range	Positions per Class						
												UU	LU	UM	LM	UL	LL	Total
1	85	82	88	44	79	86	83	75	74	89	25. –2.94			1		3	6	10
2	84	73	80	87	78	41	59	39	77	76 67	2.70–0.46			2	1	5	3	11
3	30	81	64	38	37	32	52	45	62	51	0.43–0.13			4	5		1	10
4	61	63									0.12–0.07				2			2
														7	8	8	10	33

The 56 positions having no Greek Orthodox members are: 1–29, 31, 33–36, 40, 42, 43, 46–50, 53–58, 60, 65, 66, 68–72.

TABLE 51: *Members with No Religions Affiliation*

Decile	1	2	3	4	5	6	7	8	9	10	Percentage Range	Positions per Class						
												UU	LU	UM	LM	UL	LL	Total
1	46 70	89	86	84	88	82	87	83	78	29	100. –52.63			1	1	2	7	11
2	75	45	80	52	64	15 21 27 47 85	77	61	66	79	51.86–46.70		2	1	5	4	2	14
3	50	53	72	63	74	23	37	76	33	7	46.57–40.	1	1	2	3	3		10
4	57	62	38	67	68	60	39	58	1	35	39.46–33.60	1		3	4	2		10
5	73	43	26	59	40	31	18	49	41	48	33.51–31.25		1	5	3	1		10
6	55	22	3	51	34	4	20 65	30	28	19	31.03–26.98	2	3	3	2	1		11
7	13	9	2	54	5	10 44	32	12	24	81	26.84–19.86	4	3	2	1		1	11
8	69	56	42	25	36	71	14	8	11	16	19.44–11.63	2	3	2	1	2		10
9	17										10.65		1					1
												10	14	19	20	15	10	88

Only Position 6 lacks members with no religious affiliation.

INDEX